The Pregnant Virgin

Marie-Louise von Franz, Honorary Patron

**Studies in Jungian Psychology
by Jungian Analysts**

Daryl Sharp, General Editor

The Pregnant Virgin

A Process of
Psychological Transformation

Marion Woodman

To those with whom I am sharing the journey.

With much gratitude to Daryl Sharp, Ross Woodman, Shirley Grace Jeffries, Fraser Boa, Greg Mogenson and to my analysands.

Chapter 2 is based on a lecture originally published as "Abandonment in the Creative Woman," in *Chiron: A Review of Jungian Analysis* (1985).

Chapter 3 is based on a lecture originally published as "Psyche/Soma Awareness" in *Quadrant* (Journal of the C.G. Jung Foundation for Analytical Psychology, New York), vol. 17, no. 2 (Fall 1984).

Canadian Cataloguing in Publication Data

Woodman, Marion
    The pregnant virgin : a process of psychological transformation

Studies in Jungian psychology by Jungian analysts; 21

Includes bibliographical references and index.
ISBN 0-919123-41-4 (bound). ISBN 0-919123-20-1 (pbk.).

1. Woman — Psychology. 2. Consciousness.
3. Identity (Psychology). 4. Jung, C.G. (Carl
Gustav), 1875-1961. I. Title. II. Series.

HQ1206.W66 1985   155.6'33   C85-099077-7

INNER CITY BOOKS
Box 1271, Station Q, Toronto, Canada M4T 2P4
Telephone (416) 927-0355

Honorary Patron: Marie-Louise von Franz.
Publisher and General Editor: Daryl Sharp.

INNER CITY BOOKS was founded in 1980 to promote the understanding and practical application of the work of C.G. Jung.

Index by Daryl Sharp.

Printed and bound in Canada by
University of Toronto Press Incorporated

CONTENTS

See final pages for descriptions of other Inner City Books

Flora, detail of *La Primavera* by Sandro Botticelli.
(Uffizi Gallery, Florence)

Introduction:

Frog Conjunctions

since feeling is first
who pays any attention
to the syntax of things
will never wholly kiss you;

   then
laugh, leaning back in my arms
for life's not a paragraph

And death i think is no parenthesis.
             —e.e. cummings.

The Pregnant Virgin is a study in process. In its conception, it was called *Chrysalis*. By the time it was born, the baby had outgrown its chosen name. Its skeleton—the process of metamorphosis from caterpillar to chrysalis to butterfly—was intact. The whole, however, had become more than the sum of its parts. The parts concentrate on the periods in the chrysalis when life as we have known it is over. No longer who we were, we know not who we may become. We experience ourselves as living mush, fearful of the journey down the birth canal. The whole has to do with the process of psychological pregnancy—the virgin forever a virgin, forever pregnant, forever open to possibilities.

The analogy between the virgin with child and the chrysalis with butterfly does not originate with me. In ancient Greece, the word for soul was *psyche*, often imaged as a butterfly. The emergence of the butterfly from the chrysalis was analogous to the birth of the soul from matter, a birth commonly identified with release, hence a symbol of immortality. The Divine Child, the Redeemer, the child of the spirit shaping in the womb of the virgin, finds a natural image in the winged butterfly transforming in the chrysalis, preparing to be free of the creature that crawls on its belly. This book does not, however, make the traditional body/soul distinction between caterpillar and butterfly, mortal and immortal life. Rather it explores the presence of the one in the other, suggesting that immortality is a reality contained within mortality and, in this life, dependent upon it. *The Pregnant Virgin*, that is, looks at ways of restoring the unity of body and soul.

Flora, one of the figures in Botticelli's *Primavera*, captures the paradoxical external stillness and internal kindling of pregnancy. She embodies the evanescent beauty of the maiden blossoming into womanhood. As the shy earth-nymph Chloris, she has surrendered to the breath of

Zephyr, and is now being awakened into the calm, luxuriant Flora. Like Mary, impregnated by the Holy Spirit, she stands radiant and full of grace, her femininity forthright and lyrically tender as she looks the beholder straight in the eye.

Writing *The Pregnant Virgin* has been a nine months' pregnancy. The book rejected its preconceived pattern; it evolved in its own metamorphic process. Last August in my second month, I suffered severe morning sickness. One look at an expanse of white paper made me ill. I feared a miscarriage. Then, as usually happens when I am conscious enough to ask the right question, the answer came in a dream:

> I am sitting on steps near the waters of Georgian Bay. I am attempting to roll a big lily pad into the shape of a cylinder. It won't do what I want it to do. One end keeps falling open as I hold the other end rolled. Behind me is an old hotel. Two men are fighting on the balcony. I can feel their blows in my bones. I think I should try to do something about that, but a voice says, "Fashion your pipe."
>
> I continue with the lily pad, and suddenly one man throws the other off the balcony, right over my head. Now I really must do something. I am about to rise when the voice commands again, "Fashion your pipe."
>
> Now I understand—I am creating an instrument. I see beside me and a little behind, a huge smiling frog sitting in a pool of green eggs, immensely proud of herself and waiting for me to finish the piccolo-pipe so the eggs can go through and be played into meaningful sounds.

I woke up knowing what the problem was. Instead of putting my full concentration into making the "pipe," I was allowing my energy to be drained by the blows of the two men on the balcony. Their voices I knew well enough: "Forget writing. Live your life as you always have. You can't write anyway." But there was another voice, a submerged feminine voice, tenacious and proud: "I want to write, but I don't want to write essays. I want to write my way." There was the impasse.

I walked through the bush to Iris Bay. I thought about the water lily—the Canadian lotus, whose blossom carries much the same symbolism as the rose. Its roots grow deep in the life-bestowing mud, sending nourishment up the sturdy stem to the leaves and flowers. Serene in its creamy white simplicity, the blossom opens petal by petal to the sun, symbolic of the Goddess—Prajnaparamita, Tara, Sophia—Creation opening herself to Consciousness. She is the blossom in the heart, the knowing, the dawning of God in the soul. Her divine wisdom brings release from the passion and pain of ego desire.

I picked a lily pad. I concentrated on fashioning my pipe. I remembered my grinning frog. Surely the lotus leaf was the right instrument to pipe her eggs. But how? How does one put psychological concepts through a lotus leaf? What would frog syntax sound like? How would it conjunct? Certainly not with "and," "but," and "for." It would have much more to do with leaping through the air from lily pad to lily pad, leaping intuitively with the imagination, or swimming through water. Leap—leap—out of sheer faith in my froggy instincts. Leap—trusting in another lily pad. Leap—knowing that other frogs would understand. Leap—leap—remembering my journal that looks like a Beethoven manuscript—blots, blue ink, red, yellow and green, pages torn by an angry pen, smudged with tears, leaping with joy from exclamation marks to dashes that speak more than the words between, my journal that dances with the heartbeat of a process in motion. How does one fashion a pipe that can contain that honesty, and be at the same time profession-ally credible? How can a woman write from her authentic center without being labeled "histrionic" or "hysterical"? Splat! Long Pause!

And then my frog spoke from the mud.

"Why don't you write as you feel? Be a virgin. Surrender to the whirlwind and see what happens."

"Impossible!" I replied. "I'm not going to make a fool of myself. I'm not going to set myself up to be shot down. I know the guns too well."

That conversation put *Chrysalis* into a cocoon. For weeks I tried to find a syntax that could simultaneously contain the passion of my heart and the analytic detachment of my mind.

I was encouraged by a picture of an Indian Goddess holding her hands in a gesture that would contain the lily pad. Known as "link of increase," meaning "marriage" or "coronation," its highly differentiated fingers seem to cradle a pearl or flower.[1] The tips of the two middle fingers, gently brought together, symbolize a coincidence of opposites. Some firm, gentle, androgynous style seemed to be indicated.

Further enlightenment came with Nietzsche's essay "Truth and Falsi-ty," in which he writes, "I'm afraid we are not rid of God because we still have faith in grammar."[2] Yes, I did feel answerable to that hatchet god—Jehovah, by whatever name—that god who stares down with his "thou shalts" writ in stone, a demonic parody of the creative imagination. Unaware of leaping, he keeps everything concrete and literal.

And then I read Carolyn Heilbrun's review of Lyndall Gordon's biography of Virginia Woolf. Heilbrun points out that Woolf was, like all women, trained to silence, that "the unlovable woman was always the woman who used words to effect. She was caricatured as a tattle, a scold, a shrew, a witch." Women felt "the pressure to relinquish language, and 'nice' women" were quiet.[3] She concludes that "muted by centuries of training, women writers especially have found that when they attempted truthfully to record their own lives, language failed."[4]

If that is true of the artist, it is no less true of any woman attempting to speak with her own voice. It is also true of the man who dares to articulate his soul process. The word "feminine," as I understand it, has very little to do with gender, nor is woman the custodian of femininity. Both men and women are searching for their pregnant virgin. She is the part of us who is outcast, the part who comes to consciousness through going into darkness, mining our leaden darkness, until we bring her silver out.

Anyone who tries to work creatively understands this. I remember, for example, when I was directing creative theater with high school students. We worked without a script for months before the show. Students who were trained to "give a good performance" found the process intolerable. Their rigidity, their fear of being "the hole in the program" blocked their creativity. They waited to be told what their lines were, what their moves had to be, what their attitudes should be. The quiet introverts who were accustomed to dropping into their own space had no difficulty concentrating until the images that sprang from their own bodies came alive. They loved being free. They loved to play. They loved to be challenged to go deeper into the darkness, to allow whatever wanted to happen to happen.

And things did happen. The whole theater came alive with roars, tears, laughter, movements of poignant beauty and hilarious irony. The curious visitors who ventured through the theater door shook their heads and fled from the chaos. But for those of us inside, it was contained chaos. We were used to the intensity. Two months before the show, the students, the dance director, the music director and I decided what movements we wanted to explore further, what poems, what music.[5] This basic skeleton was added to and subtracted from until the very last performance.

All of us involved, whether actors, directors or stagehands, were responsible for our own process. As our confidence grew, for example, our energies increased, and our student stage manager had to look within himself to find new ways of keeping discipline backstage without destroy-ing the fire. At the time, I had no conceptualized idea of what was going on. In retrospect, however, I see our theater as the womb of the Great Mother in which the virgin souls of the students came to birth in their own bodies and emerged to a level of psychological consciousness, confident enough and flexible enough to allow the wind of the spirit to blow through. Part of their process was to recognize in themselves and in each other whether their poem or dance was being allowed to live its own life or whether they were obstructing it with "a good performance."

What we were interested in was individual process, group process and eventually process between the audience and the cast. Since it was theater-in-the-round, the students usually seated their parents so that at some point in the program they would kneel two feet away and look them straight in the eye. More than one parent found the naked encounter with their own adult-child overwhelming, and struggled to choke back the unexpected tears.

What we were not interested in was product or external performance. In the Tostal, the theater, there was no examination, no predetermined goal, no such thing as failure except betrayal of the process. In other areas of the school we might undergo dismemberment—history student in Room 13, poor athlete in the gym, excellent flutist in the music room. Culturally, we might also be dismembered—smelly feet in the shoe store, myopic eyes at the optometrist's, armpits in the drugstore, acne at the doctor's. In that room, we took our bodies out of the culture that tinkered with its parts. There we could be whole. We came from our own place of vulnerability, and by staying with that vulnerability we perceived our own strength and our own wounds.

The Pregnant Virgin is coming from that same place. All my analysands are a part of this book. Together we have experienced death and rebirth, together we have analyzed hundreds of dreams. Many of the repetitive motifs introduced in my two earlier books are further developed here. While many of my analysands have eating disorders and hence struggle with some form of food addiction, their psychological framework has much in common with those who are addicted in other ways—to work, alcohol, drugs, sleep, futile relationships, etc. The soul material presented here, my analysands have generously agreed to share, in the hope that it will shed some light on emerging feminine consciousness. Knowing that others are on the same demanding journey seems to ease the load.

I, too, am on the journey. The process that goes on in the kitchen in chapter 1 is the same process that goes on in India in chapter 7, with one crucial difference. The butterfly on the curtain (page 13) is transforming according to the laws of nature; the butterfly on the ceiling (page 178) is transforming through the fire of conscious choice. And this book too is on the journey. Two of the chapters were originally written for lectures, two for journals, and the others are attempts to wrestle light out of darkness. Each one is a prism through which the difficulties of Becoming and Being may be looked at from different angles.

I have not yet solved the problem of frog conjunctions, but my frog is still laying eggs. I think she enjoys my syntactical pregnancy. Meanwhile, this is not an apology for a polliwog. It is a challenge to myself and my readers to listen with the heart, to hear the language that lives in the Silence as surely as it lives in the Word.

I am not a mechanism, an assembly of various sections.
And it is not because the mechanism is working wrongly, .
*   that I am ill.*
I am ill because of wounds to the soul, to the deep emotional
*   self*
and the wounds to the soul take a long, long time, only time
*   can help*
and patience, and a certain difficult repentance
long, difficult repentance, realisation of life's mistake, and
*   the freeing oneself*
from the endless repetition of the mistake
which mankind at large has chosen to sanctify.

—D.H. Lawrence, "Healing."

No bird soars too high, if he soars with his own wings.
Prisons are built with stones of Law, Brothels with bricks of religion.
Joys impregnate. Sorrows bring forth.
Always be ready to speak your mind, and a base man will avoid you.
The eagle never lost so much time as when he submitted to learn of the crow.
Expect poison from the standing water.
Damn braces. Bless relaxes.

If the doors of perception were cleansed every thing would appear to man as it is, infinite.
For man has closed himself up, till he sees all things thro' narrow chinks of his cavern.

The man who never alters his opinion is like standing water, & breeds reptiles of the mind.

—William Blake, from *The Marriage of Heaven and Hell.*

They and they only can acquire the philosophic imagination, the sacred power of self-intuition, who within themselves can interpret and understand the symbol that the wings of the air-sylph are forming within the skin of the caterpillar; these only who feel in their own spirits the same instinct which impels the chrysalis of the horned-fly to leave room in its involucrum for antennae yet to come. They know and feel that the potential works in them, even as the actual works on them.

—Samuel Taylor Coleridge, *Biographia Literaria.*

1

Chrysalis:

Am I Really?

Then Sunrise kissed my Chrysalis—
And I stood up—and lived—
                    —Emily Dickinson.

I was three years old when I made the most important psychological discovery of my life. I discovered that a living creature, obeying its own inner laws, moves through cycles of growth, dies, and is reborn as a new creation.

One day I was smoking my corncob bubble-pipe helping my father in the garden. I always enjoyed helping him because he understood bugs, and flowers, and where the wind came from. I found a lump stuck to a branch, and Father explained that Catherine Caterpillar had made a chrysalis for herself. We would take it inside and pin it on the kitchen curtain. One day a butterfly would emerge from that lump.

Well, I had seen magic in my father's garden, but this stretched even my imagination. However, we carefully stuck the big pins through the curtain, and every morning I grabbed my doll and pipe and ran downstairs to show them the butterfly. No butterfly! My father said I had to be patient. The chrysalis only looked dead. Remarkable changes were happening inside. A caterpillar's life was very different from a butterfly's, and they needed very different bodies. A caterpillar chewed solid leaves; a butterfly drank liquid nectar. A caterpillar was sexless, almost sightless, and landlocked; a butterfly laid eggs, could see and fly. Most of the caterpillar's organs would dissolve, and those fluids would help the tiny wings, eyes, muscles and brain of the developing butterfly to grow. But that was very hard work, so hard that the creature could accomplish nothing else so long as it was going on. It had to stay in that protective shell.

I waited for that sluggish glutton of a caterpillar to change into a delicate butterfly, but I secretly figured my father had made a mistake. Then one morning my doll and I were eating our shredded wheat when I sensed I was not alone in the kitchen. I stayed still. I felt a presence on the curtain. There it was, its wings still expanding, shimmering with translucent light—an angel who could fly. Its chrysalis was empty. That mystery on the kitchen curtain was my first encounter with death and rebirth.

13

Years later I discovered that the butterfly is a symbol of the human soul. I also discovered that in its first moments out of the chrysalis the butterfly voids a drop of excreta that has been accumulating during pupation. This drop is frequently red and sometimes voided during first flight. Consequently, a shower of butterflies may produce a shower of blood, a phenomenon that released terror and suspicion in earlier cultures, sometimes resulting in massacres. Symbolically, if we are to release our own butterfly, we too will sacrifice a drop of blood, let the past go and turn to the future.

It is the twilight zone between past and future that is the precarious world of transformation within the chrysalis. Part of us is looking back, yearning for the magic we have lost; part is glad to say good-bye to our chaotic past; part looks ahead with whatever courage we can muster; part is excited by the changing potential; part sits stone-still not daring to look either way. Individuals who consciously accept the chrysalis, whether in analysis or in life's experience, have accepted a life/death paradox, a paradox which returns in a different form at each new spiral of growth. In T.S. Eliot's "Journey of the Magi," one of the kings, having returned to his own country, describes his experience in Bethlehem:

> *... so we continued*
> *And arrived at evening, not a moment too soon*
> *Finding the place; it was (you may say) satisfactory.*
>
> *All this was a long time ago, I remember,*
> *And I would do it again, but set down*
> *This set down*
> *This: were we led all that way for*
> *Birth or Death? There was a Birth, certainly,*
> *We had evidence and no doubt. I had seen birth and death,*
> *But had thought they were different; this Birth was*
> *Hard and bitter agony for us, like Death, our death.*
> *We returned to our places, these Kingdoms,*
> *But no longer at ease here, in the old dispensation,*
> *With an alien people clutching their gods.*
> *I should be glad of another death.*[1]

If we accept this paradox, we are not torn to pieces by what seems to be intolerable contradiction. Birth is the death of the life we have known; death is the birth of the life we have yet to live. We need to hold the tensions and allow our circuit to give way to a larger circumference.

People splayed in a perpetual chrysalis, those who find life "weary, stale, flat and unprofitable"[2] or, to use the modern jargon, "boring," are in trouble. Stuck in a state of stasis, they clutch their childhood toys, divorce themselves from the reality of their present circumstances, and sit hoping for some magic that will release them from their pain into a world that is "just and good," a make-believe world of childhood innocence. Fearful of getting out of relationships that are stultifying their growth, fearful of confronting parents, partners or children who are maintaining infantile attitudes, they sink into chronic illness and/or psychic death. Life becomes a network of illusions and lies. Rather than take responsibility for what is happening, rather than accept the challenge of growth, they cling to the rigid framework that they have constructed or that has been assigned to them from birth. They attempt to stay "fixed." Such an attitude is against life, for change is a law of life. To remain fixed is to rot, particularly if it be in the Garden of Eden.

Why are we so afraid of change? Why, when we are so desperate for change, do we become even more desperate when transformation begins? Why do we lose our childhood faith in growing? Why do we cling to old attachments instead of submitting ourselves to new possibilities—to the undiscovered worlds in our own bodies, minds and souls? We plant our fat amaryllis bulb. We water it, give it sunlight, watch the first green shoot, the rapidly growing stock, the buds, and then marvel at the great bell flowers tolling their hallelujahs to the snow outside. Why should we have more faith in an amaryllis bulb than in ourselves? Is it because we know that the amaryllis is living by some inner law—a law that we have lost touch with in ourselves? If we can allow ourselves time to listen to the amaryllis, we can resonate with its silence. We can experience its eternal stillness. We can find ourselves at the heart of the mystery. And in that place, the place of the Goddess, we can accept birth and death. The exquisite blossom will die, but if the bulb is given rest and darkness, another bloom will come next year.

Insecurity lies at the heart of the fear of change. Individuals who recognize their own worth among those they love can leave and return without fear of separation. They know they are valued for themselves. Our computerized society, fascinating and efficient as it is, is making deeper and deeper inroads into genuine human values. A machine, however intricate, has no soul, nor does it move with the rhythms of instinct. A computer may be able to vomit out the facts of my existence, but it cannot fathom the subterranean corridors of my aloneness, nor can it hear my silence, nor can it respond to the shadow that passes over my eyes. It cannot compute the depth and breadth and height of the human soul. When society deliberately programs itself to a set of norms that has very little to do with instinct, love or privacy, then people who set out to become individuals, trusting in the dignity of their own soul and the creativity of their own imagination, have good reason to be afraid. They are outcasts, cut off from society and to a greater or lesser degree from their own instincts. As they work in the silence of their cocoon, they often think they are crazy. They also think they would be crazier if they gave up their faith in their own journey. Like the chrysalis pinned to the kitchen curtain, Blake's proverb is pinned to their study wall: "If a fool would persist in his folly, he would become wise."[3]

Courage to stand alone, to wear the "white plume" of freedom,[4] has been the mark of the hero in any society. Standing alone today demands even more courage and strength than it did in former cultures. From infancy, children have been programmed to perform. Rather than living from their own needs and feelings, they learn to assess situations in order to please others. Without an inner core of certainty grounded in their own musculature, they lack the inner resources to stand alone. Pummelled by mass media and peer group pressures, their identity may be utterly absorbed by collective stereotypes. In the absence of adequate rites of passage, ad-men become the high priests of an initiation into the addictions of consumerism. Everywhere the ceremony of innocence is exploited.

Without recognized rites, members of a society are not sure who they are within the structure. Children who have fumbled their way through puberty find themselves in adolescence raging for independence, at the same time furious when asked to take responsibility. Boys who have never been separated from their mothers and are fearful of their fathers cannot make the step into adult manhood. Girls who have lived in the service of their driving masculine energies are not going to forsake their P.P.F.F. (Prestige, Power, Fame and Fortune) for a sense of harmony with the cosmos. Even the rites of marriage are confusing. Unwed couples who have lived together for years may eventually believe that "marriage isn't going to make any difference," and then be genuinely confused when sexual difficulties do develop after the vows are spoken. Arriving at middle age is agony for those who cannot accept the mature beauty of autumn. They see their wrinkles hardening into lines, and new liver spots appearing every day, without the compensating mellowing in their soul. Without the rites of the elders, they cannot look forward to holding a position of honor in their society, nor in most cases will they treasure their own wisdom. For some, even the dignity of death dare not be contemplated.

The undercurrent of despair in our society is epitomized in a German word that first appeared in English in 1963, and is now incorporated into the Oxford English Dictionary (Supplement, 1985). It is *torschlusspanik*, (pronounced tor-shluss-panic), defined as "panic at the thought that a door between oneself and life's opportunities has shut." Words enter a language when they are needed, and *torschlusspanik* has arrived. The doors that were once opened through initiation rites are still crucial thresholds in the human psyche, and when those doors do not open, or when they are not recognized for what they are, life shrinks into a series of rejections fraught with *torschlusspanik*: the graduation formal to which the girl was not invited; the marriage that did not take place; the baby that was never born; the job that never materialized. Looking back, we recognize that it was often not our choice that determined which door opened and which door shut. We were chosen for this, rejected for that.

Torschlusspanik is now a part of our culture because there are so few rites to which individuals will submit in order to transcend their own selfish drives. Without the broader perspective, they see no meaning in the rejection. The door thuds, leaving them bitter or resigned. If, instead, they could temper themselves to a point of total concentration, a bursting point where they could either pass over or fall back as in a rite of passage, then they could test who they are. Their passion would be spent in an all-out positive effort, instead of deteriorating into disillusionment and despair. The terror behind that word *torschlusspanik* is what drives many people into analysis—the last door has shut, the last rejection has taken place. No door will ever open again. Nothing means anything.

Another reason for fearing the chrysalis lies in our cultural loss of containers. Our society's emphasis on linear growth and achievement alienates us from the cyclic pattern of death and rebirth, so that when we experience ourselves dying, or dream that we are, we fear annihilation. Primitive societies are close enough to the natural cycles of their lives to provide the containers through which the members of the tribe can experience death and rebirth as they pass through the difficult transitions. To quote from the classic *Rites of Passage* by Arnold van Gannep:

> In such societies every change in a person's life involves actions and reactions between sacred and profane—actions and reactions to be regulated and guarded so that society as a whole will suffer no discomfort or injury. Transitions from group to group and from one social situation to the next are looked on as implicit in the very fact of existence, so that a man's life comes to be made up of a succession of stages with similar ends and beginnings: birth, social puberty, marriage, fatherhood, advancement to a higher class, occupational specialization, and death. For every one of these events there are ceremonies whose essential purpose is to enable the individual to pass from one defined position to another which is equally well defined. ... In this respect man's life resembles nature, from which neither the individual nor the society stands independent.[5]

Through their initiation, for example, boys are recognized as responsible adult men. They are cut off from their mothers, trained as warriors, instructed in the culture of their tribe.

For girls, the meaning of puberty rites is somewhat different. Here I quote from Bruce Lincoln's *Emerging from the Chrysalis*:

> Rather than changing women's status, initiation changes their fundamental being, addressing ontological concerns rather than hierarchical ones.

A woman does not become more powerful or authoritative, but more creative, more alive, more ontologically real. ... The pattern of female initiation is thus one of growth or magnification, an expansion of powers, capabilities, experiences. This magnification is accomplished by gradually endowing the initiand with symbolic items that make of her a woman, and beyond this a cosmic being. These items can be concrete, such as clothing or jewelry, or they can be nonmaterial in nature, such as songs chanted for the woman-to-be, myths repeated in her presence, scars or paintings placed upon her body.[6]

The scarification is meant to provide an experience of intense pain and an enduring record of that pain. The person is rendered unique. Through this magnification, the woman "steps into the cosmic arena: she is given the water of life, with which she nourishes the cosmic tree."[7]

Such primitive rituals did not change the way people lived. They gave meaning to life. By means of ritual, relationship to the unchanging, archetypal aspects of existence was affirmed and renewed. What would otherwise have been boring drudgery or *torschlusspanik* was invested with a meaning that transcended animal survival. Through ritual, human activity was connected to the divine.

In more sophisticated societies, the church and the theater became ritual containers. Within the safety and the confines of the Mass, for instance, the individual could surrender to God and experience dismem-

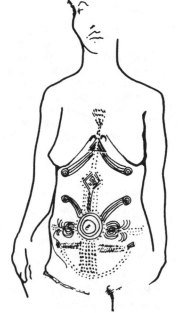

Ritual scarification (from Bruce Lincoln, *Emerging from the Chrysalis*).

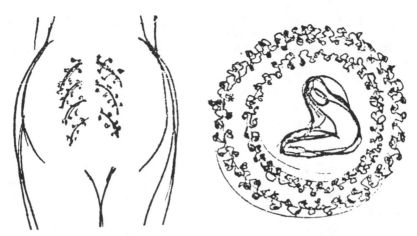

Woman's drawings of dream images, showing "healed wound-welts" on her belly, with little berries of flesh hanging from the wound (*left*). In the dream the berries transformed into wreaths of flowers forming a double circle around a kneeling woman (*right*). The fruit of the wounding has transformed into the protective love of the Goddess, symbolized in the flowering mandalas. (The dream initiated the woman's acceptance of her body, and she subsequently studied dancing.)

berment and death, descent into Hell and resurrection of the spirit on the third day. One could experience the magnification of one's own spirit by experiencing oneself as sacrificer and sacrificed. Like the primitive, the participant left the ritual with enhanced meaning, with a profound sense of belonging to a cosmos and to a community that respected that cosmos.

The theater also provided a ritual container, a public chrysalis. The plays dealt with archetypal realities. On the stage, men and women saw their own psychological depths enacted and were thus encouraged to reflect on their own human situation.

We have lost our containers; chaos threatens. Without rituals to make a firm demarcation between the profane and the sacred, between what is us and what is not us, we tend to identify with archetypal patterns of being—hero, Father, Mother, etc. We forget that we are individual human beings; we allow ourselves to be inflated by the power of the unconscious and usurp it for our own. And we do this not knowing what we do and that we do it. Liberated from the "superstitious" belief in gods and demons, we claim for ourselves the power once attributed to them. We do not realize we have usurped or stolen it. How then do we explain our anxiety and dissatisfaction? Power makes us fearful; lack of it makes us anxious. Few are satisfied with what they have. Despite our so-called liberation from gods and demons, few can live without them. Their absence makes nothing better. It may even make everything worse.

If, for example, a child has acted as buffer between his parents, he may fear his home will disintegrate if he ceases to act as intermediary. Without realizing it, he has assumed the power of the savior in his small world. When as an adult his boundaries are widened, he will tend to take on that archetypal role wherever he goes. He will also suffer guilt when he fails. He may even suffer guilt for being unable to make it snow when his family has planned a skiing weekend. Such hubris is seen as ludicrous once it is brought to consciousness, but, without consciousness, depression and despair fester inside. "I should have been able to do something. I failed." Instead of leaving other people's destiny to them and accepting his own, he attempts to take responsibility for Fate and feels inadequate when the door thuds. The resulting guilt can quickly switch to rage, rage that resonates back to the powerless childhood. "What do you expect of me? I can't do it. Get off my back. Carry your own load. LEAVE ME ALONE."

Many people, for example, think life is a meaningless merry-go-round if they are not being transported by love like Prince Charles and Lady Diana, or living for a cause like Mother Theresa, or dying for a dream like Martin Luther King. They measure their standard of behavior by comparison with figures who carry immense archetypal projections—Marilyn Monroe, John F. Kennedy, Michael Jackson. A mask ceases to be a mask. Instead, with the help of dyes and surgery, the mask becomes the face. Cosmetics are identity or character or Fate. By identifying with an archetype instead of remaining detached from it, they turn life into theater and themselves into actors on a stage, thus falling prey to demonic as well as angelic inflation. Without the container, they confuse the sacred and profane worlds.

We are the descendants of Freud and Jung, and while poets and madmen had free access to their unconscious before those two giants, the world of the archetype is now an open market for the general populace without any ritual containment. If we are blindly living out an archetype, we are not containing our own life. We are possessed, and possession acts as a magnet on unconscious people in our environment. Everyday life becomes a dangerous world where illusion and reality can be fatally confused.

A life that is being truly lived is constantly burning away the veils of illusion, gradually revealing the essence of the individual. Psychoanalysis can speed up that process. Sometimes people experience themselves as caterpillars crawling along. Externally, everything seems fine. Some deep intuitive voice, however, may be whispering, "It's not worth it. There's nobody here. I need a cocoon. I need to go back and find myself." Now, they may not quite realize that when caterpillars go into cocoons, they

What is Man!
The Suns Light when he unfolds it
Depends on the Organ that beholds it.
(William Blake, frontispiece for
The Gates of Paradise)

do not emerge as high-class caterpillars, and they may not be prepared for the agony of the transformation that goes on inside the chrysalis. Nor are they quite prepared for the winged beauty that slowly and painfully emerges, that lives by a very different set of laws than a caterpillar. Even more confounding is the fact that friends and relations who may be quite happy caterpillars have no patience with a silent, hard-edged chrysalis that is all turned in on itself—"selfish, lazy, self-indulgent." And they have even less patience with a confused butterfly who hasn't adjusted to the laws of aerodynamics.

Still, it is amazing how often other caterpillars, inspired by butterflies, sacrifice their landlubber condition, make their own chrysalis and find their own wings. Jung writes that coming to consciousness is "the sacrifice of the merely natural man, of the unconscious, ingenuous being whose tragic career began with the eating of the apple in Paradise."[8]

The chrysalis is essential if we are to find ourselves. Yet very little in our extroverted society supports introverted withdrawal. We are supposed to be doers, taking care of others, supporting good causes, unselfish, energetic, doing our social duty. If we choose to simply *be*, our loved ones may automatically assume we are doing nothing, and at first we may feel that way ourselves. We begin to look at our primeval muck as it surfaces in dreams. All hell starts to break loose inside, and we wonder what's the point of dredging up all this stuff. We argue with ourselves: "I should be out there doing something useful. But the truth is I can't do anything useful if there's no *I* to do it. I can't love anyone else, if there's no I to do the loving. If I don't know myself, I cannot love myself, and if I do not love myself, my love of others is probably my projected need of their acceptance. I am putting on a performance in order to be loved. I fear rejection. If nobody loves me, I won't exist. But who are they loving? Who am I?"

That is what going into the chrysalis is all about—undergoing a metamorphosis in order one day to be able to stand up and say *I am*. The gnawing hunger, the incessant yearning at the core of many lives, began at birth, or perhaps even *in utero*. In order to survive in a demanding environment where one or both parents projected their un-lived dreams (or nightmares) onto their children, the infants gave up trying to live their own lives. As little human beings with needs and feelings of their own, they were rejected. Their mystery was never considered, and so they grew up automatically thinking in terms of other people's response. In other words, they developed a charming persona, a mask they created with infinite care—a mask that, as adults, may be at once their greatest blessing and greatest curse. Outwardly they may be brilliantly successful, but inwardly empty. They cannot understand why their intimate relationships repeatedly end in disaster, a pattern they recognize but can do nothing to stop. They dream they are actors, the spotlight is on them, but they cannot remember what play they are in, let alone what their lines are. If their ego is barely formed, they may not even appear in their own dreams, or may recognize themselves as objects or little animals.

It is important to point out, however, that we all need several personas, that is, the right mask for the right occasion. Jung was once lecturing on the topic when a student accused him of being hypocritical if he used a persona. Jung said that he had just had a fight with his wife, and he was still angry, but that anger had nothing to do with the students, nor with their reason for getting themselves to the Institute that morning. It was neither fair to himself nor to them to show that anger there. However, he said, he intended to finish the fight when he went home. The point is that we must be conscious enough to know when we are using a persona and for what reason. Otherwise we easily identify with a particular persona, which obliges us to repress our genuine feelings and prevents us from acting on them at the right time and place. The persona is necessary because people at different levels of consciousness respond to a situation with very different antennae. Naively or deliberately, making oneself vulnerable to psychic wounding without good reason is foolish. To be wary of casting pearls before swine is not conceit but plain common sense.

As the transformation process goes on, pregnancies and new-born babies frequently appear in dreams. When the conscious ego is able to release repressed psychic energy, or reconnects with unconscious body energy, or makes a decision on its own behalf, that new energy is symbolized as new life. When the psyche is preparing to move onto a new level of awareness, or one's conscious attitude has made a new connection with the unconscious, then dreams may appear where the dream ego, the shadow or the anima is pregnant. Nine months later, so long as the process has not been aborted, there are often dreams of crossing borders, passing over into a new country, moving through subterranean tunnels or actually giving birth (see below, page 158). If the ego maintains the connection, the new-born child is nurtured with soul food. If the ego falters and fails to act on the new energy, the baby may appear mutilated, starving or dead. Or it may simply disappear.

I have found that individuals tend to repeat the pattern of their own actual birth every time life requires them to move onto a new level of awareness. As they entered the world, so they continue to re-enter at each new spiral of growth. If, for example, their birth was straightforward, they tend to handle passovers with courage and natural trust. If their birth was difficult, they become extremely fearful, manifest symptoms of suffocating, become claustrophobic (psychically and physically). If they were premature, they tend to be always a little ahead of themselves. If they were held back, the rebirth process may be very slow. If they were breech-birth, they tend to go through life "ass-backwards." If they were born by Caesarian section, they may avoid confrontations. If their mother was heavily drugged, they may come up to the point of passover with lots of energy, then suddenly, for no apparent reason, stop, or move into a regression, and wait for someone else to do something. Often this is the point where addictions reappear—binging, starving, drinking, sleeping, overworking—anything to avoid facing the reality of moving out into a challenging world.

Many delightful babies appear in dreams, and just as many little tyrants who need firm and loving discipline. One child, however, is noticeably different from the others. This is the abandoned one, who may appear in bullrushes, in straw in a barn, in a tree, almost always in some forgotten or out-of-the-way place. This child will be radiant with light, robust, intelligent, sensitive. Often it is able to talk minutes after it is born. It has Presence. It is the Divine Child, bringing with it the "hard and bitter agony" of the new dispensation—the agony of Eliot's Magi. With its birth, the old gods have to go.

Since the natural gradient of the psyche is toward wholeness, the Self will attempt to push the neglected part forward for recognition. It contains energy of the highest value, the gold in the dung. In the Bible it is the stone that was rejected that becomes the cornerstone.[9] It manifests either in a sudden or subtle change in personality, or, conversely, in a fanaticism which the existing ego adopts in order to try to keep the new and threatening energy out. If the ego fails to go through the psychic birth canal, neurotic symptoms manifest physically and psychically. The suffering may be intense, but it is based on worshipping false gods. It is not the genuine suffering that accompanies efforts to incorporate the new life. The neurotic is always one phase behind where his reality is. When he should be outgrowing childish behavior, he hangs onto it. When he should be moving into maturity, he hangs onto youthful folly. Never congruent with himself or others, he is never where he seems to be. What he cannot do is live in the *now*.

Many people are being dragged toward wholeness in their daily lives, but because they do not understand initiation rites, they cannot make sense of what is happening to them. They put on a happy face all day, and return to their apartment and cry all night. Perhaps their beloved has gone off with someone else; perhaps their business has failed; perhaps they have lost interest in their work; perhaps they are coping with a fatal illness; perhaps a loved one has died. Perhaps, and this is worst of all, everything has begun to go wrong for no apparent reason. If they have no concept of rites of passage, they experience themselves as victims, powerless to resist an overwhelming Fate. Their meaningless suffering drives them to escape through food, alcohol, drugs, sex. Or they take up arms against the gods and cry out, "Why me?"

They are being presented with the possibility of rebirth into a different life. Through failures, symptoms, inferiority feelings and overwhelming problems, they are being prodded to renounce life attachments that have become redundant. The possibility of rebirth constellates with the breakdown of what has gone before. That is why Jung emphasized the positive purpose of neurosis.[10] But because they do not understand, people cling to the familiar, refuse to make the necessary sacrifices, resist their own growth. Unable to give up their habitual lives, they are unable to receive new life.

Unless cultural rituals support the leap from one level of consciousness to another, there are no containing walls within which the process can happen. Without an understanding of myth or religion, without an understanding of the relationship between destruction and creation, death and rebirth, the individual suffers the mysteries of life as meaningless mayhem—alone. To ease the meaningless suffering, addictions may develop that are an attempt to repress the confusing demands of the growth process which cultural structures no longer clarify or contain.

The burning question when one enters analysis is "Who am I?" The immediate problem, however, as soon as powerful emotions begin to surface, is often a psyche/soma split. While women tend to talk about their bodies more than men, both sexes in our culture are grievously unrelated to their own body experience. Women say, "I don't like this body"; men say, "It hurts." Their use of the third-person neuter pronoun in referring to their body makes quite clear their sense of alienation. They may talk about "my heart," "my kidneys," "my feet," but their body as a whole is depersonalized. Repeatedly they say, "I don't feel anything below the neck. I experience feelings in my head, but nothing in my heart." Their lack of emotional response to a powerful dream image reflects the split. And yet, when they engage in active imagination with that dream image located in their body, their muscles release undulations of repressed grief. The body has become the whipping post. If the person is anxious, the body is starved, gorged, drugged, intoxicated, forced to vomit, driven into exhaustion or driven to frenzied reaction against self-destruction. When this magnificent animal attempts to send up warning signals, it is silenced with pills.

Many people can listen to their cat more intelligently than they can listen to their own despised body. Because they attend to their pet in a cherishing way, it returns their love. Their body, however, may have to let out an earth-shattering scream in order to be heard at all. Before symptoms manifest, quieter screams appear in dreams: a forsaken baby elephant, a starving kitten, a dog with a leg ripped out. Almost always the wounded animal is either gently or fiercely attempting to attract the attention of the dreamer, who may or may not respond. In fairytales it is the friendly animal who often carries the hero or heroine to the goal because the animal is the instinct that knows how to obey the Goddess when reason fails.

It is possible that the scream that comes from the forsaken body, the scream that manifests in a symptom, is the cry of the soul that can find no other way to be heard. If we have lived behind a mask all our lives, sooner or later—if we are lucky that mask will be smashed. Then we will have to look in our own mirror at our own reality. Perhaps we will be appalled. Perhaps we will look into the terrified eyes of our own tiny child, that child who has never known love and who now beseeches us to respond. This child is alone, forsaken before we left the womb, or at birth, or when we began to please our parents and learned to put on our best performance in order to be accepted. As life progresses, we may continue to abandon our child by pleasing others —teachers, professors, bosses, friends and partners, even analysts. That child who is our very *soul* cries out from underneath the rubble of our lives, often from the core of our worst complex, begging us to say, "You are not alone. I love you."

We dare not drop the tensions. In order to widen consciousness, we have to hold both arms on the cross. If we reject one part of ourselves, we give up our past; if we reject the other part, we give up our future. We must hold onto our roots and build from there. Those roots often appear as a psychic home sometimes a summer cottage that the dreamer loves, or the country of his origin, or his ancestors' origin. The longing to go Home must certainly be looked at symbolically, for it is often more than a regressive longing for the security of the womb. It can be the one solid root that goes right through one's life, becoming the point of genuine nurturance for spiritual growth.

Whether we like it or not, one of our tasks on this earth is to work with the opposites through different levels of consciousness until body, soul and spirit resonate together. Initiation rites, experienced at the appropriate times in our lives, burn off what is no longer relevant, opening our eyes to new possibilities of our own uniqueness. They tear off the protective veils of illusion until at last we are strong enough to stand in our own naked truth.

The process is mirrored in dreams, often in images of cooking, cars, cupboards and clothes. The Cinderella work is accomplished in the kitchen. Having brought the wild things of nature in, taken off their feathers, cleaned out their entrails, cooked them and made them accessible to consciousness, the ego stands firm. Mother and Father no longer drive the car. The incessant sorting through actual cupboards and drawers has ceased, and the sorting in dreams has reached a finely differentiated level of detail. What clothes to wear is no longer a constant frustration, and the incongruous shoe combinations have at last settled into pairs that are the same color with the same size heel. Or maybe no shoes at all—just good solid feet on good solid ground. Usually the Self allows the ego time to enjoy this period of experiencing its new strength—perhaps months, perhaps years. Each process is unique, moving at its own appointed pace.

The existence and continuity of the ego is essential to our lives. It is necessary that we experience the person who wakes up in the morning as the same person who fell asleep last night, despite the fact that what took place during the hours of sleep may appear so unrelated to the waking state that it never enters consciousness. One way in which the ego maintains its integrity is to remove from itself everything that does not directly offer it support. It simply excludes or suppresses everything which does not coincide with its conscious understanding of itself.

The danger in such a limited view is that the ego may harden and dry up, just as the earth will harden and dry up if it is not continually replenished with water. The ego needs the nourishment of underground springs. It requires the compensatory life of dreams if its continuity is to move beyond mere survival and perpetuation. In addition to these, it requires direction and purpose. As soon as it gives itself up to a higher goal, however, it is threatened, not only by the fear that it may not be able to achieve it, but by a dawning sense that that higher goal, because of the demands it makes, is the enemy of the ego. In some sense, the ego feels that it may be working against itself. Ultimately, of course, it is, but for a better good.

The goal of human striving in the individuation process is the recognition of the Self, the regulating center of the psyche. That recognition relativizes the ego's position in the psychic structure, and initiates a dialogue between conscious and unconscious. "The only way the Self can manifest is through conflict," writes Marie-Louise von Franz. "To meet one's insoluble and eternal conflict is to meet God, which would be the end of the ego with all its blather."[11]

If the ego rejects that conflict, then the goal is contaminated by the ego's desire for more and more power, or wealth, or happiness. The result is ego inflation. According to Jung:

> An inflated consciousness is always egocentric and conscious of nothing but its own existence. It is incapable of learning from the past, incapable of understanding contemporary events, and incapable of drawing right conclusions about the future. It is hypnotized by itself and therefore cannot be argued with. It inevitably dooms itself to calamities that must strike it dead.
>
> Paradoxically enough, inflation is a regression of consciousness into unconsciousness. This always happens when consciousness takes too many unconscious contents upon itself and loses the faculty of discrimination, the *sine qua non* of all consciousness.[12]

The inflated ego tends to idolatry. It focuses on a single image, fashions it and worships it. Determined to create that image, it is trapped in profane ritual.

Religiously speaking, all such profane rituals are contained in the worship of the Golden Calf. A fat woman's body image, for example, may be her Golden Calf. No matter how much she thinks she hates it, her rituals are taking place around it. It is this thralldom before her own body image that she may be called upon to sacrifice. The profane worship must be sacrificed to make way for the sacred. The withdrawal from the one operates simultaneously with the entrance into the other. We withdraw as we enter. Withdrawing is entering. Whether we stress the withdrawing or the entering, we are stressing the same thing.

When this process begins, it may be reflected in the dreams by a bell tolling, an alarm sounding or lightning striking. It can also be heralded by physical symptoms. It can be brought on by loss of faith, loss of relationship or the imminence of death. Something almost imperceptible begins to happen. For people watching their dreams, the bell usually tolls some weeks before the actual events occur. In real life we seem to be carrying on as usual, but a very clear inner voice may begin to comment, hinting that things are not as they seem to be. We may find ourselves singing songs that put a very ironic twist on our conscious actions. Our inner clown may be singing, "Put your sweet lips a little closer," to the tune of "Please release me and let me go." If the ego has not sufficient strength and flexibility, it will panic and either regress to its former terrors of annihilation, or regress to its former rigid framework—in either case, refusing to go through the birth canal.

The ego now has to be strong enough to remain concentrated in stillness, so that it can mediate what is happening both positively and negatively. It must hold a detached position, relying now on its differentiated femininity in order to submit, now on its discriminating masculinity in order to question and cut away. Something immense begins to happen in the very foundation of the personality, while consciousness experiences the conflict as crucifixion. Ego desires are no longer relevant. The old questions no longer have any meaning, and there are no answers. There may be a few stricken "why's," but they belong to the order of logic and discipline, and what is taking place is irrational, beyond ego control. The ego on some level knows. It knows that what is happening has to happen. It knows that its personal desires have to be sacrificed to the transpersonal. It knows it is confronting death.

It is a period of throbbing pain. It is King Lear howling on the heath, brought to submission and reunited with the daughter whose truth was her dowry. At last, he says,

> *Upon such sacrifices, my Cordelia,*
> *The Gods themselves throw incense.*[13]

It is Job covered with boils, moving from "Do not condemn me; shew me wherefore thou contendest with me" to "I have heard of thee by the hearing of the ear: but now mine eye seeth thee."[14]

It is Jesus in Gethsemane, sweating blood, moving from "Let this cup pass from me" to "Thy will be done."[15]

A woman during such a period of withdrawal and entry had the following vision:

> I was walking by the St. Lawrence one sunny, summer day. I thought I was going Home. Instantly the sky darkened; the earth grew cold. I could not see with my eyes, nor hear with my ears. I was seeing inside, hearing inside. Then I realized I was on ice, floating, suddenly not floating, but being thrust by the power of the current. The ice began to crack. I leaped from one floe to another, the ice cracking in front, behind, beside. I thought I might die in the ice-cold water, or be ground by the grating blocks. And all the time I knew I was being propelled toward the ocean. I just kept jumping and screaming, "Please, God, don't kill me. Not yet. Not this time."

At times like this, Rilke's words can be very reassuring:

> Be patient toward all that is unsolved in your heart and ... try to love the *questions themselves* like locked rooms and like books that are

The Agony in the Garden by William Blake. (Tate Gallery, London)

written in a very foreign tongue. Do not now seek the answers, which cannot be given you because you would not be able to live them. And the point is, to live everything. *Live* the questions now. Perhaps you will then gradually, without noticing it, live along some distant day into the answer.[16]

These situations, whether in analysis or in life, or both, can raise profound religious questions. Is this God confronting me? Was I on the wrong track? Am I being forcibly turned around? Is there some almighty plan that is different from mine? Am I being forced to submit? Should I accept Fate? Do I, in fact, have *any* free will? Is this God burning away the veils of illusion, or am I facing the devil? Is he making one last stand to cheat me out of my own life?

Psychologically, the questions are equally blistering. Is this the Self demanding a sacrifice? Or is this the real face of the complex that has crippled me all my life? Just when I thought I could be free, there it is to destroy me. Everything I have fought so hard to bring to consciousness is now in question. Why do I suddenly wake up every night at the same time? Why do I feel this searing pain? Why are my hands so weak? Am I really *alone*? I'm worse off now than I ever was. I'm back in the old pattern. I'm back in the matrix—back in the Garden recognizing the place for the first time. Is this who I really am? Is this who I have been running away from all my life?

Psychologically, the ego, like Lear, Job and Jesus, is penetrating and being penetrated by the archetypal Ground of Being in an effort to bring to consciousness whatever it can of that vast unknown. It experiences another law operating from within, a dawning realization that it has a destiny of its own which must be obeyed. It knows that something new is being born; it has to breathe into the pain and let it be.

Many people in our culture are attempting to suffer these transformations alone, without any ritual container and without any group to support the influx of transcendent power. Like Eliot's Magi, they experience the birth as "hard and bitter agony ... like Death, our death." They are "no longer at ease here, in the old dispensation,/With an alien people clutching their gods."

Without the container and without the group, the aloneness is almost intolerable. The individual ego has to be strong enough to build its own chrysalis in order to create a loving communication with its own inner symbols. Their numinosity brings the confidence and integrity, humor and illumination without which the ego could not survive, let alone expand. A child*ish* ego, primitive and unconscious, cannot maintain a living chrysalis; it wants to project everything, and, tuned to a natural order, it explains what happens by magic. The chrysalis becomes too precious in itself, shellacked with sentimentality. A child*like* ego can hold the tension, pull in the projections and ponder the inner mystery. At the transpersonal level, the symbols are simultaneously individual and universal. At that level, none of us is alone. New relationships, bypassing the world of transitory disguise, begin at that depth, and from there relate back to the world in a totally new way.

Hours before he died, Thomas Merton, author of *The Seven Storey Mountain*, gave a lecture which concluded with a plea for openness to the "painfulness of inner change":

> What is essential ... is not embedded in buildings, is not embedded in clothing, is not necessarily embedded even in a rule. It is somewhere along the line of something deeper than a rule. It is concerned with this business of total inner transformation.[17]

According to his own account, Merton completed his inner transformation on his Asian journey standing barefoot in the presence of the giant Buddhas of Polonnaruwa in Ceylon. "I know and have seen what I was obscurely looking for," he wrote. "I don't know what else remains but I have now seen and have pierced through the surface and have got beyond the shadow and the disguise."[18]

When Merton asked a Buddhist abbot, "What is the 'knowledge of freedom'?" the abbot replied, "One must ascend all the steps, but then when there are no more steps one must make the leap. Knowledge of freedom is the knowledge, the experience, of this leap."[19]

Voices from the Chrysalis

It's hard for me to trust life. I like to take hold of it, grab it by the neck and put my teeth into it, just to be sure it doesn't get away on me.

I try to see how far I've come, rather than how far I have to go.

Now that I'm contacting my own inner clock, I am so slow. My life is on top of me. The collision of values overwhelms me. Am I wasting my time? I don't know. ... I don't know. ... this terrible aloneness.

I've always identified with what I'm not. But who am I? My guilt and shame and fear are making me human.

I was always waiting until all the responsibilities were completed, then there would be time for me. How? I never thought about that. I've been so busy *doing*, I've missed something very important to me. I don't think I was ever a child. I have no recollection at all of being a very young child with any sense of being ME.

I wonder if it takes a holocaust, outer or inner, to help us to realize what is really essential in life.

I lived a smile-and-grin, smile-and-grin existence. I was dying.

I rage for life. I want so much to be free.

I'm trying to have faith—faith that I will be born.

I'm so off balance. I pray for daily guidance to avoid tripping over things. I can go to sleep when I orient myself to the stars.

The spirit is in the volcano inside. My relationships aren't very good right now, so I go back to work. I'm safe there. But even that isn't perfect.

I'll explode if I have to react to one more thing. I'm pulling back. I'm overwhelmed by the pressures of the outside world and the mounting pressures of the interior world are making me feel actually sick.

Used to feel capable, used to speak and write well. Now I never feel secure because I can't find words.

Am I fighting my destiny or does my destiny require I take a stand?

When I touch into that essence and recognize myself as what I've been running away from, I am humbled.

I'm Miss Compassion, Miss Humanity. I'm a missing piece. I'm also a child of God.

To get rid of one's past one has to forgive —confront and forgive—and move into the present. Forgive oneself too, and God.

I hated my father. I imitated him so I knew I hated myself.

Illustration by Barbara Swan for Anne Sexton's "Sleeping Beauty," from *Transformations* (Boston: Houghton Mifflin Company, 1971).

2

"Taking it Like a Man":

Abandonment in the Creative Woman

Each night I am nailed into place
and forget who I am.
Daddy?
That's another kind of prison.
—Anne Sexton, "Sleeping Beauty."

For many women born and reared in a patriarchal culture, initiation into mature womanhood occurs through abandonment, actual or psychological. It is the identity-conferring experience that frees them from the father.

Some women can accept their destiny in a traditional, patriarchal relationship, finding within its obvious limitations—social, intellectual, spiritual—compensations that are important to them. Others who accept that destiny but nevertheless resist its limitations are forced for financial, political or social reasons to stay within its framework.

However, an increasing number of women whose psychic center has always radiated around the father, real or imagined, are determined to go through the initiation. These women are by inner necessity creators in the Keatsian sense of "soul-makers";[1] that is, their quest for meaning drives them to find their own inner story. They reject collective masculine values as an intrusive imposition, but their search for a personal identity from within almost inevitably brings them into collision with the very forces they are struggling to integrate. In the effort to liberate themselves from the very real restrictions of a patriarchal culture, they ironically, even at a highly conscious level, tend to become its victims. The internal father, who in the soul-making process they sought to please, turns on them—or appears to—as soon as that father-image is projected onto a man, or they seek recognition and reward in those creative fields still largely dominated by men.

While this situation is now changing, there is still a long way to go. The psychic dynamics involved in the change are still far from understood. Men and woman caught up in those dynamics, and even consciously committed to so-called enlightened relationships, are still not getting through to each other despite their heroic efforts to do so, efforts that refuse to admit failure even when failure is all they experience. This can become vividly clear in the analytic relationship, often a microcosm of what is happening on the cultural level.

33

The word abandonment comes from the Old English verb *bannan*, meaning "to summon" (O.E.D.). To be among those summoned was to relinquish oneself to service. Abandonment means literally "to be un-called," symbolically "to be without a destiny." If one's destiny has been dictated by the father, however, then to be uncalled may be a blessing rather than a curse. Free of the father, the daughter may then truly *abandon herself* to the process of her own soul-making. This rite of passage contains within itself the double meaning of abandonment. Emily Dickinson sums this up in her usual elliptical style:

> *I'm ceded—I've stopped being Theirs—*
> *The name They dropped upon my face*
> *With water, in the country church*
> *Is finished using, now,*
> *And They can put it with my Dolls,*
> *My childhood, and the string of spools,*
> *I've finished threading—too—*
>
> *Baptized, before, without the choice,*
> *But this time, consciously, of Grace—*
> *Unto supremest name—*
> *Called to my Full—The Crescent dropped—*
> *Existence's whole Arc, filled up,*
> *With one small Diadem.*
>
> *My second Rank—too small the first—*
> *Crowned—Crowing—on my Father's breast—*
> *A half unconscious Queen—*
> *But this time—Adequate—Erect,*
> *With Will to choose, or to reject,*
> *And I choose, just a Crown—*[2]

The "half unconscious Queen," as I see her, is bonded, for better or for worse, to her creative imagination, a situation that originated in the psychological bonding to her father. Even in childhood such a woman is outside the ban (i.e., calling) that contains other children. In adolescence, while her sisters are conspiring about bangles, babies and bans of marriage, she is banished by her own decree. Her creativity is of a different nature: plays, canvasses, sonatas or chemical experiments. On some level she always feels banned from life and yearns for what other people take for granted. Yet while part of her feels abandoned, part of her knows that were she to forsake her own creativity she would be abandoning her own soul.

Many variables are involved in defining the creative woman. Some women are creative in their homemaking, creating a loving, spontaneous environment for their husbands and children—a place to go out from, a place to go back to. Others are creating in an extraverted professional situation. Some are successfully doing both. In this discussion, however,

I am thinking of the creative woman as one who is compelled from within to relate to her own creative imagination.

While the lights and shadows in individuals vary greatly, a basic pattern of such a woman's psychology can be outlined. As a little girl she loves and admires her father, or her image of what her absent father must be. And apparently for good reason. He is courageous, intelligent and sensitive, a man of high ideals, a man of vision committed to his own search, a man who in many cases never found his place in the patriarchy. His vision of the perfect woman quite naturally took him into marriage with a woman who loved his vision, usually a "father's daughter" whose dream for herself was cut short by the reality of marriage and family. Thus the *puer* man typically finds his mate in the *puella* woman.[3]

In such a household there is no place for the chaos of unruly children, the "filth" of the chthonic or earthy feminine, nor the energies of conscious sexuality. Ostensibly, the father may be "the man around the house," but the wife and mother "wears the pants." Full of repressed sexuality and resentment, she deals stoically with a disappointing world and projects her unlived life onto her children.

The father, meanwhile, blessed with the comforting presence of his wife-mother, is then free to project his own unfulfilled feeling values—his young anima onto his little girl. Together they build a Garden of Eden. The child is trapped in spiritual incest, even more dangerous than actual incest because neither he nor she has any reason to suspect that something is amiss. Called to be "Daddy's little princess," the daughter is at once his spiritual mother, his beloved, his inspiratrice. With her he will have thoughts and feelings that never come up with anyone else. She instinctively knows how to act as buffer between him and a judgmental world; she instinctively knows how to connect him to his own inner reality. Indeed, this is the only world she really understands—this world where she acts as the connecting link between her father's ego and the collective unconscious. Feeding on his vision of Light, Beauty and Truth, her young psyche can plumb the depths of his anguish or soar to the heights of his dream. That dynamic interplay continues to be her life-source as a creative woman, and without it her life becomes empty.

If her father accepts her inner life, then they genuinely share the eternal world of the creative imagination. Its values become her reality. Quick to recognize the illusions of the temporal world, she sets her sights on what is authentic, often becoming a veritable Cassandra, outcast by both her peer group and her parents' friends. Her security lies in her commitment to *essence* (a commitment, incidentally, which may lead to anorexia because she either forgets to eat or her throat refuses to open to the food of a world of which she is not a part). Such a woman lives on the archetypal edge, where life is exciting, fraught with danger—all or nothing, perfect or impossible. She knows little about bread and butter living and does not suffer fools gladly.

If her father is not mature enough to value her for herself, but, consciously or unconsciously, forces her into becoming his star performer, then her trap is a very different one because it involves his rejection of her reality. Unable to recognize her own responses, she simply relinquishes herself to trying to please Daddy.

Daughters of both types of men will be so-called anima women (good hooks for men's unconscious projections), though of a very different tempering. Both will have dreams where they appear, for instance, in well-lit glass solariums, in perfect blue apartments without kitchens, in plastic bags or coffins that threaten to suffocate them. Both will realize there is something between them and the world, something that cuts off their own feeling, a veil that is seldom penetrated. Both will strive to make life into a work of art, and vaguely realize they have not lived. Because of that primal relationship, the father's daughter walks a thin line precariously close to the collective unconscious, unable—like Rainer Maria Rilke, for example—to separate her personal angels and demons from the transpersonal.

And demons are as immediate to her as angels, because she lives so close to her father's shadow. Unless he has worked on himself, as in analysis, and gained some insight into his *puer* psychology, he is probably quite unaware of his ambivalence toward women. His bonding to his own mother may have created a Prince Charming, but a prince who is nevertheless dependent on women's approval. His chthonic shadow hates that dependence and hates the women who make him feel vulnerable. Unless he has worked hard on his own feeling values, he may function on a conscious level as an ascetic scholar, a priest, or even a carefree Don Juan, while his unconscious shadow is a cold, violent killer, intent on destroying any "witch" who would seduce him into her power. Men who live close to the unconscious quite legitimately need to protect themselves from the seduction of the lamia (see figure below, page 167), as the Romantic artists, many of them dead before forty, make painfully clear. The *puer's* shadow, however, may murder not only witches but the femininity of his little daughter as well. On the one hand he may be mothering, nourishing, cherishing, while on the other creating a *femme fatale* whose attitude toward men is kill or be killed.

The *femme fatale* lives in an unconscious body: her femininity is unconscious, her sexuality is unconscious. Often promiscuous, she manipulates "lovers" to prove her power as a woman, but her love is unrelated to her lust. Thus she may consciously love her father (or her father surrogate) and be committed to her own creativity through that incestuous bonding, and at the same time be lured into violent and dangerous adventures.

Her sexuality and femininity foundered on the reef of her primal relationship to her mother. The *puella* mother who has never taken up residence in her own body, and therefore fears her own chthonic nature, is not going to experience pregnancy as a quiet meditation with her unborn child, nor birth as a joyful bonding experience. Although she may go through the motions of natural childbirth, the psyche/soma split in her is so deep that physical bonding between her and her baby daughter does not take place. Her child lives with a profound sense of despair, a despair which becomes conscious if in later years she does active imagination with her body and releases waves of grief and terror that resonate with the initial, primal rejection.

The body that appears in dreams wrapped in wire, encircled by a black snake or encumbered by a fish tail from the waist down, may be holding a death-wish too deep for tears. The security of the mother's body world is not present for her in the original matrix, nor is there reinforcement for her maturing body as she moves toward puberty, attempting to differentiate her own boundaries from those of her mother and the external world. Unable to establish these fundamental physical demarcations, she often literally does not know where she begins or where she ends in relation to Mater (mother). During her developmental years, when she might otherwise be consolidating a sense of her physical identity, she is instead responding to the unconscious rejection by her mother.

The following is a recurring childhood dream which continued to haunt a fifty-year-old woman until it was worked through in analysis:

> I am four or five years old. I'm with my mother in a crowded building, probably a department store. My mother is wearing dark clothes, a coat and hat in brown or black, and throughout I see only her back. As we leave the building, I am slowed down by the crowd, and my mother, unknowing, moves ahead and disappears among the people. I try to call to her, but she doesn't hear me, nor does anyone else. I'm very frightened, not only at being lost but at my mother's not noticing we've been separated.
>
> I come out of the building onto a long flight of broad steps, rather like those outside the National Gallery in London, but higher. The steps lead down into a large square, empty of any objects, but with similar steps leading to buildings on the other sides. The square, the steps and the buildings are very clean and white. From my vantage point I look around the square, hoping to see my mother. She is nowhere to be seen. I am alone on the steps. There are other people in the square, but they are unaware of me. I know nothing I do will make them notice me.
>
> I am panic-stricken and overwhelmed with a sense of loss, of having been abandoned. It's as though I've ceased to exist for my mother, that she won't bother to come back for me, may even have forgotten about me, that in fact I can't make anyone aware that I exist.
>
> For a moment, and at the same time, I'm an adult observer across the

square who sees the small child standing alone at the top of the steps, trying to call out. This is also I, a grown woman who feels enormous pity for this child, longs to comfort and reassure her, but is unable to reach her. Something—the unconsciousness of the other people or the child's own panic—prevents communication between the child and the adult who cares and understands.

The woman associated this dream with Edward Munch's painting *The Scream*, which evoked in her a similar panic. "The background is dark and murky," she said, "while in my dream the environment is very clear, white and hard-edged, dotted with dark, ill-defined but equally hard-edged figures. The screamer is trying to escape from his environment; the child on the steps is trying to connect with hers." Many men and women are trapped in lives of quiet desperation until they turn to help that child within.

The body's memory, stored in muscle and bone, fuses the desire to connect and the desire to escape so they are simultaneously present in an undifferentiated form. The result—an identity of opposites—manifests as despair: nothing can be done and everything must be endured.

The above dream, with its "very clean and white" panorama of steps and square surrounded by buildings, while the dreamer is effectively alone and unable to "make anyone aware that I exist," is a characteristic dream of an anorexic. (This woman was not anorexic, but her adolescent son suffered from a severe eating disorder.) It shows her inability to connect with the strangers in her own psyche. They are present but they cannot communicate. It is as if Mater is concretized outside the body because it cannot be incorporated: the baby could not assimilate milk and physical intimacy from a mother who "won't bother to come back" and "may even have forgotten" her.

Psychic intimacy and physical intimacy go together naturally, but, where they have been split apart at a pre-verbal level, the instinct is isolated. The emotional food that should be incorporated with the physical food is not present; thus the instinctual pole of what Jung called "a psychoid process" receives a different message from the psychic pole.[4] Without the experience of the instincts, neither the feminine soul nor the masculine spirit is embodied; consequently in later life emotional intimacy, including love-making, may be undermined by a sense of betrayal. The body is not present. *She* is not there.

The woman who is whole resonates both physically and psychically. The soul, that is, is incarnate. Women who are robbed of that feminine birthright may have to experience physical acceptance by another woman, whether in dreams, in close friendship or in a lesbian relationship, before they can find security within themselves. (In rare cases, this can happen in relationship with a man, depending on the maturity of his anima.)

The Scream (1895), lithograph by Edward Munch.

The distortion in the body/psyche relationship is compounded by the symbiotic relationship between father and daughter. There is a primal confusion between the spiritual and instinctual depths because the love she received from her father is the very energy which sustains her life. With such confusion between spirit and matter, she may experience her body as a prison to be lugged around while her spirit hovers somewhere above her head, at any moment ready to leap into "the white radiance of eternity."[5]

Her body becomes a prison because the symbiotic matrix—here more accurately termed the patrix—is with the parent of the opposite sex. From her mother she has learned rejection of her body; from her father she has learned emotional withholding, for although she knows she is his beloved, and knows her mother is no real rival, she also senses there is a line she dare not cross. In her adult years, the gender confusion may manifest in the compulsion (or at least the preference) to be held by a man not as a lover but as a mother. She needs a "cuddle bunny" because her sexuality is not sufficiently embodied to respond to mature masculine penetration.[6]

Such a woman's terror of abandonment, then, lies not only in the loss of a meaningful relationship, but also in the loss of the physical contact that grounds her in her body. Locked in her musculature, her feminine feelings are not available to her; thus, if she is threatened with abandonment, she may become virtually catatonic with unexpressed terror, and subject to strange physical symptoms. She is losing herself, physically and spiritually. Abandonment becomes annihilation because her body with its welter of undifferentiated feeling cannot provide the *temenos*, the safe place, to protect her ego. Nor can the collective world offer support. Her preoccupation with the world of the imagination makes her view the mundane world with scorn and fear. It is a cruel, illusory world in which unreal people clutter their lives with superfluous objects, and clutter is unendurable when the inner world is dismembered.

A woman whose survival is thus tied to the masculine spirit has unconsciously sacrificed her femininity to what she believes is the best in life. In relationship to a man she appears at first to relate superbly because she can so adroitly become what he is projecting onto her. She in turn loves what she projects onto him. Their relationship assumes suprahuman dimensions: loving father, loving mother, hardly less than god and goddess. When father/god fails to live up to the projection, or decides to reject it, he deals the "imperial thunderbolt" that scalps her "naked soul."[7]

Cut off outwardly from her environment, cut off inwardly from her positive masculine guide, the woman identifies with the dark side of the father archetype—the demon lover. There is no one to mediate between her terrorized ego and the chaos through which it is falling. The abyss is bottomless. Her masculine solar consciousness asks questions for which there are no answers; her feminine lunar consciousness is not sufficiently mature to accept apparent meaninglessness.

She has done everything to make herself acceptable and she has failed; she is "unlovable" and that verdict resonates right back to the primary abandonment. Life becomes a prison where the password is "renunciation"; the animus-magician becomes the trickster with whom she has colluded in relinquishing herself. Describing this feeling of loss of soul, Emily Dickinson writes:

> And yet—Existence—some way back—
> Stopped—struck—my ticking—through—[8]

Suicide in that situation may become a fulfillment of her destiny. In Sylvia Plath's last "Words":

> Years later I
> Encountered them on the road—
>
> Words dry and riderless,
> The indefatigable hoof-taps.
> While

> *From the bottom of the pool, fixed stars*
> *Govern a life.*[9]

Suicide is a final stroke of vengeance against the savage god who has abandoned her. Paradoxically, it is affirming what he has done to her ego: God has taken her out of life, so killing herself is affirming him. Suicide is a *Liebestod*, a death marriage in which she embraces the dark side of God—a negative mystical union. Psychologically, it is marriage to the demon lover. The relationship of the woman to the demon is sado-masochistic, and her battle with him fascinates because it has within it the elements of violent eroticism. As Shakespeare's Cleopatra says when she puts the asp to her breast:

> *The stroke of death is as a lover's pinch,*
> *Which hurts, and is desir'd.*[10]

Inherent in such a vision, however, is a sense of total defeat. One battles against a power which is inexorable. The father animus demands order, justice, meaning. However, the crucial events in her life—the loss of a lover, loss of a child or childlessness, the inability to create—may defy human comprehension. Without a compensating feminine consciousness, which would accept the deeper mysteries of Fate, life becomes a losing battle against meaningless suffering. The demon lover lures the woman into blind, egotistical pride that rejects the creative possibilities inherent in inner tension. Outwardly, she may perform as usual, but in the subterranean depths she knows the battle is being lost and yearns for release from despair. It is the last collision of the opposites—the desire to be a part of life, the desire to escape. The heart breaks, overwhelmed by rage against the inevitability of loss.

Suicide is the ultimate abandonment, and while few women have a conscious propensity for suicide, many are dealing with abysmal despair which may manifest unconsciously in a fatal accident or a terminal illness. They repeatedly go through the anguish of losing men onto whom they have projected their savior; they fail to recognize that the passionate interaction of their relationships is based on narcissistic need; they will not sacrifice the complex and accept the "boredom" of being human. They are forsaking their own souls and their own creativity—personified as the neglected little girls and boys who repeatedly appear in their dreams. Essentially, they are afraid to take responsibility for their own lives. If the object of loss is introjected and sealed off, it becomes, in Emily Dickinson's words:

> *The Horror not to be surveyed—*
> *But skirted in the Dark—*
> *With Consciousness suspended—*
> *And Being under Lock—*[11]

If, on the other hand, loneliness leads to insight and illumination, the ego may establish a creative relationship with the inner world and release its own destiny.

Martha, the middle-aged woman whose recurring childhood dream was quoted earlier, is a tall, stately woman with a studied air of confidence. Born into a professional family, she did all that was expected of her at university, married her high school sweetheart, had her family, divorced, and then held a careful balance between work, children and men for some twenty years. She would go out with men but nothing would last. She came into analysis to find out why the pattern of loss kept repeating itself.

Some time later she fell in love with a highly respected leader in her community; he fell in love with her, and soon marriage seemed inevitable. After one year things began to go wrong; after two years he left her. At that time, now in the habit of paying close attention to emotional events, Martha carefully articulated her feelings:

> I don't know where I've been. I am numb. I projected everything I ever wanted in a man onto him. And he left me for another—for an ordinary woman. All I want to be is ordinary. But I don't know how to be ordinary. I am a stranger to others, to myself.
>
> I think back to my childhood, to that terrible sense of abandonment. I was never at the center, the living center of anyone's life. That's all I want—to share my life in its deepest essentials with another. My parents didn't share their deepest core with me. My husband said he loved me, but the most important things of life he did not share. And he went off with a woman who could share the ordinary world with him. I don't know how to do that.
>
> I know what the man is projecting onto me. I become what he wants me to be, and at the time it feels natural and real to me. I feel totally alive. And then something goes dead in the relationship, usually in the sexuality. I feel he is manipulating, using power, forcing me to be what he wants me to be. He is making love to his image of me, not to me. I too am projecting. It is not he who is making love to me. Everything swings into unreality. I hate myself for enduring it. I hate him for forcing me. It is intolerable. I go unconscious. Nothing has happened between us. We are both disappointed, resentful, confounded by the seeming intimacy which wasn't intimacy at all.
>
> I know this lack of intimacy exists between me and my children. They too have developed magnificent personas—lively, efficient, able to cope with anything. Underneath there is grief; it comes out in their poems, their songs. That essential part of themselves they do not share with me. I feel there is a veil around me. When I write, when I am alone, the tragic side of myself surfaces, but I cannot share that with others.
>
> I know in this situation I could go into my act. I could fly into activity, busy myself with any number of creative things, but that would be choosing the persona again. I won't do that. It's not quite as it was in

the past. I'm not incapacitated. I'm not being swung helplessly around. I know something terrible has happened to me, but there is a quiet place at the center.

It's the ordinary things that hurt so much, the little human acts we shared together. I stumble along in my numbness. I see the plum blossoms and I'm overcome with slivers of pain. At least the pain is alive. At least I know I am somewhere feeling the reality of what I am going through. Behind that numbness is blind terror. It is the terror of the child within me—the child who knew everything was going wrong, that she was unacceptable, and frantically attempted to try to figure out what to do in order to be loved. It's the terrible aloneness of standing at the top of the stairs crying and no one pays any attention, of knowing that who I am is impossible to those around me. It is standing bereft, hearing mocking laughter in the empty corridor behind me, trying to contort myself into someone who could be loved. I have rejected that child, as everyone else has rejected her. She's still standing there crying, "What do you want me to be? I don't understand. I don't understand. I'll do anything you want, but don't reject me."

Well, this time I won't build up my false persona. It can't relate because it can't feel. I know I have to stay with the feeling. I have to experience my vulnerability. I have to allow others to know how vulnerable I am. This is the loss of everything I ever wanted in a man. I am ashamed to be so naive. I respected and loved everything he was. He is gone. I am not young. I may never have such a relationship again. I do not trust that God has something new for me. I do not hope. Hope in me is an illusion. Honest despair is better than a fantasy of hope. This is the confrontation: the abandoning of all I hoped for.

Martha, like other women of her type, can be an enigma to men. Functioning without a strong feminine ego, she nevertheless gives an appearance of being, as she says, "some kind of iron lady who can take anything, and take it alone." And she *can* go on, but behind it all "there's a black rock in the heart."

The man who carries the positive projections of such a woman may feel himself quite unnecessary in the relationship, may even feel his masculine ego and his potency threatened. If he withdraws or leaves her, he may well be astonished to see her collapse. He probably had no idea of her dependence on him, her need for grounding. (As Martha put it, "He thought my energy was all going into the analysis and I didn't care about the relationship. What does he think analysis is about?") If in addition to withdrawing he takes up with the opposite type of woman (a shadow sister of the first), the situation illustrated in Barbra Streisand's *Yentl* may arise, where the masculine-oriented Yentl projects her femininity onto her rival and sings, "No wonder he loves her," thus passively surrendering what is crucial to her existence.

The projection of a woman's unconscious femininity onto a shadow sister is a typical trick of the magician animus. When he feels he is losing her to another man, he will do everything he can to destroy the possibility of authentic relationship. Once her shadow energy is projected onto the other woman, her lover's anima may also split: he loves *her* for her strength, her shadow for her sexual vulnerability.

Instead of acknowledging her appropriate rage and jealousy, such a woman may retreat into her abandoned child, harangued by her negative animus: "This is the way it always ends, will always end. When the chips are down, never trust a man. You can stand alone. You always have. You're a better man than he. You're not sweet and feminine like she is. If only you hadn't stood your ground in discussions. If only you'd pretended the issues didn't matter. If only you hadn't tried to make him more conscious. If only you had been more sensitive to his needs. If only ... if only ... if only. Never mind. Take it like a man."

If she were to withdraw her projections, she might be able to look the man straight in the eye, honoring his manhood and her womanhood, and say, "What the hell is going on here?" Instead, she is helplessly crippled by self-recriminations. She looks at the situation with rational understanding, thus ignoring her true feeling. She does not fly into a "childish" tantrum. She does not whimper and cry. She knows she's not dead because she's still standing up. She plays the role of "the perfect gentleman."[12]

Analyzing Daddy's Little Princess

While many women attempt to work out their destiny through their own creative work or their own life experience, others enter analysis when they see a destructive pattern undermining their relationships with men. Sometimes they are shocked by their own *femme fatale*; sometimes they are grieved when the sexual relationship with a husband they love has failed, although it may have been fine *until* they married. Often they are driven into analysis by mysterious body problems which medical science has termed psychosomatic but can do nothing to relieve. Sometimes they are despairing in their separation from life; sometimes they are stricken because their creativity is blocked; sometimes they are terrified of madness.

Working with such a woman is like working with anyone else except that the ambushes are more immediate, precipitous and treacherous because the unconscious is her home and native land. The analyst must take full cognizance of the power of her imagination, her capacity to abandon herself to the archetypal world, and her lack of relationship to her own body.

The analyst, whether man or woman, will become her inspiratrice, her connecting link to the unconscious. If her father was her companion rather than her guide on the inner journey, then the analyst is treated as a partner, a *frater* or *soror*, daring the dangers and sharing the triumphs. Together they explore a world of imagination, rich with imagery and insights. She makes an exciting analysand because she is not afraid to enter the underworld and she regularly brings back to the analyst riches, both personal and transpersonal. She understands Silence, and if the analyst can endure the intensity of her world, every session becomes a happening.

If she is an Ariadne, betrothed to the god before her birth, but side-tracked by her love for the sun-hero Theseus, then, like Ariadne when she was eventually abandoned, she may give herself up to death. She may surrender to deep depression, and, at the nadir of that experience, recognize the light in the darkness. She may in fact find her true destiny: surrender to the god. Not many modern women want to face the nun in themselves, but not a few in analysis are forced to put the archetypal projections where they belong; they must separate personal relationships from archetypal, and work out their own salvation in harmony with the inner god and goddess without the support of a church or the containment of nunnery walls. The woman who knows she has a "calling," artistically or spiritually, may sometimes question her commitment to her inner marriage, but essentially she *knows* she dare not betray that inner reality.

The woman who has carried the idealized projection of her father all her life, however, may question whether she is called or whether she is trapped in an illusion—an inner marriage that is itself unfruitful, yet forces her to seek the perfect marriage in the outer world. "Called or uncalled" can be an anguished decision, but if the woman concludes she is not called then she needs to look carefully lest she abandon herself to an illusion of perfect union in the human world, an illusion that repeatedly lures her into inevitable abandonment in her relationships with men. Then she may recognize that her problem lies in falling in love with her own projection and attempting to create herself in an image which is being projected onto her, thus abandoning her own Being. As human intimacy develops, she herself rejects that image and cannot continue the pretense. As she reveals more and more of herself, the man experiences *her* as the betrayer because she had withheld so much of her true nature in order to win him. Unconsciously, her rage toward the man and toward herself (as self-betrayer) unites with his rage, creating the bomb which must inevitably explode.

The two shadow figures will have their revenge. If healing is to take place, she must not act like a gentleman; she must not try to understand why he is abandoning her. She is angry and her rage is killer-rage and killer-jealousy that needs an acceptable channel. The pent-up fury of a lifetime has to be released from the body to make room for the healing love. That personal rage has to be acknowledged and experienced before the transpersonal understanding and compassion can flow in.

Somewhere in that anguish and anger, the woman will realize that she has *not* been abandoned by the man she loves. The man she loves does not exist in human form. He never did. She has been projecting an inner image of her own. Her mirror has shattered, and now she can either die or accept reality. And the reality is that she does not grieve for that actual man. She grieves both for her perfect lover and for the beautiful woman she was when she was in love. Taken to her naked truth, she grieves for her own child, the child she herself abandoned when she first set out to please Daddy.

That child in all its childish and childlike faith, hope and love is the one that cries out in its aloneness. In spite of its vulnerability, it has to trust life if the woman is ever to bring her essence to maturity.

The original abandonment by her mother and the creative relationship with her father may make her feel that women are a waste of time. She may know, however, that she does not want to go through "the hassle" of falling in love with a male analyst, and therefore choose to work with a woman. In the transference the analyst then carries the projection of the loving mother the woman never had. Together they nurture and discipline the abandoned child, giving it a safe place to play and cherishing it into maturity. It is that child who has suffered outside the limits of society, yet is still holding to its own innate wisdom, refusing to die. Its vulnerability and strength, born of its aloneness, give it the detachment necessary to the artist and the clown. In my experience, that detachment, simultaneously personal and transpersonal, is the only energy strong enough to depotentiate the trickster.

Let me illustrate this with a brief story. One Christmas Eve I happened to be in the Chalk Farm underground station in London, England. The trains were nowhere to be seen. A few prodigals stood shivering in that dank cave, dreaming of the fireside they were heading for or the one they didn't have. Suddenly a drunken, high-pitched roar echoed through the vast cavern. A massive, slovenly woman lurched through the entrance with two little girls, perhaps six and four. They had no coats; their thin little arms clutched at this heaving mass roaring her obscenities into the emptiness. Her Cockney humor was outrageous—so frank, so visceral, so true. Shocked laughter bounced off the walls. In one crystal clear cry, the four year old stood to the full height of her tiny frame and shouted, "Don't you laugh at my mom!" There was silence—and not a dry eye on the platform.

That little girl's innate wisdom ripped the veils off every onlooker. She was the only one, at once detached and connected enough, to see the Reality. She was the unexpected guest that Christmas Eve.

The creative woman's body may be an unaccepted guest. Because it has so often been the scapegoat, loving attention needs to be paid to its attempts to make itself heard. There may be severe digestive problems, migraine headaches, skin rashes and allergies. These can be a part of any analysis, but the artistic temperament, flying with its intuition, may overlook an ulcer and be possessed by a pimple. Old patterns of avoidance and repression, often involving eating disorders, may re-emerge. With increased body awareness, the feeling values that are being differentiated verbally are being reinforced by the emotions released from the muscles—a reinforcement that comes as a shock to the woman who is a stranger in her own body.

If she falls in love with the analyst, that must be dealt with openly because the mourning in relation to the mother repeats itself and now that grief can be handled consciously and perhaps creatively. If the analyst touches or embraces the analysand, both need to be very aware of the difference between personal and transpersonal touching; that awareness can come only from the analyst's own sense of detachment. As the analysand learns to listen to her own body, her sexuality gradually becomes connected to real feeling and the lesbian dreams are either replaced by heterosexual dreams or she consciously chooses a lesbian relationship. It is a period of building a strong ego, well-grounded in the feminine body and the emotions springing from that body. This woman particularly needs a strong foothold in the everyday world, in order to be able to surrender to her creative imagination with the full assurance that she will be able to return to her own ego and relate to others.

As the analysand gains confidence, the analyst may find herself increasingly in the role of inspiratrice. The woman may ask for critical appraisals of her creations, looking for encouragement to dare to put her work before the public. There is a double danger here: first, the analyst could quickly turn into negative mother; second, she could make the fledgling artist totally dependent on her, both creatively and critically. Rather they must agree to leave critiques to the critics, and not risk contaminating the *temenos* of the analysis.

In my experience, there is one very dangerous passover to be made with the creative woman. If she is in a mid-life crisis, has recognized that she has not yet taken responsibility for her talent and has lived a basically persona-oriented—or animus-dominated—life, she may suddenly reclaim her abandoned child and attempt a 180-degree turn, with all the determination of the outcast about to come into her kingdom. Either the archetypal influx is too much for her immature body, or the ego is not sufficiently related to the body energy, or the psychic shift is too sudden for the body to move in harmony with it. Whatever the cause, there may be serious physical symptoms. It is as if the initiation rites that were not assimilated at puberty have now to be integrated before the rites of menopause can be endured.

During this period the forsaken body has to be claimed, cherished, inhabited, before it surrenders to becoming a vessel for creativity. In this situation it is often difficult to distinguish the adolescent from the menopausal woman, but careful differentiation of the two phases of lunar consciousness will help her to own her own life, instead of bitterly yearning for what in fact is hers for the claiming. This can be a very threatening passover. Unless solid body work has embodied her emotions, she may once again feel herself doomed to abandonment.

This type of woman working with a male analyst will constellate a very different situation. In him she sees the positive father, whom her psychology naturally makes into her own positive animus. The outcome can be confusing and destructive largely because of the peculiar strength of the male ego in the Western patriarchal world. While the male analyst is encouraging the healing activity arising out of the analytic constellation, his countertransference may go well beyond encouragement to become a father's pride in his daughter's achievement.

Since historically the daughter's achievement has always counted for less (being measured by quite different standards), the father-analyst's pride in his daughter-analysand's creative work now, with the new feminist ethos, takes on an added dimension. There is the sense of breaking ground, establishing a new alignment between the sexes, building a new cultural matrix. What may not be seen is the regressive re-enactment of the old patriarchal dominance, with all the incestuous undercurrents that energize it, giving the illusion of healing, creativity and change. What may in reality be constellated is the father complex that brought the woman into analysis in the first place. If this is the case—and it need not be—then the moment the countertransference is realized and withdrawn (as eventually it must be) the analysand will not only be back where she started, but what is worse, she will feel herself to have been seduced or deceived in the most treacherous manner possible.

What the male analyst may fail to recognize in the psychology of the creative woman is the profound split between her imagination and her body. For her, the imagination is the real world, and the father-man who can penetrate and impregnate that world brings "light to the sun and music to the wind."[13] He is her beloved. Here is where her intimate intercourse is. Here is where incest is permitted. Since her physical sexuality is basically unconscious, she may have relationships outside the analysis which she does not bother to mention. Ordinary men are outside her sphere, barely worthy of her *femme fatale*.

The model of the alchemical vessel, involving harmonious cooperation between the adept and his *soror mystica*, is tailor-made for her. And tailor-made for her destruction if the male analyst becomes frightened, is seduced or misappropriates his power. If the vessel explodes, she has no body to return to, no world to return to. Putting her animus to work is no answer; he has driven her all her life to please Daddy—university professors, husband, boss, virtually any male authority. His laughter can be diabolic when he has vanquished another rival. She needs rather to be finding her own life in her own body, differentiating her own femininity (which will involve her unconscious rage against men) and integrating her own masculinity and femininity.

Unless the analysis has opened up space for the trickster father—that is, made room for the trauma at the center of her psyche—she is eventually going to be abandoned again, and nothing, not even incest, so arouses the full range of patriarchal feeling as the abandoned daughter.

Historically, in ancient cultures, daughters were often abandoned because only male offspring were valued. When the analysand experiences her abandonment, the whole patriarchal myth at its most primitive origins is constellated. The urgency with which the unconscious takes hold to effect the sacrifice (Thomas Hardy's *Tess of the d'Urbervilles* at Stonehenge, for example) is apparent in the abandoned and sacrificial role of the woman in Western literature. To find oneself abandoned to, or at the mercy of, this myth can evoke a profound passivity on the part of both persons involved, as if what is happening is both necessary and inevitable. Fate, Destiny, Karma—everything comes into play to support what has happened and is happening.

What needs to take place is a profound, revolutionary realignment of the relationship—a realignment that is as huge a challenge to the male ego as it is to the father complex that feeds that ego. The analyst who has been "the best little boy in the world" and tried to be the most loving father in the world may have a very caring professional persona, but when it comes to real feeling he may find himself at a total loss. A woman who is fighting for her life is going to demand genuine feeling and she has a right to an honest response; otherwise she is trapped, with her inner, spiritual animus contaminated by her projection onto the analyst.

The truth can set both her and the analyst free. The unexpected may happen; something new, unknown to either—what Jung called the transcendent function[14]—may emerge. Abandonment, in the negative sense of betrayal, loss, exposure, death, may become abandonment in the positive sense of open, spontaneous, free. To go with that is to break out of the magician-father constellation into the unknown, where true creativity resides. Then and only then is the delusion of the old pattern seen, because the illusion it contained is now seen as a reality struggling to break out of the trap that imprisoned it. Herein lies the new ground now being cultivated by psychologically conscious women, a ground that requires a radical re-examination of timeworn attitudes.

The dangers lurking in the transference-countertransference between female analyst and the creative male analysand also deserve close attention. This is not the place for a full discussion of those dynamics. Let me point out, however, that the female analyst regularly constellates the positive mother in the man. If the unconscious is his native land, then together they may mine that configuration for all the energy it contains. Together they may tap into a geyser of creative life that erupts with poetry, music, drama, pottery. Then she becomes the muse of her spiritual son, as Venus-Urania was the muse of Adonis. That such a relationship can be fatal—Adonis assuming a strength that is not his, which leaves him unprepared to confront Ares the boar, the more incestuous, more instinctive lover of Venus—may not be seen in the first flush of creative renewal. Releasing and containing the analysand's dynamic Ares shadow requires of the female analyst a fine differentiation of her own virgin, a feminine consciousness no longer identified with the mother, a consciousness that is receptive to her own creative masculine, freed from the tyranny of the father.

If the analyst, male or female, recognizes from the beginning the psychic dynamics inevitable in the relationship and can handle the countertransference, then the process need not be traumatic. Somehow the power of the dark magician and the omnivorous witch must be depotentiated. While these negative complexes can act positively in that they force the analysand to do the inner work necessary to escape their clutches, they can also destroy before the individual is strong enough to withstand their energy. A flash storm, a tornado, a searing fire—such dream images regularly alert one to a dangerous situation—can rip the center out of the psychic house.

In terms of the Jungian model, there is little difference between the ego of an unconscious woman and the anima of an unconscious man; there is a similar analogy between a man and the animus of a woman. In any intimate relationship, the love/hate dynamics among these four are going to constellate. If the analysand falls into persona identification, the persona and the defensive ego will operate at all costs to hide the inner world, and that inner world includes the instincts. If passionate eroticism is not consciously discussed, the body is once again abandoned and the shadow will takes its revenge in physical symptoms. At the point of highest tension between analyst and analysand, one or the other may fall into unconsciousness and accuse the other of wanting power. Each may accuse the other of wanting "more and more and more," and both be saying, "That's not true."

Such conflicts arise because the shadow projections are constellated: the negative mother's "more" wants quantity, whereas the negative father demands quality. The feminine feels it is being psychically raped and the masculine feels it is being sucked dry by the terrified child. Enormous hostility built up in the unconscious toward the opposite sex may erupt. Unless the analyst can instantly move to a strong ego position, a position well fortified by authentic feeling, there is no mediator between consciousness and unconscious. This is no time for ineffectual masculinity, nor masochistic femininity, nor tyrannical father, nor positive mother, nor any musical-chairs combination of the four. Both analyst and analysand must speak and both must be heard. The old map is useless in new country.

The woman who is in touch with her inner virgin has passed the frontier of the anima woman operating out of a male psychology.[15] She finds herself saying things she never said before, verbalizing questions she never asked before. She tries to speak from her feminine reality while at the same time aware of the masculine standpoint. Often she is caught between two conflicting points of view: the rational, goal-oriented and just, versus the irrational, cyclic, relating. Her task is not to choose one or the other, but to hold the tension between them.

A woman who has devoted her life to examinations and scholarship, or politics or the business world, knows how to organize her mind in obedience to the laws of unity, coherence and emphasis. What she too often has lost in such training is faith in the values that come from the heart. When she attempts to speak from that place she contacts her abandoned soul. Fearful of appearing "childish and stupid," she feels her face going red, clutches at her neck to try to get the words out; breathlessly she plummets on, hoping she won't be stopped, hoping she won't lose her vocabulary and collapse in confusion. She is trying desperately to articulate her feminine Being, trying to transcend the either/or prison that locks her into contradiction.

The either/or model is now as untenable as Newtonian physics. Just as the world of science has come to accept that light is at once both wave and particle—depending on the experiment used to determine its nature[16]—so women must learn to live in a world of paradox, a world where two mutually exclusive views of reality may be held at the same time. The rhythms there are circuitous, slow, born of the feeling that comes from the thinking heart. Many people intuitively know that such a place exists; few have the confidence to talk or walk from that center.

*

Martha did eventually confront her own abandonment of all she had ever hoped for in relating to men. Commenting on the disintegration of her last relationship, she wrote:

> Maybe I am too strong. He said he experienced me as critical; I experienced him as judgmental. I know my inner little girl is too needy, too demanding. She is so uncentered she attempts to find her center in a

relationship—man as god and mother. I was trying to let her grow up. I can't help feeling that I did the right thing. I told him honestly what I felt. I tried to understand how he felt. We could not communicate. I was true to my feeling values, but he wouldn't rise to the challenge. He recognized his persona problem, but he didn't want to work on it. He wanted to go back to his uncritical mother. He did. He married her. So long as we had our paradise, it was fine. When it came to the real problems of relationship, he wasn't there. Yes, it is the same old pattern, but I'm more conscious this time. Consciousness makes it worse, also makes it better. Maybe it is Fate. Maybe we weren't meant to be together.

After these reflections, still contaminated by an attitude of judge and blame, she had the following dream:

> I'm sitting up in my very first bed. I'm facing the head as a child might in play. Leaning against the headboard is Laurence Olivier, the object of my most varied and detailed adolescent fantasies. He is old, but still enormously attractive, with an abundance of snow-white hair. We are in a relationship, have been for some months at least—a settled sort of thing. The thought comes to me that it's rather delightful to have my adolescent fantasy come true almost as I imagined it. At this point we are both assailed by an overwhelming sexual desire, which we are about to give in to when I awaken.

"I awoke with a boot in my stomach," Martha said. "I felt crushed, overwhelmed. Then relief. At least I know now what I've been living with all my life. I recognize the fantasy world." The dream suggests that the fantasy world has been with her "for some months at least," a poignant understatement in light of the setting in her "very first bed." Laurence Olivier, the elegant father-figure, is very old, clearly suggesting that this fantasy attitude is outworn.

The dream clarifies in no uncertain terms the cross Martha has been on all her life, and at the same time delivers "the boot in her stomach," the transcendent that can release her. Here is the same conflict that was inherent in her recurring childhood dream mentioned earlier: the desire to escape, the desire to connect. Escaping into the complex (abandoning herself to Sir Laurence, the consummate actor), protects her from the pain of connecting to life. It also separates her from her own authentic Being in her own body. It is the actual experience of the kick in the stomach that makes her wake up to where she has been all her life—in a compromise with an illusion. That fantasy world is a pact with the devil. The kick is the wound from the Self through which the god can enter. The dream has thrown the ego out of the crib and into the fire. Having seen and abandoned the fantasy, the dreamer is now the abandoned one, free to abandon herself to her own life.

Martha, like so many of her contemporaries, is now attempting to consolidate her insights. She is attempting to be nothing more nor less than who she is, determined to put her energy into her creative work. With such an attitude she is more likely to be able to accept the next man in her life as *he* really is, while the contradiction at the core of her own life becomes more clear:

> I am still split on some level. I am still angry, unreconciled. Intellectually I realize I set up an impossible situation for him. I think I was unconsciously very negative. I think he read the real message, which was very critical. I think I was demanding perfection. My anger is directed not at him but at all men. It's an intellectual construct: deflect my anger off myself by making him wrong. It's myself I'm angry at. I betray my own soul, my own little girl.
>
> It's horrendous, really. There is no mature femininity there at all. It's still a matter of commitment. I'm still trying to escape when I'm trying so hard to commit. All the time my arms are out begging to connect, something else is pulling me back, not wanting to commit. That is irresponsible. I'm waiting for someone to say, "You're great. What you're doing is worthwhile." I look for reinforcement from outside. Rather than waiting for my own inner authority to come up, I shift into pleasing. I'm terrified to connect because I'm sure I'll be found inadequate. I keep trying to justify my existence instead of just Being.
>
> You know what it is? It's a problem of loving. I don't love myself enough. I understand love in my head, but when it comes to opening my heart, I don't know what that means. When I feel myself tight, I relax, I breathe into my heart. Then I can take the chance. I listen with my heart. I can feel what I'm feeling. I want, I want so very much, for that little girl to grow into mature womanhood.

Feminine consciousness, not to be confused with mothering, is evolving in many men and women. While a few great individuals in the past have articulated its territory, it is now coming to consciousness as a cultural phenomenon. It is our responsibility not only to hear it, but to act on it and accept the consequence of our lives being turned inside out. If we choose to abandon it, it turns its dark face—revengeful, depressed, suicidal. If we abandon ourselves to it,

> *the faithfulness I can imagine would be a weed*
> *flowering in tar, a blue energy piercing*
> *the massed atoms of a bedrock disbelief.*[17]

Throughout my whole life, during every moment I have lived, the world has gradually been taking on light and fire for me, until it has come to envelop me in one mass of luminosity, glowing from within . . . the purple flush of matter imperceptibly fading into the gold of spirit, to be lost finally in the incandescence of a personal universe. . . .

This is what I have learnt from my contact with the earth—the diaphany of the divine at the heart of a glowing universe, the divine radiating from the depths of matter a-flame.

—Teilhard de Chardin, *Le Divine Milieu*.

The aim of psychoanalysis—still unfulfilled, and still only half-conscious—is to return our souls to our bodies, to return ourselves to ourselves, and thus to overcome the human state of self-alienation.

—Norman O. Brown.

In the self-same point where the soul is made sensual, in the self-same point is the city of God ordained from without beginning.

—Dame Julian of Norwich.

We did not think of the great open plains, the beautiful rolling hills, and winding streams with tangled growths as "wild." Only to the white man was nature a "wilderness" and only to him was the land "infested" with "wild" animals and "savage" people. To us it was tame. Earth was bountiful and we were surrounded with the blessings of the Great Mystery. Not until the hairy man from the east came and with brutal frenzy heaped injustices upon us and the families we loved was it "wild" for us. When the very animals of the forest began fleeing from his approach, then it was that for us the "Wild West" began.

—Chief Luther Standing Bear, *Land of the Spotted Eagle*.

3

The Kore of Matter:

Psyche/Soma Awareness

According to quantum mechanics there is no such thing as objectivity,
We cannot eliminate ourselves from the picture. We are a part of
nature, and when we study nature there is no way around the fact that
nature is studying itself. Physics has become a branch of psychology,
or perhaps the other way around.
                                    —Gary Zukav, *The Dancing Wu Li Masters.*

Body awareness has become an important focus in my analytic practice because of my experience with both women and men who, despite earnest commitment to their dreams and to their own growth, are still unable to trust the process. Their souls are dislocated in bodies so wounded that the ego's willingness in itself is simply not enough.

Failure in travailing life's junctures is not necessarily the failure of the ego to adopt a new attitude toward the Self by sacrificing the old. Many of my analysands have what I believe to be appropriate ego attitudes; their bodies, however, have at some point been traumatized. While their egos can be approached through confrontation, challenge or humor, their bodies cannot respond. The more quickly the ego moves ahead, the more terrorized the body becomes. The task then is to find some means of going back to the point of wounding to reconnect with the abandoned child. The body, like the child, tells the truth, and tells it through movement or lack of movement.

A trained observer can discern whether the soul has taken up residence in the body, or whether the body image is so intolerable that the flesh is barely inhabited. The body can be so retarded that it cannot even imagine itself as an adult. If, as James Hillman says, "the image by which the flesh lives is the ultimate ruling necessity,"[1] then some means must be found to create an adequate image—physically as well as psychically. Body awareness, as I understand it, has nothing to do with the technology of the body. It is not fitness or longevity that is at stake, although these may be by-products. What is at stake is the integration of body, soul and spirit.

So long as we are in this world, the psyche is enacted through the medium of the body. William Blake described the body as "that portion of Soul discerned by the five Senses."[2] The soul is, of course, much more than the bodily "portion" of itself. It is not limited to manifesting in the physical body; ít manifests also in that infinite body which constitutes the "body" of the imagination, a body that includes the entire visionary world of the arts—music, sculpture, painting, poetry, dance, architecture. Each of these visionary or imaginary worlds may be thought of as larger human bodies, or a single giant human body. That it may act in another world, of which the arts are an expression, is one of the oldest speculations about the immortality of the soul, and art as an expression of it.

The soul, then, manifests in a multiplicity of forms. While it is on earth, it must have a body image as its home, as its primary medium of expression. The soul will not naturally reject its body image any more than the mother's breast will naturally reject her baby. The body mirrors the soul. Where rejection occurs, something has gone seriously wrong. But no matter what went wrong, the soul will do everything in its power to correct it. How then do we explain the blockage of the body as the soul's medium of expression? Seen from this point of view, anorexia nervosa and bulimia, for example, are the result of an abnormal release of psychic energy in an effort to overcome body blockage. Obesity is a manifestation of a soul that has more energy than the body can deal with.

Blocked bodies, metaphorically (sometimes literally), have hardened arteries, arteries blocked by too much cholesterol that makes it hard for the heart to pump blood through the system. They place mounting obstacles in the way of psychic energy. The result is that the energy has to find other modes of action, other modes of expression. Some of these are very creative and make for brilliant careers in the professions and the arts. But always, people whose psychic energy has had to carve out other channels of expression because their bodies were blocked, are haunted by their refusal, conscious or unconscious, to permit their souls to take up residence in their bodies. The result is that, without quite understanding what they are feeling or why they are feeling it, they are possessed by homeless souls who wander like ghosts in a bleak twilight zone where they cannot find shelter or rest. They are haunted by their own wandering souls that hover somewhere near the earth, crying in vain to be let in. Refusing them entrance into their own bodies, such people become the enemies of their souls. They unconsciously realize that they have sentenced their souls to perpetual exile. For this reason, they find no real satisfaction in the other outlets, however creative, that the soul in exile from the body finds for itself. Temporary release from despair through total immersion in work leaves them, when the work is done, in ever deeper states of despair. Indeed, in certain cases the creative work leads to suicide.

Any wounding in the body will produce a tremendous discharge of healing energy at the point of blockage. That goes on in the sick body.

The aim in body workshops is to help individuals to recognize what the soul is trying to do, and then to relax the body so the soul can do it. It is to bring about an alignment in which the illness is understood in a very different light.

Disembodied

The woman who has been a "Daddy's girl," for example, has seldom if ever experienced her "dark" side, her rage and jealousy, lust and ecstasy. Alienated from her body, she does not know the magnificent energy that is blocked from consciousness, so blocked that it rarely manifests in dreams. She can spend the analytic hour in a euphoria of golden dream images, then awkwardly pull herself together and sadly resume the unbearable burden of her own body. Her dreams often mirror this self-alienation: she may appear as an animated object—a golfball, a cloud, a sausage with a head; sometimes a head moves two inches above a severed neck; sometimes a tight rope or scarf blocks communication between head and heart; sometimes her father's rotting head putrifies her abdomen.

While such images clearly demonstrate the enormity of the shadow problem, as analyst I cannot simply say, "There, you see, there is the severance from your own feelings. There's where your evil witch is separating you from yourself." That approach could only fall on deaf ears because a soul that has chosen to cut itself off from a "filthy" world is not going to recognize a self-murderer in its midst, nor will it acknowledge such demeaning human passions as greed, lust, power, and "the thousand natural shocks that flesh is heir to."[3]

Body work can release the witch. She dare not be confronted directly through facing the eating disorder with forced feeding or deprivation, but she can be beheaded through skillful maneuvers with shield and sword, as Perseus dealt with Medusa, while bringing the body to consciousness.[4] Body work accelerates the process and creates a strong container for the ego.

Analysis attempts to uncover the complexes in which repressed energy is held. If the analysand has a relatively harmonious body/psyche relationship, the shadow material is obvious in the dreams. In many people, however, body and psyche were split apart at a very early age. In cases where a person was unwanted, or unwelcome because of gender, the body/psyche split began *in utero* or at birth, as if the soul had chosen not to enter the body, but instead remained in exile from it. The energy is centered in or above the head, and the person has to make a concentrated effort to stay out of a fantasy world in order to deal with the simplest details of everyday reality. Denied a bodily home, such people are possessed by a longing for some home that is not of this earth. Their early dreams in analysis are usually very positive, full of numinous visions of golden cities, golden birds and specific places where they are assured of security and love. It is as if the Self knows their hold on the everyday world is tenuous and gives these magnificent dreams as anchor points to which they can return when suicidal despair manifests, as it inevitably does in the later stages of analysis.

The death wish becomes conscious when they are forced to recognize the fantasy world of Light, Beauty and Truth that they have woven around themselves, a world of illusion that does not tally with the real world, a world of archetypal proportions that has protected them from the despicable reality they have chosen to ignore and disdain. They are like Tennyson's Lady of Shalott, who daily wove her magic web while watching the "shadows of the world" reflected in her mirror. She knew she would die if she dared look down to Camelot. Then one day a "bearded meteor, trailing light"—an actual man—streaked across her mirror.

> *She left the web, she left the loom,*
> *She made three paces thro' the room,*
> *She saw the water-lily bloom,*
> *She saw the helmet and the plume,*
> *She look'd down to Camelot.*
> *Out flew the web and floated wide;*
> *The mirror crack'd from side to side;*
> *"The curse is come upon me," cried*
> *The Lady of Shalott.*[5]

The death wish has its own etiology in each individual, but two factors are almost always present in women who consciously or unconsciously long to escape from this world. First, the mother has not been related to her own female body, has disparaged her own sexuality, and has therefore been unable to cherish the female body of her baby daughter. The child has grown up making the best of an impossible situation, performing for her parents, teachers and the world to the very best of her mental and spiritual endowments, but at bottom feeling rejected in her own personhood, blaming her "ugly" body for making her "unlovable." Second, the constellation in the home has usually created a situation in which she is bonded to the father, either the actual father or her imaginary vision of the perfect world that would exist if only Father would come home.[6]

Where the emphasis in the family was on perfect performance without any genuine recognition of the Becoming or Being of the child, she very early learned that her instinctual responses were not acceptable; thus her anger, fear, even joy, were driven into the musculature of her body, chronically locked in, and inaccessible to everyday living. When the authentic feeling is cut off from the instincts, genuine conflict either remains in the unconscious or becomes somatized there.

Esther Harding, referring to the ego complex preceding the formation of a conscious ego, writes:

> Where the ego is inadequately developed in modern adults and is not made conscious, we find that the ego complex remains in the unconscious and functions from there. In consciousness an individual representing this level of development may be conspicuously lacking in that concentration and centeredness which is characteristic of the person with more conscious ego development; yet egotism and will to power, of which the unevolved person is unaware, may function nonetheless and produce their inevitable effects on all with whom he comes in contact. ... [Where] egotism and self-will are in the unconscious ... they manifest themselves in somatic, that is, in prepsychological form.
>
> When the ego comes to consciousness and the individual becomes aware of himself as I, the reaction to difficulties or obstructions will no longer appear in physical form as symptoms but will be recognized in consciousness as emotions. That is to say, the reaction will be a psychological one. ... The emergence of the ego from the unconscious brings with it a new problem, the problem of the will to power.[7]

Reclaiming the Body

Months may pass in the analytic process before the conflict appears in dreams. Body work, which must be handled with considerable patience and love, reaches out to that lost infant whose little body—strong, tender, sure—was never allowed to develop. The body is suspicious and terrified, and only gradually can it learn to trust its own instincts and discipline them into a firm steady base for the maturing psyche. Unless the body knows it is loved, that its responses are acceptable, the psyche does not have the ground of certainty in the instincts that it requires; sooner or later in the analysis the person will become stuck because the ego is afraid to trust; at the point of surrender the ego becomes paralyzed. Unless the body knows that there are inner loving arms strong enough to contain it, however fierce or broken it may be, it will hang onto its own rigidity in an effort to survive. That rigidity is echoed in the rigidity of the persona and the ego.

A woman whose mother did not love her own femininity, and who therefore rejected the female body of her daughter, almost inevitably goes through a period of lesbian dreams or lesbian acting-out because her body requires the acceptance of a woman. Usually this is only temporary and the woman's energy gradually turns toward men. If the lesbian phase has been carefully integrated, insuring that the feminine ego is firmly located in the female body, then the woman who has never been able to surrender to orgasm experiences a new world of sexuality. Energy blocks that were knotted into her pelvis and thighs from early childhood and puberty are released and energy flows naturally into ecstasy. Once that release is achieved, a woman who formerly looked for cuddling and holding in a man's embrace no longer attempts to turn her lover into a mother. Her man is free to experience his own masculinity in the giving and receiving of the sexual relationship.

Body work must be approached with the same respect and attentiveness that one gives to dreams. The body has a wisdom of its own. However slowly and circuitously that wisdom manifests, once it is experienced it is a foundation, a basis of knowing that gives confidence and total support to the ego. To reach its wisdom requires absolute concentration: dropping the mind into the body, breathing into whatever is ready to be released, and allowing the process of expression until the negative, dammed energy is out, making room for the positive energy, genuine Light, to flood in. After body work, the dreams bring to consciousness the complexes that have been threatened or released. Ancient toilets that have been overflowing, broken or plugged begin to flush; animals that have been dead, disabled, frenzied or starving begin to be healed; automobiles with faulty starters, flat tires and smashed-in rear trunks are repaired; houses with defective wiring, where short circuits amass too much energy in one socket with no current in another, are recircuited. Often new windows replace little old garret slits, or big secret rooms are discovered in the old house.

If the individual is ready, and if the experience has been one of trust, a powerfully numinous dream of the Great Mother as nourishing, loving protector is often given. Rarely does she show her face, but her love infiltrates the body with a soft, luminous Light, an experience so powerful that the woman returns to that moment again and again when the Gethsemane days of the analysis seem unendurable. Repeatedly, analysands say, "I don't know what happened. I am not a religious person, but I know Somebody loves me."

Such an experience can turn an addiction around. The emptiness at the center of the psyche that has heretofore been experienced as nothingness—an abyss to be avoided with as much anesthesia as necessary—can be transformed into Beingness, respected and cherished as the abode of the Goddess. Concentration then becomes a movement around the center, and the frenzied, forsaken hours that were formerly spent binging, vomiting, starving, working, drinking, cleaning can be transformed into the most creative hours of the day. Addictive personalities are often highly energized people who are lost in a maze because their search for essence has failed. They run around like gerbils on a wheel finding whatever transcendent experience they can through the euphoria of starvation, the orgasm of vomiting, the spirit in alcohol, the "reality" in drugs. If they can once touch into the reality at their own center, and learn to nourish it through breathing, dance, T'ai-Chi—whatever works for them—then they are in touch with their own creativity. Their energy now has a creative, rather than a self-destructive, direction.

As the body becomes more conscious, its messages become clearer and more trustworthy. Many intuitives who have trusted their intuition all their lives realize through body work that their bodies are just as intuitive as their psyches. One woman, for example, was with a male friend one night when suddenly her body began to shake. Formerly she would have ignored it; now she recognized its dread. The next day her friend phoned to tell her he wished to end the relationship. Her body had *known*. The body is the medium through which the soul enacts itself. No matter how blocked the medium is, unless it is completely destroyed the body will still register the soul's activity. (Whether the signals are picked up or rejected is another question.) This kind of intense body response has to be taken into consideration in analysis because the feeling function is so crucial to ego development. If a person is doing his or her best to establish a standpoint based on authentic feeling values, and trying to develop the courage to act on that standpoint, then the body must reinforce that stand. What I have discovered in many of my analysands, however, is what I call a "possum psychology," where the body either cannot or will not reinforce the feeling value. It experiences life as a magical minefield in which it alone is knocked down by inaudible explosions. If there is unconscious hostility in the environment, the inner body, acting autonomously, falls over "dead." Having experienced this inner collapse all their lives, these people have learned to keep up the social chatter and use the polite persona as a decoy to beguile danger away from the fallen ego. When the crisis subsides, the ego attempts to stand up, but if it senses an unseen enemy, it automatically falls "dead" again.

Where the body is so intuitive and so unconscious, the ego has never functioned properly because in any threatening situation, the autonomic nervous system has said *No*, and the ego has withdrawn. Until the body responses are brought to consciousness so that the individual can recognize what is happening both internally and in the environment, one cannot act with normal aggression, cannot respond to everyday challenges, and the ego cannot mature through normal interchange. The sensitive body sets up a defense mechanism that may manifest in fat, in swelling, in blushing, in vomiting; it will do what it can to keep the poison out. If the individual lives close to the unconscious—e.g., is a psychic or an artist—then the body responses require acute observation and must be dealt with consciously. Otherwise, the isolated ego will seek some soporific to escape the unfocused dread.

When the ego does become conscious enough to hear the possum's warning ("Mines here somewhere"), it must take the responsibility for defending itself; otherwise it is mindlessly vulnerable to psychic poisoning. Once it recognizes where the danger is, it can decide whether to withdraw or to stand firm. Since there is no visible threat, no confrontation is possible. Either defense mechanism creates encapsulated fear or anger which requires an appropriate vehicle and place for expression. Instead of scratching, eating, drinking or some other compulsive behavior manifesting in random motor movement, the body needs time to return to its own rhythm. If it is allowed to dance, for example, in the quietness of its own living room, the displaced reaction will find a natural outlet in rhythmical movement. Thus the energy, instead of becoming self-destructive, is channeled creatively. Psychic energy manifesting in this kind of rhythmic movement is the beginning of the spiritual form of instinct.[8]

Integration of Body and Soul

The task, then, is to bridge "the seeming incommensurability between the physical world and the psychic."[9] Jung himself attempted to bridge this "seeming incommensurability" in his concept of the psychoid nature of the archetype. "Since psyche and matter are contained in one and the same world," he writes in his essay, "On the Nature of the Psyche,"

> and moreover are in continuous contact with one another and ultimately rest on irrepresentable, transcendental factors, it is not only possible but fairly probable, even, that psyche and matter are two different aspects of one and the same thing. The synchronicity phenomena point, it seems to me, in this direction, for they show that the nonpsychic can behave like the psychic, and vice versa, without there being any causal connection between them. Our present knowledge does not allow us to do much more than compare the relation of the psychic to the material world with two cones, whose apices [apexes], meeting in a point without extension—a real zero-point—touch and do not touch.[10]

That zero-point where the apexes of the two cones "touch and do not touch" is the object of exploration in workshops I have given with three body specialists: Mary Hamilton, a dance and movement educator; Beverly Stokes, who trained with Bonnie Bainbridge Cohen in developmental processes and experiential anatomy; and Ann Skinner, a voice teacher who has studied with Kristin Linklater.[11] Our desire to lead workshop participants to that zero-point required us to discover new ways of investigating and penetrating the mysteries of the psyche/soma relationship.

Through deep relaxation, for example, a participant can find a specific area of unconsciousness in the body, and then through concentration implant a numinous symbol from a dream in that area. The symbol is recognized as an individual gift of healing that works on three levels, emotional, intellectual and imaginative, appealing to body, mind and spirit. The dream image planted in the body acts as a magnet attracting the energy, transforming it and releasing it as healing power. Vibrant energy is released into the dark, chronically blocked muscles; ensuing dreams articulate the complex that has had that area in thrall. The psychic energy frees the physical; the physical illuminates the psychic. As I have noted previously, although a person may have conscious insight into the way a complex cripples his or her action, if the body does not let go of the conflict created through years of habitual tension, half the problem is not solved and the former distorted pattern is quick to reestablish itself.

Moreover, it is the contained energy of the images that constitutes what Jung, drawing upon an ancient tradition, called "the subtle body" or "breath-soul."[12] In bringing the apexes of the psychic and physical cones to this zero-point where they "touch and do not touch," we acknowledge it. The subtle body denies neither psyche nor soma, but brings them together in a *tertium non datur*, a third which holds the physical and psychic tensions and acts as a catalyst releasing energy to both sides. Once the subtle body begins to become conscious, it cannot be treated as if it did not exist; severe physical and/or psychic symptoms will erupt if it is disregarded. The laws governing the subtle body have to be recognized, usually requiring radical changes in unconscious eating and drinking habits, breathing, sexuality, etc. One of the functions of analysis is to create a conscious container appropriate to the subtle body.

If an obese woman realizes that she images her big body as a defense against the world, she may also realize that she imagines her defensive wall in a circumference two feet around herself. Her physical body then holds enough weight to fill that space. If she transforms her defensive attitude to one of inner strength, then she can concentrate on a shaft of inner light within her body that cannot be invaded from the outside. Once she has achieved this, her posture noticeably changes and gradually her body takes a more definite shape and substance. In other words, the perceived and the perceiver influence each other.

Another form of body work is movement based on human developmental patterns and evolutionary origins. Since human movement has its foundation in the early patterns that we learn and develop as infants and is rooted in our evolutionary inheritance, reexperiencing these movement sequences can open a greater depth of physical and psychic experience. The dreams of fish and human embryos that emerge reaffirm Jung's statement that "the lower vertebrates have from earliest times been favourite symbols of the collective psychic substratum, which is localized anatomically in the subcortical centres, the cerebellum and the spinal cord."[13]

It is also possible to approach the authenticity of the body and psyche through the voice. By releasing the body from its chronic conflicts and permitting the breath to reach into the body depths, we allow the voice to come naturally from its own instinctual source with full resonance. Few people hear their own voices because their fear and blocked rage keep the voice in the throat, unrelated to the real energy of their imagination and their emotions. In those brief moments when we do manage to free our own authentic voices, the whole being resonates with that truth, and a marriage of personal and transpersonal is palpable in the environment.

The possibilities of discovery in this area are beginning to open in many directions. It may be the meeting point for the intuitive wisdom of the East and the conscious knowledge of the West. In *The Tao of Physics*, Capra writes,

> He [Bohm] sees mind and matter as being interdependent and correlated, but not causally connected. They are mutually enfolding projections of a higher reality which is neither matter nor consciousness.[14]

Integrating Body, Dream and Active Imagination

One example will illustrate how body work can resonate with a dream image, immediately bringing to consciousness powerful repressed emotions which, without embodiment, might have fallen back into unconsciousness. Louise was in her early forties, had a history of eating problems, had done intensive body work for several years and had been in analysis for three. Her father died when she was three, leaving an ideal image of masculinity with which no ordinary man could compete. The dream came after an intense body session. It is written exactly as it was recorded on her tape cassette. Here is the first part:

> I notice a light streaming through a partially open door. I go in. It [a room] is empty of furniture, has polished hardwood floors, blue pale painted walls with white wood trim and floor-to-ceiling windows, high ceiling, much light. Back wall had built-in white cupboards like in church halls and two toilets. Also a little back staircase where workers were. They wondered why I was there. I asked if there was a kitchen. They replied, "No." Just like that. "No." I figured that it was still a perfect studio, just the right size, wouldn't need a kitchen if I didn't live there. But as I went back up and into the studio it seemed bigger, and bigger, and probably too much rent. As I passed through, it got even bigger and I left.
>
> There appeared then a shape of an arm on a map. It looked like an erect penis. It cut a swath on the map. It's the part to remain open from the experience. Then I'm in the bedroom, originally the studio, with my husband and the worm. ...

At that time in her life, Louise was in the process of choosing a teaching studio and was so concerned that the space be right that she considered eating her meals out rather than paying for a kitchen and bothering with cooking. In the dream the studio has an elegant, classical quality: it is spacious with excellent light, pale blue with white trim. The setting suggests high ideals, a work space in which she is not in touch with everyday reality. There is no furniture for her, no food for her. It is a place where she can minister to others. The aesthetically beautiful room suggests an idealized father and, as it grows bigger, she realizes the price of such perfection may be too high. The open door suggests an opportunity—the possibility of surveying that space in order to recognize that it is negative space, that she cannot live there, that this world of cold, perfectionistic thinking needs two toilets and leaves no room for the reality of her personhood. This kind of psychological space is judgmental, at the same time self-sacrificing, indifferent to ego needs. The workers on the stairs stress the fact that there is no kitchen. Nothing can come in to be transformed. While she may become more aware of her neurotic conflict in such a well-lit space, the raw energy necessary for healing and transformation is not there. Here she may become a martyr to her own ideals without ever being grounded in her own instinctual reality.

Suddenly an arm cuts a swath across a map, a giant penis rips into what has been her archetype of the way; that rent is "the part to remain open from the experience." Something bigger than her known experience is smashing in, demanding a larger awareness. She thought of it as the hand of God, Fate, the Self, opening her to a larger circumference. No longer will she be able to live in terms of pleasing others in her blue room. (The impact of the dream was so powerful that I felt it might be the critical turning-point of her life.) Now she must really ask, "Who am I?"

Through the neurotic split comes the experience; through the experienced conflict comes the truth; through the wound comes the healing. The penis is the creative principle. (Jung writes, "The phallus always means the creative mana, the power of healing and fertility, the 'extraordinarily potent.' ")[15] Through it the male and female are united; through it the semen is injected. If it is not erect, there is no immediate need for union. The question, "What do I really want?" creates the erect penis. "What do I really feel?" creates the wound. When she decides to leave that room, the penis is erect. But the problem is, "Who am I outside that room?" As Louise discussed the dream, a sob of terror and recognition broke from her when that last question was repeated. "I don't know," she whispered, "I do not know." In the dream that moment constellates the worm.

The dream continued:

I and my husband brought him up from an early age. Just a funny, tiny, wee, little thing at first. Like the marsupial babies out of the womb when barely conceived and crawling around in Mother's pouch. No hair, just wet skin, like little worms. My husband was very in tune with it; it was very necessary to him.

We were in the bedroom where my husband looked after him. I was holding him but he moved so quickly on my hands that I was terrified I would lose him. So I thought it would be interesting to let him crawl on the floor because then he wouldn't move so much on me. It was a polished wood floor. He moved so quickly I was really worried I would lose him, that I wouldn't be able to catch him again, or would lose him under something. He was so small we wouldn't see him under something. He was so small we wouldn't see him very well. So I scrambled to get hold of him again and he scurried into a corner by the floor boards, but there was a lot of dust and lint there and he got caught in it. It stuck to him, so he became like a dust ball. I was panicking. I couldn't get a hold of him.

My husband never panicked. I finally got him but he looked awful. He was stiff as a board, dry, and covered in dust. The dust and lint had dried his skin and him up. And I thought, "Oh my God, this is terrible!" His eyes had gone white like a fish when it's over-cooked and he had another white eye on his belly (like the poking place of the Pillsbury Dough Boy).[16] I poured water on him and nothing happened. I said, "God, he's dead. I'm so sorry, he's dead, he's dead, he's dead!" Nothing happened, nothing happened! My husband left the room. As I watched him in my hand there was a metamorphosis. His eyes became whiter and then he was cradled in a corn husk; his whole back felt like a corn husk, was a corn husk. Suddenly he became alive. He got bigger and bigger and came out of the husk. He was very frightening and I yelled for my husband to come to come *to come*.

He was standing on the bed as we faced off. I kept looking at this monkey/child that was growing. I had a knife in my left hand very sharp and pointed and the beast grabbed a knife as well. I think he had a knife. I screamed for my husband who came to the door and I got just to the doorway and said, "You've got to call the zoo. You've got to call the zoo. Call the zoo. Call the zoo." And so he went to do that.

I kept the chimp/ape talking. I considered him quite dangerous; I thought him quite hostile. He had leapt off the bed and ended up in the closet.

I said, "Do you remember Grandpa?"

And he was hostile about the past. "I hated him."

I said, "Remember school?"—which my husband had taught him.

And he said, "I hated it. I hated it."

"Do you remember before school and being little?"

"I hated it! I hated it all."

My husband returned with this enormous meal on a tray for him and put it on the bed. I thought it a very improper meal for a *champ* (chimp)—all soups, mashed potatoes, carrots, green beans, all cooked soft.

He then left the room and I ran after him leaving the door ajar to keep an eye on the chimp. I said, "Have you called the zoo yet?"

He said, "Well, I did the food first."

And I said, "Oh, my God, that's crazy! You should have called them first! They should have been here by now!"

So as the dream ended he was picking up the phone nonchalantly to call the zoo.

Now she is with her husband in their bedroom, which had been the studio. The setting reinforces the theme of masculine-feminine relationship in her unconscious. Her husband is "very in tune" with the little worm who crawls around in Mother's pouch. The worm reflects the person she has been, the person who appears meek and mild, being what other people want her to be, Daddy's little girl doing the right things for the wrong reasons, attempting to please the established order. That worm is "very necessary" in partnership with this kind of gentle masculinity.

The truth is revealed, however, when the worm is born out of the corn husk, when it is released out of the mother principle. Suddenly a totally unknown part of her grows at a terrifying pace. Because she had not known her ape, she has not realized that what she is nursing inside her masochistic view of herself is rage. Her hatred toward her grandfather, school, being little, everything, has been repressed in her body. She has "aped out" what others wanted of her, identified with the mother who does everything right but cannot act out of her real feelings. The inner man in such a situation is a wimp but he has the common sense to feed the ape soft feminine foods. The ego recognizes the danger and wants to put the rage in the zoo. While the situation is not resolved in the dream, the masculine is in no hurry to lock the energy behind bars. Does the "aping" belong in the zoo? Or is this the instinctual energy necessary for the maturation of both masculine and feminine?

In her notes after a yoga workshop on the evening before her dream, Louise had written:

I had been working on my pelvis, trying to move it, trying to move the sacrum, the bottom of the spine, trying to connect to *hara* and bring the energy into my legs and arms. When I lay down at the end of the class I felt my right side (weak) balancing with my left in strength. My left softened. My whole body felt huge—good huge, energy flowing through toes and fingers. I enjoyed my bigness. But what was I to do with this balance and strength and calm energy? Something panicked in me; I felt terrible panic.

When she internalized the ape in active imagination in my office, she began,

I am aware of lower back pain in my fifth lumbar, also in my neck. It's characteristic of my family. It's the hatred, loathing, despising of everything that happens to a child when things are out of its control. It's hatred of the patriarchy, hatred of school. I never learned anything that had to do with me. School was a bore except for specific teachers.

As she singled out various objects of her loathing, her body vibrated uncontrollably. That rage climaxed in waves of energy moving from feet to head. There was a pause, then hysterical cries somewhere between laughter and sobbing, then crystal clear laughter rippled all through her body for some moments. Then her body fell, her forehead on the ground. She remained in this reverent posture for some time, then sat quietly on the floor and said,

> I feel such joy, such calm. All the body work I have done, all the screaming out of anger and pain was personal. I thought that was over. Even when I had the dream I did not connect to the rage. I am shocked. I didn't know it was there. Only now do I recognize the transpersonal quality of that rage. I feel it. It is a relief.

When she poked "the poking place" of her Pillsbury Boy, she was quite unprepared for the numinous energy that poured out of her dough—first negative, then positive. Through the place of her wounding, physically and psychically, the numinous energy entered and the transformation began.

Looked at as a rite of passage, this dream and the ensuing body session make quite clear the meaning of Esther Harding's remark that the conscious person's reaction to difficulties will be psychological rather than physical symptoms (above, page 59).

Louise has outgrown the blue studio, the life of feeding the idealized father while depriving her own marsupial baby ("barely conceived"), at the same time unconsciously compensating with food. Without that blue womb and the womb of her mother's pouch, she is terrified. The great "arm of God" sweeps across her territory and destroys the old map. She is psychologically born—her psychologically conscious femininity, her Kore, is released from unconscious matter. She becomes aware of herself as *I*, with her own needs and her own emotions, and with that awareness comes the problem of the repressed rage and the will to power.

Like Louise, many men and women have been hungry all their lives. But hungry for what? For food, for recognition, for power, for righteousness? Like hollow Young Man in Edward Albee's *American Dream*, they feel they were separated, when they were still very young, from their twin, "inasmuch as you can separate one being." They were "torn apart, thrown to opposite ends of the continent." Like him, their soul, their "twin bumble," has been gouged out, and they are left saying,

> I have been drained, torn asunder ... disemboweled. I have, now, only my person ... my body, my face. I use what I have ... I let people love me ... I accept the syntax around me, for while I know I cannot relate

Martha Graham never claims to have invented the contraction of the body. Rather, its very organic aspect in human life is what she chose to formalize and dramatize. At its most basic, she explained, "The release is the moment in life when you inhale; the breathing going out, when you exhale, is the contraction. It's the first and last moments in life and it's used as technique, to increase the emotional activity in the body—so that you're teaching the body, not teaching the mind."

Angular, sharp, and stunningly percussive, the Graham contraction always originates in what Graham calls "the house of the pelvic truth."— Anna Kisselgoff, *New York Times Magazine,* Feb. 19, 1984. (Photograph by Barbara Morgan, from *The Notebooks of Martha Graham;* New York: Harcourt Brace Jovanovich, 1973)

... I know I must be related *to*. I let people love me ... I let people touch me ... I let them draw pleasure from my groin ... from my presence ... from the fact of me ... but, that is all it comes to. As I told you, I am incomplete ... I can feel nothing. I can feel nothing. And so ... here I am ... as you see me. I am ... but this ... what you see.[17]

Whatever ego they have operates at all costs to hide their inner world or lack of it. They have no kitchen, no way of taking nature's wisdom in, no way of processing and integrating it. Because their egos are so frail, they have no way to mediate what is going on between conscious and unconscious. They are identified with their personas, each building a body beautiful that gestures and performs, cut off from instinctual and imaginative roots. If these roots are never nourished, they are never gratified. They are abandoned, ravenously hungry, incessantly attempting to reach their natural satiation point—which never comes. Until the abandoned soul is allowed to return from exile, there is no possibility of physical or spiritual peace.

*

The fury of the neglected Goddess often manifests when individuals begin to experience their genuine femininity. When their virgin soul has been ravished from the grip of the mother complex, they become conscious of how they have betrayed their outcast whore and may be angry with everyone in their past who has ever denied their totality. They need to recognize, then, that their forebears were probably never initiated into *their* femininity, and therefore left their children a heritage of unconscious feminine outrage. Each generation labors in the shadow of its predecessors.

It is important to recognize the difference between personal anger in intimate relationships, and transpersonal rage that erupts from an archetypal level, the level at which the Goddess enters. When that differentiation takes place and the rage is appropriately released, the Goddess can turn her other face. Then the soul can take up residence in its vastly enlarged home and go about its own creative life. The density of matter is infiltrated by Light so that the individual, instead of lugging around a heap of dark flesh, experiences both the calm, rich wisdom of the conscious ego in the conscious body and the authenticity of the transpersonal love that impregnates Being.

Redeemed matter is the container confident enough and flexible enough to magnify the creative imagination.

Voices from the Chrysalis

It's difficult work trying to remember in my body the beatings I took from early childhood, through my adolescence. I know the events took place. I remember the preambles, the aftermaths, but have no memory of a single blow to my body. I've always seen these blank pages as a saving grace, a necessary mercy, but I begin to perceive the price my body has paid for its amnesia. It has lost consciousness of itself, anesthetized itself too well. The work is terrifying. I feel it in my throat, my chest, my pelvis. But my choice is made. I won't give up.

Incest made me a radioactive child. It activated guilt, sexuality. Fantasies protected me from the pain. I always pretended I was asleep.

I decided to let go. I let my lungs open themselves and let the breath come into my diaphragm. I learned to breathe into my backside, and my God, what I discovered there! Terror. My diaphragm was holding a murderer down.

I always believed in God. I always had the gift of faith. Now, with my wife's death I feel this terrible emptiness that nothing can fill. I tried food. I tried alcohol. But I refuse to be buried alive. I want to trust again. I'm doing some very difficult work—trying to remember in a physical, body memory.

I've never learned to be angry except in a very negative raging way. Now it is hard to feel legitimate in that.

Living with my mother was like living with a star that was so awesome, so beautiful, I just wanted to breathe her in with my eyes. I became more aware of my own plainness, my own insignificance. Cold and unapproachable as she was, I drank her through my eyes. She was a wonderful knife in my side.

I finally found my little girl. I let her dance—spontaneous, free. Loving her, I love myself. I am worthy of love. I can give love.

My throat and chest were always full of phlegm. One day I was able to roar. Then I could sing.

Breath is the secret of letting go. It won't allow me to lock into one thing. Breath reinforces images or allows them to change. It allows me to be receptive, flowing, balanced.

I never lived my own life. I pray for the dignity to die my own death.

I look in the mirror. I see the lines. I put on makeup. Lipstick doesn't make me look vital. I see a tired painted face. I'm sixty, I've aged ten years in two. I've never felt my age before. Now I want me—no veneer—just me. I won't pretend. I want to live before I die.

"There are two kinds of people," she once decreed to me emphatically. "One kind, you can just tell by looking at them at what point they congealed into their final selves. It might be a very *nice* self, but you know you can expect no more suprises from it. Whereas, the other kind keep moving, changing. . . . They are *fluid*. They keep moving forward and making new trysts with life, and the motion of it keeps them young. In my opinion, they are the only people who are still alive. You must be constantly on your guard, Justin, against congealing."

—Gail Godwin, *The Finishing School.*

You make me feel shiny and new,
Like a virgin,
Touched for the very first time,
Like a virgin.

—Pop singer Madonna.

The fate of fire depends on wood; as long as there is wood below, the fire burns above. It is the same in human life; there is in man likewise a fate that lends power to his life. And if he succeeds in assigning the right plan to life and to fate, thus bringing the two into harmony, he puts his fate on a firm footing.

—Ting (The Cauldron), *I Ching,* Hexagram 50.

There is one elementary TRUTH—the ignorance of which kills
countless ideas and splendid plans:
The moment one definitely commits oneself, then Providence
moves too. All sorts of things occur to help one that
never otherwise would have occurred. . . .

Whatever you can do,
Or dream you can do,
Begin it.
Boldness has genius, power and magic in it.
Begin it now.

—Goethe.

4

At the Right Time:

The Ritual Journey

He who tiptoes cannot stand;
He who strides cannot walk.
—Lao Tzu, *Tao Te Ching.*

If you enjoy watching caterpillars, you may someday be lucky enough to observe the moment when the crawling stops. Delicate membranes are attached to a twig, the old skin is shed and the pupal skin begins to harden. The caterpillar has chosen the kind of food the butterfly will need; it has chosen the exact space the butterfly will require to inflate its wings. Without that space immediately available, the wings would stick together and the butterfly would never fly. Instinctively, the creature that crawls on its belly meticulously prepares for the winged flower that will emerge.

If we look back on our own lives, we see a similar process. In our mother's womb, we develop the hands and feet, the eyes, the ears, the lungs—all the physical attributes which, in the fullness of time, will be essential to us as human beings during our stay on Earth. As we mature, we are astonished at the accuracy with which Fate uses one situation to develop the attributes necessary for another. From the soul's standpoint, it is possible that life as we know it now is a uterus in which the subtle body is preparing itself for the world into which it will be born when our physical body dies. Many of us, at one time or another, have felt a propensity for wings.

I was once meditating on T.S. Eliot's "intersection of the timeless moment."[1] I drew my own Celtic cross encircled by flame in the center of a large piece of paper, and then (whether it was Eliot's image or my own I've never been able to ascertain), I drew a necklace of cameos around the cross and in each of the first few cameos I painted an image of a moment in my life when the divine had intersected the human. Whenever another "timeless moment" occurred, I filled in another cameo. Now, with three cameos yet to be filled, I see those moments as the eternal thread that illuminates the necklace of my life. I see each as a distilled essence: stripped to bone, antennae still unfolding.

Most of us—if we are not in permanent jet lag, our bodies flying ahead while our souls are left behind—are trying to make a meaningful pattern

73

out of the random incidents of our lives. We sense that we have lost our birthright. We don't know exactly what that is. We do know we want to find it. Since ritual is inherent in our nature, participating consciously in our own ritual journeys is a reliable way of recognizing our own needs, our own destinies.

Primitive man, driven by instinctual energy, made his slow and dangerous way up the mountain into the cave. There he wrestled, out of his own darkness, images that capture the very essence of the animals they portray. By going back into the uterus of the Great Mother, he reconnected with the seeds of his own creativity.[2]

In societies where ritual was and is a part of the social structure, the ego of the individual is dissolved in the group ritual and the participants reestablish their bond with the transcendent power. Only when the person is in a state of *participation mystique* (identification) with the group and the numinous power released in the unconscious does transformation occur. Having surrendered one's ego to the transpersonal energy of the group, one is enlarged, no longer isolated in a private world. The rites of passage are accompanied by elaborate preparations: purification, sometimes masks to suggest a change of personality, a ritual garment, tattooing, and symbolic dance routines that are accepted individually and culturally as part of the transformation process. The purpose of the ritual is to bring the individual, through intense concentration, to a point of psychological intensity where the archetype will burst through to consciousness, manifesting in an image that releases powerful energy (primitive man creating the essence of the animal on the cave wall). The places in which the image appears are thereafter revered as holy places and religiously maintained as sanctuaries where the divine might again intersect the human.

In genuine ritual, the journey is both inner and outer, which means that the body as well as the psyche is involved, often with both being extended to their utmost limits. The individual is attempting to transcend the present ego position: by allowing oneself to drop into the unconsciousness of one's emotionally charged body, one can break through the present ego barriers into the transpersonal energy infusing the group. Thus one's relationship to oneself and to the world is restored, and life has meaning within a mythical framework.

The upheavals of the twentieth century have left many people without ritualistic containers. For the individual attempting his or her personal path, fateful moments occur when the ego is gripped by the Self. In all honesty, one says, "I feel I am dying." The confrontation is indeed a confrontation unto death because a new gradient is being released into the conscious psyche, and the ego has no alternative but to follow unless it resigns itself to psychic death. The confrontation has to be dealt with in some ritualistic manner in order to find out what archetype is behind the assault and how the ego can cooperate in shaping its own destiny. By bringing the archetype to consciousness through ritual action, writes Erich Neumann, "the potentially spiritual character of the hitherto unconscious act becomes transparent, the archetype or symbol reaches a new level of efficacy," and the individual achieves a new level of awareness.[3] When the god or goddess appears—that is, when the symbol is made conscious—consciousness and unconscious are thus connected, and the repetitive ritual behavior is no longer necessary. In fact, for introverts, meditation in place of ritual acting out may be sufficient to generate the energy necessary for an image to manifest in consciousness. Whether through meditation or through ritual, individuals find themselves in a position where they must be their own priests, and it is most important that they understand what they are enacting or what is being enacted in them.

Modern men and women, pulled by the same magnet that drew the Ice Age man up to the cave, are journeying through the dark labyrinth of their own souls. In spite of the pain and terror involved, the archetype of the way lures them; they yearn to bring the unconscious to consciousness. Penetrating into that tunnel of death and potential rebirth demands supreme effort, tenaciously holding on with no conscious orientation until a light shines in the darkness. Only if the tension between the anxiety and the fascination is held, will the combustion point occur—the point when the tearing apart ceases and a sense of unity is experienced. With the unity there invariably comes an image. If it happens to be an archetypal image of the Great Mother, then one can assume that the unconscious situation, behind the anxiety and the compulsive fascination that demanded the journey, is made visible in that image. Unless the tension is held until the image appears, the energy will regress into unconsciousness and the gold of the experience is lost. That particular initiation has failed.

In twentieth-century society, a form of group ritual is enacted at rock festivals. Pop music has always been an accurate barometer of the currents of its own time, and rock lyrics today no longer appeal only to teenagers. The accouterments of ritual are all there—masks, jewelry, tattooing, ritual garments, suggestive symbols, dance—all these held together by the insistence of the musical beat and the shriek of heavily amplified guitars. While drugs were part of the ritual scene in the sixties and seventies, Grandmaster Flash and the Furious Five warn eighties' listeners, "Don't do it." At the center is the rock star who stimulates the participants into a ritual frenzy until a combustion point is reached, and symbols appear in the minds of the believers. If the listeners have been thoroughly gripped by the experience, they will return enhanced and enlarged. The problem, however, as it was with the earlier "flower children," is that if the ego is not strong enough to integrate the archetypal images, one gains no enlightenment from the ritual, and far from being enlarged, the individual has merely succumbed to collective activity. In that case, the robbery of the birthright is further enacted. Instead of moving into larger consciousness, the ego is absorbed and made vulnerable to mass poisoning.

Much can be learned from modern rock stars about emerging archetypal images. Cyndi Lauper throws herself into *Time After Time* with no apologies for her female auto-eroticism. In her gypsy garb, charged with manic energy and gentle sensitivity, she is the outsider, the lost little girl who made it. She is who she is. And then there is Madonna herself, a woman whose birth certificate actually bears the name Madonna, a woman whose body conveys all the action-packed activity of "the trash queen of the hop."⁴ Whatever else she is doing, she is exploiting the emerging archetype of the virgin, the woman who, in Esther Harding's phrase, "does what she does ... because what she does is true."⁵ She is playing the paradox (virgin/whore) for all it is worth—and it is worth well into the millions. Her Boy Toy, one of her famous accessories, competes with her rosaries and crucifixes as part of her image. Together they are blatant in their message: if you can't deal with me, that's your problem.

Cyndi and Madonna are at the moment (March 12, 1985) the two most popular feminine icons of the pop world, and as symbols they are playing a decisive role in constellating millions of unconscious virgins, male and female. They are concretized versions of an archetype that is carrying a huge emotional charge, an archetype that is still in the process of becoming conscious in the culture as a whole. The point is that they do embody an image from the unconscious, and they do act as magnets for that emerging image in their listeners. Both are exploiting their outcast condition and the fierce and poignant energy the outcast embodies. Both are concretized symbols carrying new energy and releasing new energy—the virgin forever pregnant with new possibilities. Surely one of those possibilities burst into cultural consciousness when rock singers, in response to the Ethiopian famine, banded together to declare, "We are the world, we are the children."⁶

Now, where is the fixed point of renewal for people who are neither pop music fans nor faithful believers in church dogma nor participants in church ritual? Where is their ritual journey? What does it look like?

In *Symbols of Transformation*, Jung points out that dogma was essential at one stage of man's mental development.

> The barrage of materialistic criticism that has been directed against the physical impossibility of dogma ever since the age of enlightenment is completely beside the point. Dogma *must* be a physical impossibility, for it has nothing whatever to say about the physical world but is a symbol

Pop singer **Madonna** in the film *Desperately Seeking Susan.*

of "transcendental" or unconscious processes which, so far as psychology can understand them at all, seem to be bound up with the unavoidable development of consciousness. Belief in dogma is an equally unavoidable stop-gap which must sooner or later be replaced by adequate understanding and knowledge if our civilization is to continue.[7]

Many people without church dogma and ritual are now being thrust into such "unconscious processes which ... seem to be bound up with the unavoidable development of consciousness." In their dreams they arrive at some border or port; they find themselves in Vancouver or San Francisco, or Buffalo lies in darkness across the river. Something may be impeding their crossing. Perhaps they have lost their identity card, or they are carrying too much luggage. Sometimes they arrive at a well-beloved threshold (the demarcation and meeting place between the outer profane world and the inner sacred space) and some crisis blocks their entry. They cannot pass over into the new world. They need to go to the bathroom, but there is a long line before them, or someone persists in stepping ahead.

What does one do when everything rational inside says, "Let it go," and everything emotional says, "I cannot"? What does a widow do with her debilitating sense of loss over a husband who died six years ago? What does a man do with his yearning for the wife who left him four years ago? What does a mother do with her incapacitating grief for her child who died two years ago? How does one rechannel love into fresh, creative outlets? How does one reopen oneself to the flow of each new day? How does one become a virgin again? Or perhaps a better question: How does one become a virgin at all? That is the crucial question where private rituals are being considered because unless one has the strength of a virgin, private rituals, like public mass rituals, can degenerate into total loss of consciousness, or worse, find a collective demon at the center. Such rituals can end in hysteria and the collapse of the ego structure.

As I understand the virgin archetype, it is that aspect of the feminine, in man or in woman, that has the courage to Be and the flexibility to be always Becoming. Rooted in the instincts, the virgin has a loving relationship to the Great Earth Mother. But she is not herself the Great Mother. Men and women who can consciously relate to this archetype do not make mothering synonymous with femininity, nor are they hampered by unconscious material from their own personal mothers. They have been through the joy and the agony of the daily sorting of the seeds of their own feeling values in order to find out who they authentically are, and they continue to do so. They are strong enough and pliable enough to surrender to the penetration of the Spirit and to bring the fruit of that union into consciousness.

Sorting the seeds is a daily process of ruthless honesty that allows us grain by grain to discover our Being. The Latin verb *esse* means "to be"; thus in discovering our Being we are discovering our essence. This is a monumental task when we have spent our lives Doing, especially when Doing has become an escape from Being because Being is experienced as nothingness.

Again and again we have to say to ourselves: What was my feeling. in that situation—*not* my emotions, my feeling? My emotions may support my feeling, but emotions are affective responses determined by complexes, momentary reactions to an immediate situation. Feeling, on the other hand, evaluates what something is worth to me. What am I willing to put energy into? What is no longer of value to me? What did I really feel when the boss fed me Smarties today? I've always enjoyed them before, but today I felt him saying, "Be a good little girl. Keep quiet. Don't bother me." Why am I depressed? (Follow the depression back to where I betrayed my own feeling and turned my energy against myself). Is it possible my lover is not the man I thought him to be? Does he see me at all? Am I projecting my own inner man onto him? Am I forcing him to take responsibility for my undeveloped talents? Am I treating my body as my mother treated hers? Am I thinking like my father? Where am I blindly reacting as they did? Where am I still reacting childishly? Is my anger coming from my gut or from my head? Is it feminine anger or animus anger? (Feminine anger cleanses; animus anger

Madonna and Child by Michelangelo. (Uffizi Gallery, Florence)

leaves me tense.) Guided by the response of the unconscious as revealed in dreams, we differentiate grain from grain, question after question, until one day we find our own authentic voice.

In his study entitled "The Incest Taboo and the Virgin Archetype," John Layard makes clear that the word "virgin" was not synonymous with "chaste" in either its Greek or Hebrew origins. Referring to the Virgin Mary and to other mothers of divine heroes, he says,

> It would appear that to be a virgin in the mythological sense the woman must conceive outside or before the marriage bond. ...
>
> What then do we mean by "virgin"? It may help us to examine those ways in which we use the word which are not directly concerned with sex. We speak of a "virgin forest" as being one in which the powers of nature are untrammelled and untouched by man. But we can think of this from two diametrically opposite points of view. We can think of it either from the view of the agricultural pioneer, who would regard it as something to be destroyed and uprooted as soon as possible; or else we can think of it from the point of view of a nature lover who would regard the virgin forest with awe as a supreme manifestation of pregnant nature, and who would oppose all the most enlightened efforts of the agriculturalist or town-builder to destroy its primitive beauty,—who would, in fact, treat it as inviolably holy. The one would represent "law and order" and the other "nature". So that we have here two opposite principles, both valid, the law of man in apparently open conflict with the law of God. Yet it is the law of God, the untrammelled law of pregnant though as yet chaotic nature that we dub "virgin", and it is the reduction of that chaos which we call Law and Order.
>
> Thus in this sense *the word "virgin" does not mean chastity but the reverse, the pregnancy of nature, free and uncontrolled*, corresponding on the human plane to unmarried love, in contrast to controlled nature corresponding to married love, despite the fact that from the legal point of view sexual intercourse within the marriage bond is the only kind which is regarded as "chaste".
>
> It will be seen that this argument has landed us in the midst of a paradox, a paradox only to be solved either a) by regarding the whole biblical story of the Virgin Birth as purely allegorical, which the Church asserts it is not, it being, as she maintains, a unique historical event; or else b) by reconciling the two through the realization that instinct wants to be transformed into spirit, and that the Virgin Birth is the supreme example of this having been achieved, that is to say that Our Lady's womanhood was so complete and so closely united with God that it became self-reproductive.[8]

If we can tear off the old glasses and look at the symbolic meaning of the Virgin Mary, without the prejudices put upon her through centuries of church history, we can begin to see the significance of the virgin archetype. If that is impossible, then we can call her by another name: Leda, Danae, Semele, or any other of the human women who were ravished by a god. We have also to broaden our understanding of words like "chaste," "pure," "undefiled." We have also to remember that the symbolic content of myth, including Christian myth (and I am speaking mythologically, not religiously) has its roots in the human psyche. Mythically, Mary (unlike the earlier Greek maidens) was immaculately conceived, from the womb of Anne, a mature woman who, fearing she was too old to have a child, meditated and was visited by an angel. In response to him, Anne promised, "As the Lord my God liveth, if I bring forth either male or female, I will bring it for a gift unto the Lord my God, and it shall be ministering unto him all the days of its life."[9] In that tradition, the virgin, like the Divine Child, is the soul child of the spirit.

It is the virgin's meditative strength that is crucial in individual rituals. Without it, the ego can become inflated and then confused, and ultimately in danger of refusing to be a chalice of the divine will. Surviving as an outcast requires being strong enough to stand alone, trusting in one's own individual truth. Pondering in the heart is no sentimental journey to the Goddess. Modern women can learn much from the mistakes of the virgins described by Marion Zimmer Bradley in *The Mists of Avalon*. Fanatic in their beliefs, weaving their webs and plotting against their men, they sabotaged their personal lives by failing to open their eyes to a broader vision. Morgaine, having given herself totally to what she believed was the will of the Goddess (even when it went against her own feeling values), and having left a trail of death and destruction behind her, resignedly concludes, "The Gods move us as they will, whatever it is that we think that we are doing. We are no more than their pawns."[10] She dare not believe she had a choice, for the destruction she has left behind would drive her mad. Rituals to the Goddess can bring an influx of archaic energy and participants have to have sufficient ego strength to honor where they stand in relation to it. Otherwise, inflated with power, they fall into concentrating on what they want and magically making it come about. That is sorcery, locked in its own selfish possessiveness. In man or woman, the mature feminine, while grounded in the Goddess and open to her guidance, has honed its own personal value system. It knows its own authentic truth and has the courage to take responsibility for that truth and to act on it. That truth springs from the perpetual *now* of "letting go."

When we are strong enough to surrender to transpersonal energy without being shattered or possessed by it, ritual can bring to consciousness the spiritual meaning of otherwise unconscious acts. The symbol is the key. Through the symbolic image, the opposites are brought together, consciousness receives new life from the unconscious and we contact our essential being—our own wholeness, ourselves as both human and divine. If the concentration is not maintained (as in compulsive ritual) until the reconciling symbol appears, then the opposites are separated further apart, and instead of contacting the divine within, the participant is drawn deeper into unconsciousness. Although at first we can but vaguely comprehend the meaning and feeling value of an image, we *know* its value to our understanding of ourselves.

Committing ourselves to ritual involves total concentration (as distinct from possession). Concentration directs the energy toward consciousness and away from the unconscious flow back into the instincts. Relating to the inner images becomes a natural part of life's sustenance as the ego learns to take direction from the inside. It discovers there a world that has its own order, a world that operates through a set of laws very different from those of the transitory world. There every minute is new, every minute is *now*. Nothing is fixed. What is right in one moment may be wrong in the next. Learning to resonate with that world physically and psychically is a continuing process of listening to the inner dialogue and allowing the blossoming, petal by petal, in the heart.

Some of my analysands have severe eating disorders involving compulsive ritual behavior. Repeatedly, they are compelled into solitary rituals in which, fascinated and at the same time repulsed by food as a ritual object, they are captured by an overwhelming anticipation that drives them to eat, to eat and vomit, or to steal and hide food. Many of the elements of ritual may be present—ritual dishes, dress, repetitive gestures, and most important, the compulsion to surrender the ego to some inner driving force that will take them out of the bread and butter world, metaphorically, but into it, literally.

Grain, honey and milk are traditionally the foods of the Goddess; they are also the foods consumed in most ritual binges and bulimic vomiting. Behind the food compulsion may be a desire to consume the Goddess, a compensation for the driven, rational attitudes of daily life. Or the compulsive behavior may sometimes be evoked by another compulsion, even more dangerous, the compulsion to go with the beloved masculine spirit (often symbolized as the Light), which would take them away from the reality of a world which does not interest them. Enthralled by that spirit world, euphoric with starvation, they may suddenly be thrown into compulsive eating. It is as if the Goddess will not let them go into spirit and the death that awaits them there. However great the desire to escape, she calls them back to reality, back to the daily pressures of work, the bills to be paid, the essays to be written—and the food to be devoured. In her negative aspect she can call them back into sheer stupor, which is another kind of death. The compulsion, with its rigid, repetitive ceremony, blinds its victim to the larger reality of what is happening. Profane ritual becomes a parody of sacred ritual. The compulsive behavior which began as an attempt to find spiritual meaning ends in identification with the dark side of the mother archetype. Bulimic vomiting may

Painting of "the reconciling symbol" by Mindy Vosseler.

be an attempt to break that identification and return to the spirit.

If the addict can bring to consciousness what the ritual object symbolizes, rather than become possessed by it, then the energy which is moving into ego-obliteration through possession by a false god or goddess can be turned around and find its transcendence creatively. If the ego container is strong enough, the energy released from the destructive drive can be rechannelled into life-enhancing meaning.

Through ritual, human beings can free themselves from a purely instinctual drive in the unconscious. The more conscious we are, the more we recognize that we are not bound by a merely instinctual existence. We are not meant to be possessed either by instinct or spirit. Possession makes us blind to our images, thereby obliterating the soul and leaving us in the nonhuman realm of pure spirit or pure matter. The function of images is to mediate so that we are not possessed either by spirit or by matter. They allow us to dwell in an intermediate world which is the world of soul-making, the domain of ritual. Ritual is the soul's journey through images, images which, while partaking of both spirit and matter, belong to neither, are possessed by neither.

Transforming an Eating Disorder

Lisa was a thirty-five-year-old professional woman who had been in analysis for three years. She had gradually lost seventy-five pounds; she wanted to lose fifty more. Having devoted herself to her studies and her profession, she had never had an intimate relationship with a man. She had worked hard to free herself from her psychologically incestuous relationship to her father, and her anger toward her mother. She was no longer ashamed of her body, but the touch of a man would fill her with terror and despair, so much so that she would freeze, rigid and inarticulate. After such incidents, she would binge. She wanted the comfort of food, the swallowing down of sweetness to combat the rising fear and rage. More than that, she was terrified to give up her big body, her shelter, her armor, her constant excuse for everything that had been denied her. Her dreams began to circle back to her early childhood, the point where she had abandoned her creative child. She was breaking out in rashes, her lower back was in constant pain. Most disconcerting was her nausea when she defiantly ate chocolate. But she was too terrified to let go.

She was moving toward a threshold. Her skin rash was telling her the old snake skin had to be sloughed off; her lower back was weary of carrying her rage; her stomach was experiencing chocolate as poison. Her dreams were asking her to go back and reclaim her abandoned creativity. She was coming up to the threshold where she might step into her own womanhood. If this threshold were missed, she might regain all the weight she had lost.

And it would have been missed had preparations not been in the making for months beforehand. She and her cultural milieu were convinced that by dieting she was moving toward her own salvation. An inner voice, however, was not convinced. "What if I do get thin, and what if life still isn't worth living? That's the last 'SO WHAT?' " There was the ultimate hurdle. She was facing the loss of the illusion that had fed her all her life. Fear could escalate into panic, panic that was hard to identify because Lisa seemed to be accomplishing exactly what she set out to do.

Preparations for the threshold were in the making, physically and psychically, as described in other chapters of this book. Here I want to focus on the terror of giving up the known body. Anyone who has not lived in a body that does not correspond to a social norm finds the anguish hard to comprehend. It is easier to understand a rich man's grief when he loses his fortune, or a socialite's dread when she becomes allergic to makeup. These people are operating within society's value system. What happens, however, to people who have never held society's values, whose physical body has forced them to develop values of their own? When others rejected it, its occupant in one way or another has taken care of it. To forsake it, without consciously dealing with the grief, is like forsaking a retarded child. Moreover, whatever the body has been, it has taken center stage in almost every decision. To lose it as an habitual preoccupation is to make room for free-floating anxiety. To be free of a compulsion is to stare into the abyss.

Nor is life in a fat body without its compensations. Whether her innate temperament, family situation or peer group rejection has created her outsize body, the fat woman has had to develop enough inner strength to walk alone, and a degree of ironic detachment that simultaneously attaches her to, and separates her from, the rest of the human race. What that does to her authentic feelings and to her body is another question, but it does give her a certain psychological strength. Secretly she may be an Artemis, the virgin huntress, wild, free and unapproachable, or she may be an Athena, the virgin idealist, sensitive, energetic, a lone leader fighting for a cause. This is the other side of the virgin—aloof, untouchable, undefiled, unawakened to her own sexuality. A fat body is the armor of Athena, the arrows of Artemis. To give it up is to become defenseless. A new whirlwind of questions rips into a consciousness accustomed to solitary pride: Do I want to join the masses? Am I remotely interested in Aphrodite's sexual intrigues? Do I want to worry about my bust-line or the newest makeup? How could I commit myself to a man? Could I degrade myself with Hera's jealousy? I see the messes the Aphrodites and Heras make of their lives, and I don't think I'm so badly off. I want my freedom.

A woman at this threshold is dealing with the paradox of virginity. Part of her clings to the lower innocence of the unconscious virgin; part of her yearns for the higher innocence of the mature virgin who is confident enough to be consciously vulnerable. Incorporating the whore side of the virgin—the outcast for whom there is no room in the inn—is saying YES to the body, YES to the passions, at a level the disembodied spirit does not know. It is the pure feminine energy that allows a woman to be in love with her body; it is the energy that surges from the soles of her feet to the top of her head. Unpossessed and unpossessing, its strength is its vulnerability, vulnerable to life, to love, to otherness. It is the energy of the sacred prostitute who surrenders herself to the Goddess, allowing herself to be filled with female spirit. In sexual intercourse, the man who can surrender himself to that energy is reborn through it. Yang meets Yin, Yin meets Yang, and in the interchange both are reborn and empowered. Initiated into womanhood without losing her virginhood, the pregnant virgin gives birth to herself, to the man, and to all creation—a new world radiating with new light. Then they separate and return to their own source.

Paradoxically, accepting the higher innocence brings the body to life.

The lower innocence is terrified of change, terrified of fertility and growth. Its reaction to any threshold is NO. Unless consciously dealt with, its reaction to this threshold that will take it into life is NEVER.

When Fate starts knocking on the door, in dreams and symptoms, then a ritual may evolve out of an inner demand. The sense of carrying a load that no longer needs to be carried becomes increasingly unbearable. What was, is finished; what lies ahead is unknown. Compulsive personalities do not turn energies around easily, even when they recognize that their habitual rituals have become sterile. They have immense psychic energy invested in one object or person and letting go of that, taking up a new orientation to life without substituting another false god, is no easy task. It cannot be done unless the individual recognizes that the regressive energy has become destructive and needs to be redirected into new creative outlets.

Going back into the womb to annihilate the ego is one thing; going back to attend to the seeds is another. It is the difference between infantile regression and what Jung called *reculer pour mieux sauter*—a step back, the better to leap forward.[11] The walk on the tightrope between compulsion and creativity is always precarious because the source of both is the same. When the ego is vulnerable enough, in other words conscious enough and strong enough, to surrender to the healing power of the new life that is attempting to break through, then ritual naturally makes the connection. The time has to be ripe.

If the possibility of the intersection of human and divine is recognized in daily life, then ritual does not seem foreign. Older cultures always left room for the gods at the threshold and fireside, and in other parts of the home. Altars are set up in our lives whether we realize it or not, and unconscious altars encourage demonic visits. The refrigerator can be a cold altar for an icy god. Altars that are consciously set up create a container that can hold an influx of spiritual energy. One has to search for the right place in one's environment to create a sacred spot for the purpose of concentration.

When Lisa felt the right time encroaching on her, she took three days off work plus a long weekend. With very little formal knowledge of ritual, she allowed herself to do whatever was dictated from within. She stayed alone in her apartment. She took the phone off the hook. She fasted. She bathed and put on fresh clothes. She chose a sacrificial object—her beautiful mother's wedding veil which she had played with reverentially in her childhood, a veil that had effectively shrouded her from ever making a marriage of her own, free of the shackles that bound her mother. She put it on her small altar and left it there. Every time she passed it, her breath caught at the thought of losing it. She wrote in her journal for hours about what her body had meant to her, about her father, her mother, her brother. She assessed her sacrifice: her illusions of grandeur, her need to control, her proud isolation. She wept. She allowed herself to mourn for the person she had been. She cleaned out cupboards. She thought. She wrote some more. She danced. She washed and waxed the floor. Always she was circling the inevitability of allowing the infantile Lisa to die. That circling she brought to consciousness in her journal.

> Can I let her die? She's dead. The truth is she is dead already. Binging doesn't give me a high anymore. It doesn't deaden the pain. It's become soul destroying, self-betrayal, distracting me from responsibilities to myself. It forces me to face the despair of no longer respecting myself. Still, I'm trying to conquer the extremes—all or nothing. That feels like real energy.
>
> But the terror—the terror of living with her, the terror of living without her. What now? If I go with my real feelings, I'll have to go back to university. I'll have no money. I'll have to face the interminable essays. I'll have to give up some of my friends. They'll feel betrayed. They think they know me, but they don't. We really have little in common. I'm not the person I pretend to be. I thought I was alone before. Now I'll really be alone. There won't be anybody.
>
> And my poor body. Every time I lie on the floor it curls up in the foetal position. It goes rigid, won't let anything in. It's stubborn and resistant. It's always been this way; it's never going to be any other way. This is my fate. I've tried and tried and tried to make things happen. Nothing ever happens. I no longer expect anything to happen. It's defeat, defeat, DEFEAT.
>
> I force my arms and legs to open. I smash the floor. I'm afraid of my own rage. What is this spasm that makes me curl up this way? I cannot stay open. I cry, but this crying is different from the other crying. This is a tiny baby that cries from its gut—heartbroken sobs. It's so alone.
>
> What does this baby want? I can't go on hating her. My hatred makes her whine and she whines until she's hysterical. The more she whines, the more I hate her. I've got to listen to her. Whoever I am, she's part of me. Who am I? Am I old enough to be responsible for myself? I'm only 35. Do I want to be responsible?

She wrote her answers in terms of the present and compared them to the past. She painted images that called out for color and allowed them to transform in their own impetuous way. Then she was startled by a mature feminine voice that controlled her pen.

> You have to decide whom you serve. Are you still accepting her death sentence? Are you still bound to the complex that tried to suck out your young life and would now try to take it away again? Decide whether what you've been writing is real or fantasy. Recognize what ground you're standing on. What Goddess are you worshipping? Are you bound by the law or are you living in the spirit? Are you going to continue in fetters

or are you free? Can you step into the authenticity of your own life? Your own death? Most of what you've written no longer applies. Your responsibility now is to your new life.

Lisa tried then to hear her abandoned child's voice, and received two responses.

I am your body. My mother did not want me. I huddled in her womb as still as I could be. I was terrified of being thrown out. I survived the rupture of birth. I was unwelcomed when I got here. Had I been a boy the story might have been different. My parents gave the name they chose for me to my brother. I tried to be no bother. I was always afraid of being killed so I tried to do everything I could to be loved. I do not want to live because I am not loved. I have always been hated. Whoever it is that hates me never ceases to punish me for a crime I know nothing about. It's as if my very existence is a crime. I am punished because I exist. When I am hungry, I am not fed. When I am exhausted, I am not allowed to rest. When I need to move, I am forced to stay still. Sometimes I go wild with freedom, but I know it won't last. Whoever is doing this must hate me. But I do not know why I am hated. The punishment would stop if I ceased to exist. I am tired of being punished for a crime I never committed. I AM NOT GUILTY ... No one listens to me. I want to die because I have been sentenced to life imprisonment for a crime I never committed.

Then she heard another voice:

Lisa, Lisa, hear me. You do not understand. That is the voice of my despair. I do want to live. I am your soul. When I say I don't want to live, I mean I do not want to live in this disembodied state. I do not want to live like a ghost. I mirrored your mother. I mirrored your father. They used me to see themselves. I could not enter your body because you could not endure the anguish of your mother's rejection and your father's possession of your body. She was never yours. Now you are conscious of her anguish. Together we can love her and bring her to life. I am immortal. I cannot die, but I must have a home. I must see and hear and taste and smell and feel if I am to grow.

For the first time in her life Lisa was not angry with her body. Instead, she found she had taken up residence inside and was listening to her soul from within. For her, this was an extraordinary reversal and recognition: she had walked in her shadow's shoes all her life. Her real ego she had never lived.

The rhythm of her solitary days crescendoed as she became physically more tired and psychically more conscious. Part of her was avoiding the ritual; part was moving inevitably toward it. She became what Victor Turner calls one of the "liminal entities" who

are neither here nor there; they are betwixt and between the positions assigned and arrayed by law, custom, convention, and ceremonial. As such, their ambiguous and indeterminate attributes are expressed by a rich variety of symbols in the many societies that ritualize social and cultural transitions. Thus liminality is frequently likened to death, to being in the womb, to invisibility, to darkness, to bisexuality, to the wilderness, and to an eclipse of the sun or moon.[12]

Without quite understanding what she was doing, Lisa allowed the instincts to guide her body and the archetype to guide her psychic rhythms. Sensing their inner order and trusting it, she knew she was protected from too great and too fast an influx of spiritual energy. As she allowed the old world to go, the new was moving in. Unconscious ritual behavior associated with her compulsive eating was rechanneled into conscious awareness of what she was trying to do. This led to surrendering to the transpersonal energy that supported and directed in ways she never dreamed of.

On the fifth night, her energy had reached its zenith. She threw her ritual binging dress down the garbage chute, lit the candles and began her dance, allowing her body to circle, creating her sacred space. She had prepared her own ritual. Moving in and through and around the images of her own inner world, she arrived at the moment of sacrifice. She was subject and object—sacrificer and sacrificed. She sacrificed Lisa as she had been. She burned her ritual object, her mother's wedding veil, and in the burning she saw her own abandoned child. She took her in her arms and sat on the floor rocking her own body as she would have rocked a real baby. Then she opened her whole body to new possibility. She blew the candles out. She slept. Dawn came, not golden, but clear.

That is the bones of ritual. The transformative power of the love released cannot be articulated. Therein lies the mystery. For Lisa, being able to nourish and cherish her own spiritual child was the beginning of her own life. She as a woman was born.

Months later, she dreamed that she was looking into a starry sky. White Northern Lights began to whisk with gossamer veils from the horizon to the dome of heaven. As she looked, the veils parted and there, her head covered with stars, stood an image of Sophia, her powerful body moving with the lights, her hands sweeping her veils about her as she vanished. The sky swirled with light, and again the draperies parted and her soft feminine body sat, clothed in white samite, already evanescent among other veils, already gliding into another glimmering image.

Such an image can counterbalance a woman's derogatory feelings of her femininity as heavy, dark, stolid and earthbound. Shimmering with silver light, ever shifting, ever serene, the Goddess in the sky suggests the spiritual essence of womanhood. Refusing to be fixed, this Queen of the Night with her diadem of stars plays in and around and through the imagination, infusing darkness with light—a bridge between heaven and earth.

By nature, most addicts are involved in intercourse with the transpersonal, whether with devils or angels. If with devils, the self-destructive drives will become evident. If with angels, their ego will sooner or later be forced to submit to the fire of transformation, in which case their greedy wolf energy can become an unquenchable lust for life, with the intelligence and power of the wolf in the service of the sun-god Apollo (the god to whom the wolf belongs). Ritual demands concentration and discipline as the participant endeavors to wrestle consciousness out of unconsciousness, providing a channel for the libido lest it be lost in the instincts and the chaos of the unconscious.

The greatest threat to a successful transition is the possibility of abortion. What is sacrificed must be recognized and its loss acknowledged and mourned for as long as that may take, before final, irrevocable burial. Burial represents the conversion of subjective identification into objective facts, the *separatio* of the alchemical process. The possibility of outworn patterns reestablishing themselves is always present, and if they are resurrected they tend to become more stultifying and less relevant than ever. But when depths of subtlety capable of handling new and different energies are ready to be opened, grief that has hardened into despair can be unblocked and its energy rechannelled into vital springs of renewal. This potential energy needs to be recognized immediately in order to ensure its flow.

Lisa's experience is a good example of how ritual can act as a transformer of energy. Released from her compulsive rituals, she was also released from the terror of being whirled into the vortex of the dark side of the mother. Through her human endeavor, she brought herself to a point of submission, a vacuum, a womb ready to be fertilized by the spirit, ready to bring forth the transforming image. Using her knowledge of yoga, she stretched her whole Being that extra stretch, then released and allowed the new energy in. By going with her body to its farthest extension and letting go, by going with her psyche to its farthest extension and letting go, she cooperated with nature and spirit in allowing herself to be born. Her sacrifice released her forgiveness: loving her body, formerly seen as her enemy, she recognized it for what it was, her friend. Through her wounded body, her abandoned soul was returned to her. Through her wound, she became conscious of her inner virgin.

An Unexpected Initiation

Initiation ceremonies, in primitive tribes, in mystery cults and in the Christian Church, traditionally fall into three distinct phases: separation, transition and incorporation.[13] Bruce Lincoln suggests that for women these phases are better described as "enclosure, metamorphosis (or magnification), and emergence."[14] The person who enters a state of being at variance with the one previously held becomes "sacred" to those who remain in the profane state. "It is this new condition which calls for rites eventually incorporating the individual into the group, and returning him to the customary routines of life."[15]

A woman who suddenly becomes a widow, for example, is in sacred space, while her friends are in profane space. In ritual, she becomes "sacred"; she is in an altered state of consciousness, her ego is weakened, she is in direct contact with both the personal and archetypal unconscious. The isolation hut in primitive tribes provided the privacy essential to that condition; it provided a chrysalis in which the healing could take place. Who of us when we are suddenly thrown into sacred space—when we are no longer daughter, or mother, or husband—who of us in our bewilderment or grief has not yearned for the dignity of an isolation hut or a veil to protect our naked soul? Primitive or modern, people who have been separated from the tribe are in sacred space, transitional space in which they are vulnerable to gods and demons, vulnerable to transpersonal energy that changes their lives. Individuals who are carrying out rituals alone, or with a sensitive friend, or a strong support group, need to recognize the power of that energy.

Bea's ritual was a happening. Consciously she was focusing all her available energy on her inner journey; unconsciously, she was leaving space for the unknown. Without any church affiliation, she was attempting to find her own way.

Bea was in her fifties, attractive, efficient, with a good balance between her professional and personal life. She came into analysis because she realized that her divorce and her repetitive failures in relationships had something to do with her own psychology. After one year of analysis, not knowing there was another long one to come, she wrote in her journal:

> For many months, almost a full year, I am filled with anxiety, a stress I've never known before, a feeling of oppression I can barely cope with. My work suffers. I laugh less. The house becomes unbearable, so oppressive I can barely take the confinement of the rooms. For a while, I blame the house, work, the very cold winter. Then I realize it's not my house, my surroundings. It's something in me I'm struggling with. Then I start to bless the house. In the early morning hours, I play again and again my favorite music. I fill the house with flowers and go around like an ancient priestess. Finally some of the terrible anxiety leaves me. I am able to concentrate a bit more, pay more attention to my work, my [grown-up] children. The clouds look lighter. I sleep better. However, I don't entertain or go out much. Already living alone, I can't do anything else but be alone.
>
> Going to analysis I cry. I'm not used to crying. I didn't cry when my

marriage broke up. I didn't cry when my child died. Now I cry. Then
the feeling of oppression comes back. Something is weighing on me that's
so heavy that at times I can barely move. I feel it everywhere. It's deep
inside of me. It's like a cloud around me, a heavy cloud, unseen to the
eye. Being pure nothing, it weighs me down. I try to forget, laugh, change
scenery, go to the movies, to concerts. It's with me like a mantle, an
invisible cloak. I cannot bear the weight. I try. I fight it all the time, tell
it to go away, do my best to mentally will it away, to rise above or around
it. I do physical exercise. It does not go away.

Strain starts to show in my face. My family and friends are concerned.
I'm not ill even though I can barely move at times. It exhausts me so
much it's hard to believe it's me. I was the woman who could work and
play a lot and do many things at once. When will it end?

Bea was single-mindedly devoted to clearing out her own garbage and
releasing herself to live a full life. She was fearless in stripping away
worn-out attitudes and tenacious in her search for her own truth. One
day, approximately nine months after she wrote the above, she left my
office, walked into the street and heard an inner voice (a voice she had
earlier named "Lady") saying, "Follow me, and I will take you to God."
She was so startled she stopped; although she had no eating disorder,
she immediately decided it was imperative to have a cherry tart. This
was the voice that initiated the months of agony in which everything
in her life seemed to go wrong. Her splendid persona was slowly stripped
off. The "right" way for her to go became increasingly dubious. An
incalculable force seemed to be moving against her. Her ego was sufficiently strong, however, to hold the tension, to intervene in what seemed
disaster, and through cooperation with the Self she came through to a
new level of spiritual awareness. The journal continues:

Saturday before Palm Sunday. I went to the market to shop. The market
is a solace for me—all the food products, meat, fish, fresh vegetables,
the people. I'm feeling all right. Then it comes again—with great force,
the heaviness. I walk inside my house, up the stairs with all my shopping.
I go slower. I have no thoughts. I go into my kitchen. I walk and act
as if in a dream. I put down the many bags of groceries on the floor,
on the counter. Then very slowly, still wearing my coat, I go on my knees.
It's not good enough. Somewhere within me, I'm aware that for the first
time in my life even if I have knelt down before, I'm now going on my
knees for the first time. This! What's happening inside of me brings me
to my knees. It's stronger, much stronger than I am. I very slowly bend
my head and crouch down even further. (This is no dream. It's real. It's
unbelievable.) I now hold my head in my hands and I am bending down
low, still on my knees, of course, and words come from the very depths
of my being saying, "You win. I cannot do this alone any longer. God,
I give in to you." I bend deeper. I am absolutely silent, I don't know
for how long.

Finally I get up. I take off my coat and sit down in the living room.

So that's what it is ... God ... I'm not just me. I'm part of what is named God, for that I'm forced on my knees. I'm so overwhelmed that I dare not get up. Actually God, my God!

I stay in for the rest of the day, overwhelmed. It's God, God within that weighed, and before whom I, Bea, had to go down. I realize I'm not coping or knowing anything yet, but that I have to kneel from now on. Every day, or most days, even in the bathroom if it so happens, I start to pray. So it's God.

After four days of quiet, on Maundy Thursday morning, she awoke in terror from the following dream, written here as she wrote it down.

It's after the bombing of my city during the war. I'm walking on the road with my few belongings. I am an adult. In the next town we come outside the hospital where patients (victims of the bombing) are spread out on the grass. I walk around them and I start to pretend I am a part-time nurse. I even put a white kerchief on my head. I decide to walk away alone.

Everything now turns grey. I walk on this street, more a lane. Then there is a grey square building, not of brick or stone, but grey blocks. There are doors. In my dream I know it is a church. I knock on the door, open it and go in—sick people, half dead, no air. Br-r-r!

Then I walk out again and from the church comes this cripple (no legs man). He's dressed in grey pants, grey sweater. We walk. I'm concerned that he has no legs, like a cut-off statue on some pedestal, a moving square pedestal. When he moves his hips, the damn thing moves. It's so very weird. I walk close to him. If I walk close enough I notice that I feel his hip movement against my hip and think it's almost real, but I *know* he has no legs. However, I decide to ignore this; some pity for him, I suppose.

Then I look around me. He takes me into an alley way and then I look at the man again. He has opened his fly and it's a bloody mess, pieces of flesh, some small pieces, some bigger chunks, cut off and cut up meat. It's pink, bloody, and he's masturbating. I don't see a normal penis. I just think it might be there in that mess. He continues to masturbate, obviously enjoying himself. He has slightly toppled backwards in his cut-off state. He *knows* he's abusing me but likes that too.

I start to feel very disgusted, but also know that I want to feel that I'm a good girl, and so in spite of the mess he's in, I decide to ignore that. I'm not sure why but I also think that maybe I ought to make love with him. It's really disgusting. I'm sick of the sight and yet I think that by giving myself to him, he might not know he's that awful. ...

Then everything goes black. I'm still dreaming but it's solid black. I do not black out. I'm aware of this black-solid, solid. It's quite a while, this black.

Then light starts to come in very slowly, and there on the ground is Bea. She's in pieces, totally charred, smaller than my real body, but without doubt that's me there, not one connecting piece, totally smashed up and broken—in a way that a plate drops and totally breaks in pieces. Then I notice that the man is gone and I wake up.

Dear God help me.

"Never have I known such anguish of soul," she wrote. "When my neighbour saw me, she asked, 'Has someone died?' How could I explain to her who had died? My friend came over. I could not be alone. I was so delicate until Easter, I couldn't move. My soul was in such pain."

The setting of the dream after a bombing suggests the ordeal through which the dreamer is being initiated. Bea was actually a child when her city was bombed, but in the dream she is an adult; thus the dream's emotional impact resonates with her childhood experience. "I had to step over and on the dead to get into a sunny road," she recalled. "That was the kind of experience that took me into puberty. I was the teenager who never giggled." The dream suggests she did not then make the passover. In fact, unable to cope with starvation and massacre, the child was traumatized by what she saw and was too young to absorb the horror. She felt she must be of service, a nurse perhaps, but she was too young to nurse herself, let alone others. In order to survive, she had to sleepwalk through the occupation, hiding within herself from the world, an Anglo-Saxon version of Anne Frank in the attic waiting for a knock at the door. The energy of the dream is circling back to reconnect with the forsaken girl.

Now the attitudes and illusions which had dominated her life were being stripped away. Her sacrifice of herself in caring for others, that is, her acting like a nurse, had taken her into disastrous relationships with men, including alcoholics. "Men live out their negative side with me," she said. "I know I am sado-masochistic. 'You love me,' they say, and as soon as I think I do, I'm finished. I feel I have to give myself to them in spite of their narcissistic selfishness. I know they are afraid of my vulnerability, afraid I will become dependent on them. It's a false appearance. I give off the little girl—take care of me. But that's not me. I learned never to give my soul to a man; my money, everything I have I give, but not my soul. So I am never destitute."

In her actual life, men were attracted by her beauty and by her giving of herself. The dream suggests that she was simply going through the motions, a still traumatized bride whose quietness was a bomb left behind after the occupation, a ticking time-bomb that never exploded. What is ticking is the realization that as a child she was taken over. With a mother who was unable to love her and a father who could give her no support, she was occupied by the Nazis and left for dead. That experience of herself lies behind the nurse, the caring mother. She confronts this "mother" in a dream of a legless, masturbating male whom she wants to give herself to in an effort to heal him. The stone church building that appears as a suffocating tomb full of sick and dying, she leaves behind; the self-righteous pretense of the moral Christian is not for her. Pity can no longer masquerade as love. Her masculine side—crippled, ungrounded, locked in stone—is at the same time self-indulgent and auto-erotic. He victimizes her through his perverted power principle, and she, through her childish desire to be a good girl, becomes his victim. She betrays her own instincts in her desire to make this crippled tyrant feel good about himself.[16] The sword exactly fits the wound. The blackness ends that way of relating.

Many women who have not been through the trauma of war dream repeatedly of being victimized in concentration camps. They collude with their own inner power principle and with the men in their lives in destroying their own femininity. When in dreams they finally throw their purse over the wall or dig a tunnel out of the camp, ready to leave, the Gestapo shows its real face. It is as if the devil himself is saying, "You'll never get away from me. You sold your soul to me years ago and you are mine." The woman is then more frightened than she has ever been and in deeper despair. Her body may be wracked with pain. This is the moment when she and her analyst, or priest or very dear friend, must release all the love they possibly can to accomplish the birth.

Call it Fate, God, the Self—by whatever name, some invisible power had dismembered Bea. "I was charred," she said, "charred by the black, but it wasn't the black that did it. The black made me unable to witness the process. I would have died. The result was bad enough. From that day on, I prayed to that God inside." Bea was taken back to the point where, having lost touch with her own reality, she had put on a mask in order to survive. Now it was smashed. Her failed relationships were rescuing her from being smothered by her "nurse" persona. Free to choose whether to undertake the journey or not, she found herself destined to move in the direction the Self determined. Instead of balking in fear, she walked with as much dignity as she could muster. Through dialogue with the unconscious, the creative unity was born. At this stage, the goal and the way to the goal became one.

Following the unconscious intention of the way, and guided by her inner figures, two months later Bea had the following dream.

> There is maybe an offering to be made. I'm in this black body, and there is (or I see) no head, no face, and this black body is to be carried up or sacrificed. Obviously the black body is dead. It's a beautiful naked body and I'm carrying it up to a hill to an altar. I don't know for sure, but there is in my mind for a second the thought that I carry it to a man.
>
> I carry this body in my arms like a shawl. I then put the body down. It's so obviously me, my shape, my nakedness. I know it's me. It's a very strange me. The white woman knows that the black body is me as well.

I am that black woman too. I start to caress her, very softly. I kiss her breast, I put my hand between her legs. She is warm and wet there, and while I touch her there I look up and now I see her face. A smile appears, a beautiful very soft smile. WOW! I think she's dead but she likes to be loved. She's so terrific I can't believe it. I bend down again, either to pick her up or to cover her body with my body. I love her so. I don't know. I just know that black body is mine, whole and beautiful, and obviously loves to be loved.

The body has no head until I make love to her. WOW!

In the first section of the dream, Bea is about to sacrifice her own black headless body. Its blackness suggests her unconsciousness of it, its primitive instincts unconnected to the head. Momentarily, she thought she was carrying it to a man as in reality she had done in her sexual life.

This dream came after many months of working on her mother complex, her "feeling of being always left alone," her acceptance of having little support. For weeks she had been waking up every morning at 4 a.m. Instead of taking sleeping pills, she decided to stay awake and struggle—with something in herself, "something to overcome, or to accept." She often danced, "slow, very slow movements, all this in flannel pajamas, and bright, red socks as it was very cold." The love which she bestowed on her body during those fearsome nights culminates in the exquisitely modulated embrace imaged in the dream. "I feel I carefully have to carry this black girl, woman," she wrote. "She's delicate unless she's loved. She's dead unless she's loved. And then she smiles. I feel, know, she's me, my soul. Loving her is holy for me." The rhythms of the dream and the exclamations reveal the power of the emotional experience that brought head and body together. The intensity of the ego's love touches the soul buried in the dark flesh and the soul smiles and is resurrected.

Looking at Bea's experience as ritual, we can see what appeared to be the willed decision of the dreamer taking her up the mountain to the cave. In reality, the archetypal situation was constellated: the journey was inevitable. Her attitude to her home, and to herself in sacred space, became a rite of purification and entry, a catharsis, purging her of the fear and rage that she no longer needed to carry. Going about like an ancient priestess, she moved into a ritual change of personality. Invoking the body self as a transpersonal entity, entering the dance with utmost physical exertion and total concentration, she gave up her conscious orientation, thus opening the way for a new attitude to break through. Dance provided a ritual container that allowed the spiritual side of the unconscious to hold a higher charge of tension than it could otherwise have endured. By holding the tension until it peaked, the ego not only made room for the archetypal energy to break through, but also gained conscious ability to endure the confrontation without identifying with transpersonal power.

In the dream, Bea is at first perplexed at herself in a black body. But she stays with the perplexity, cherishing the body until the black woman has a head. Then she is gripped by love for this unknown part of herself, her instinctual side that was outcast at puberty. Again there is the paradox. The unconscious makes it quite clear in the dream that only her love for herself can redeem. As she begins to make love to her unknown shadow, she opens herself to deeper resonances of love and, like the sacred prostitute in ancient Greece,[17] submits to the love that is pouring through her. Fear gives way to love. Consciously enduring the pain, and consciously allowing her body to do what it needed to do, Bea found a new beginning, a new creation in a world with a fixed center. She was free to live in the *now*, secure in the knowledge of the divine love at the center.

Two months later, Bea had an initiation dream in which she herself was cared for by loving women:

> It seems that I have to take a bath. I'm in a large room with people sitting around a large bathtub that's set on a platform in the middle of the room. It looks like a large jacuzzi. I walk slowly through the room. I'm naked, I walk to the bath, up steps and go in. It's rather pleasant. Then women appear dressed in white robes, and I'm helped out of the bathtub and am led to a room where there are many beds, white beds, women in white. It takes a while to find my bed. We walk through several rooms; it looks like a hospital, but it isn't and people aren't sick. I'm then swaddled in white pieces of material, and gently I'm helped into my bed. I'm then served food and white wine.

The unifying motif in the dream is baptism—going into the water, stripping to her essence, dying to the old life and being born into the new. Swaddled as a newborn infant, she is welcomed to the ritual feast by women initiates who care for her. Instead of the gift of physical fertility, the mature initiate receives the gift of spiritual fecundity.

Bea's long vigil took place over a period of a year. What went on between her and her body, between her and her God and Goddess, is a mystery that cannot and should not be articulated. The mystery is sacred. The soul abides. The rest is silence.

Without cultural containers to give meaning to the death and rebirth cycles in the psyche, we can either be dragged like squealing pigs to the slaughter by a Fate we bitterly resist, or we can try to understand the cycles as they manifest in our dreams. "Only what is really oneself," writes Jung, "has the power to heal."[18] Enclosure, metamorphosis and emergence are natural cyclic phases in the individuation process. The psyche is like a rosebud that petal by petal unfolds into full blossom.

When I am in a great city, I know that I despair.
I know there is no hope for us, death waits, it is useless to care.

For oh the poor people, that are flesh of my flesh,
I, that am flesh of their flesh,
when I see the iron hooked into their faces
their poor, their fearful faces
I scream in my soul, for I know I cannot
take the iron hooks out of their faces, that make them so
*   drawn,*
nor cut the invisible wires of steel that pull them
back and forth, to work, back and forth to work,
like fearful and corpse-like fishes hooked and being played
by some malignant fisherman on an unseen shore
where he does not choose to land them yet, hooked fishes of
*   the factory world.*

—D.H. Lawrence, "City Life."

Every content of the unconscious with which one is not properly related tends to obsess one for it gets at us from behind. If you can talk to it you get into relationship with it. You can either be possessed by a content constellated in the unconscious, or you can have a relationship to it. The more one represses it, the more one is affected by it.

—Marie-Louise von Franz, *Redemption Motifs in Fairytales.*

The mistake began when God was created in a male image. Of course, women would see Him that way, but men should have been gentlemen enough, remembering their mothers, to make God a woman! But the God of Gods—the Boss—has always been a man. That makes life so perverted, and death so unnatural. We should have imagined life as created in the birth-pain of God the Mother. Then we would understand why we, Her children, have inherited pain, for we would know that our life's rhythm beats from Her great heart, torn with the agony of love and birth.

—Eugene O'Neill, *Strange Interlude*

If you look straight ahead into the darkness for your enemy, you won't see him. His movements give him away only on the periphery of vision where sight and intuition meet, where the senses are most keen. You either learn this, or you don't survive.

—Advice to combat troops in Vietnam.

5

The Dream Sister:

Further Thoughts on Addiction

Narcotics cannot still the Tooth
That nibbles at the soul—
—Emily Dickinson.

On a clear evening we look into the sky. We see a few stars. As darkness
deepens, we see the separate stars relating to each other—the Big Dipper,
Orion's Belt, the Pleiades. *Stella* is the Latin word for star; thus a
constellation is a coming together of stars made visible through darkness.
Sometimes it takes years for the separate points of light in our own dark
unconscious to constellate into a meaningful pattern. This chapter is
based on the experience of women in midlife who for most of their lives
have endured the anguish of an addiction, until finally the darkness has
become deep enough to perceive the pattern constellated within the
obsession.

For years they have known they are in the presence of something
stronger than they—a mystery that renders them powerless. Already
constellated is a "god consciousness"—awesome and holy—that has
nothing to do with the church or with groups. They know they have
to engage in a different arena of reality. That arena is the psyche. By
virtue of their temperament, training, consciousness, these women are
blessed (or cursed) with an introspective nature, an exploring mind, an
invincible curiosity about themselves which connects them to their own
inner microscope. For better or for worse, they are convinced that the
solution to their lives is in submission not to an externally imposed
authority which they cannot understand, but to a truth that abides in
themselves.

Truth is what they search for, and painful and perverse as the way
may be, the addiction is their way to truth. It is the opening to themselves. Profoundly committed to becoming conscious, they will not,
cannot, give up until they know what it means. In the addiction is hidden
the treasure—the knowledge of themselves—and they can take no other
path toward it. It is their particular sacred journey, their Tao, their
Way.

Their Way has taken them to the despair that lies at the core of the
addiction. Until the cause of the despair is uncovered, permanent healing
cannot take place. In dreams, that despair is often personified in a

99

symbiotic figure I call the "dream sister." In real life, this symbiotic figure is often the repressed side of the mother that the addict has absorbed without realizing it; it may also be the repressed femininity of the father or husband. The dream sister personifies this repression in one or both parents—a repression inherent in the psychic environment in which the addicted woman unconsciously experienced her childhood. Bringing that unconscious psychic environment into consciousness can be furthered through an understanding of the dream sister. The addict who realizes the various ways in which the dream ego relates to that "sister" is gradually bringing to consciousness her destructive, unconscious relationship to the negative mother complex.

By consciously breaking the symbiotic bond between the ego and the dream sister, the addicted woman releases herself from the death wish imposed upon her by the negative mother. Her submission to that complex, which denied her feminine reality, was her despair. In dreams her release may be imaged by the death or disappearance of the sister, who is replaced by a young femininity often personified as a vibrant adolescent. The dream sister who has stood "guilty as accused" is transformed into a pregnant virgin—open to life and love and destiny. The woman has repeated on the psychological plane the agony of the Virgin Mary, an agony that is only hinted at in the New Testament.

As we shall see later in this chapter, the Virgin Mother in her human bewilderment, rather than in her deified glory as the Mother of God, is appropriately symbolized in the Black Madonna. She is the awakened positive mother who is constellated after the purging of the negative mother complex. She is the natural patron saint of the freed "bondwoman," the released addict. The Black Madonna is black because she has literally or figuratively been through the fire and has emerged with an immense capacity for love and understanding. What the Virgin of the New Testament lost when the Church Fathers meeting in council decided to put her human anguish into the Apocrypha, the Black Madonna embodies. Like the addict who undergoes the humiliation of staying with the addiction in order to find the hidden gold, the Black Madonna suffered the miracle of the fire. The hidden treasure that filled her with shame and led to accusations of whoredom and adultery was nothing less than the Divine Child, her own spiritual identity, the *I am that I am.*

This chapter is about the alchemical fire in which femininity in our culture is burning in order to give birth to the psychologically conscious feminine.

The Closed Virgin

Most of the women I have in mind came from "good homes." Their parents were affluent, middle-class professionals whose collective values were shaped and confirmed by, for instance, *Vogue* and *Architectural Digest* and *Better Homes and Gardens.*

In order to achieve the money, cleanliness, beauty and brains necessary to live the affluent middle-class life, the household had to run like clockwork. All members were expected to take responsibility and to perform according to their collective roles. Dad—perfect scholar, perfect athlete—was once the perfect son of perfect parents living by the power principle that originally drove him to his perfect goal. Mom, likewise bewitched by appearances, was typically a highly intelligent, ambitious woman who sacrificed her own career for her children, and then more or less unconsciously expected them to achieve what she did not. Her energy went into making her body, her brain, her life, her children into works of art.

The children's accomplishments were not the result of their own self-determined goals. They knew what they ought to do, needed to do, had to do, in order to please others. Mother cut her toast in half and used saccharine in her coffee and frowned if her daughter reached for the cream. She treated her own body like a machine and expected her children to perform like perfect machines. If the machine suddenly manifested a life of its own, she was shocked. Her creation was imperfect, perhaps sick, and regarded with veiled distrust. The family members clung to each other symbiotically, so that the individual egos did not mature. Their lives were so circumscribed by the family emotional system that they could not see themselves outside of it. Rather they looked into its mirrors and were caught by its reflections. Perfection in that world became a moral issue to which every member of the family was expected to adhere. No one mentioned that Mom was subject to debilitating depression, nor that Dad often stayed out very late. Fidelity to the family secrets, implicitly demanded, created the strangling bond.

A girl child in this situation will often have been a silent witness to her mother's castration of her father. She lived with her mother's resentment of her father, resentment that surfaced when he failed to be the hero-husband her mother thought she married. A little girl caught in the middle may consciously decide that whatever her mother is, she will not be. She will never be a shrew who wages constant war with men. She will never be a cold and sexless body. She will never be "boss" in the household. Rather, she will be a cherishing, supportive wife and mother. In other words she identifies with her mother's shadow, the part of her mother that married her idealized masculine counterpart. Later, a mother in her own household, she attempts to be Earth Mother, abandoning herself to maternal instincts, natural childbirth, breast feeding, health foods and all good things for her children. As queen in her own home, she tries to be the sexy wife her father never had, and hopes her creativity will blossom through her family. The fact is, however, she is not an Earth Mother. Nothing in her background supports what she is attempting to do, nor is she sufficiently in touch with her body to rely on her instincts. She does her best, but she, her husband and her children know it is artificial.

This kind of woman is a powerful magnet to a man until the babies start to arrive. The scenario works quite well so long as she plays out her husband's anima and takes care of the feelings between them. Once she becomes involved with the first child, however, her energy cannot focus exclusively on her husband. As the child begins to develop an ego, the mother-child relationship is turned around, since the feminine side of the mother has not matured. The woman lacks grounding in the feeling values that would support her individual identity. She cannot cope. Genuine relationship she does not understand, and when the child asserts itself the woman cannot affirm her own standpoint. She tends to accept the projection of the child, its evaluation of her. Whatever it wants, it gets. If it strikes out at her, she goes down. She cannot enact the loving discipline that any creature of nature needs in order to build its own strong container. Without boundaries, the child loses its sense of security and becomes tyrannically demanding. If, for instance, a mother loses her sense of identity when her child rejects the natural orange juice she has prepared, she is setting herself up for martyrdom. She becomes depressed and thinks the solution might lie in having another baby. The cycle repeats. That baby too begins to be a little person; it exhibits unexpected emotions, "filthy habits" and boundless energy. Again the stress is too much. The woman again regresses into her Earth Mother fantasy, seeking to heal her injured ego by having yet another baby.

Eventually she may say, "Having a baby is setting out to destroy myself. The efficiency I hated so desperately in my mother is the same efficiency I see in myself in a different guise. I'm chauffeur for skating, swimming, dancing, and all the time there's this hole at the center. And all the time I feel my husband's criticism of my inability to cope." If her husband is not in fact critical, her inner man is. Her sole desire in becoming good wife and mother had been to please men, to compensate for her mother's lack of femininity toward her father. Her overwhelming desire to please makes her into a walking power principle because by pleasing others she is better able to manipulate them, albeit unconsciously. Her persona mask is saying, "Please Daddy by being Earth Mother." At the same time, her shadow is saying, "Stop the chaos. There's got to be order or I'll die." This kind of woman is another version of "Daddy's little girl," and her shadow sister "takes it like a man." Without the feminine strength to be who she is, her energy swings from the instinctual pole to the spiritual, unable to take a stand as a human being at the center—even as she is unable to stand firm at either pole.

While the family background varies from individual to individual, one aspect seems to be constant. The feminine principle was missing from the family, and this loss was suffered by father and brothers as well as by mother and daughters. "Where love reigns, there is no will to power," wrote Jung, "and where the will to power is paramount, love is lacking."[1] The opposite to love is not hate but power. Power obliterates another's individuality. Where power dominated the household, Dad's feminine soul was as devastatingly raped by the power principle as was that of his wife, especially if he was the beloved son of a domineering mother whom *he* tried to please. Moreover as a leader in the community he tried to please Mother Society. From a psychological point of view, the whole family—mother, father, daughters, sons—were motherless children who did not receive positive mothering and were, therefore, themselves powerless to give it. In performing their perfect roles, acting out "the good life," life itself was somehow neglected.

Children from this kind of home feel they have been waiting all their lives for something to happen, but it never comes. And in the perpetual waiting they are missing the *here and now*. While the parents may genuinely have felt they were doing their best for their children, they were unconsciously repeating what was done to them—molding their children into a collective image.[2] In order to survive, the children may conform, but underneath there is constellated a "heart of darkness."

Such children may unconsciously develop eating disorders as a defiant rebellion against becoming clones. In a culture whose media extols thinness as the great panacea that will bring happiness, sexuality, self-respect and social acceptance, they are blind to the insidious lies of the false goddess. Possessed by their own damaged instincts, and ironically driven by the same desire for power that their parents used in raising them, some children wolf down food, or reject it, or vomit it out. Whether that rejection of life is concretized in 200 pounds of armor, or 90 pounds of bone, or vomit in the toilet, the surest way out of the neurosis is to try to understand what food symbolizes in the individual psyche and why the energy is pulled in that direction.

Imagine two magnets. The energy field in one reacts to the energy field in the other. As they come closer, the pull between positive and negative becomes more intense until they leap together. If the magnets have the same energy field, they repel each other. They refuse to connect. Similarly, something in addicts reacts to the food and they are compulsively drawn to or repelled by its energy. "I'll die if I eat, I'll die if I don't." They may be trapped into going with the compulsion (binging), rigidly withstanding it (starving), or be alternately attracted to and repelled by it (bulimic eating and vomiting). Whatever their reaction, food is the magnet around which their lives circulate. In that context, food symbolizes the life force, the Great Mother, with which the wisdom of the body is desperately attempting to connect.

Attraction and repulsion are clear in the following diary excerpt. This woman had worked her way through to seeing food as a symbol of power—power she had learned from her mother. Eating had been simultaneously an identification with her power drive and an avoidance of looking at it. Food fed her fat animus and her tyrannical child. It did not feed her soul child, starving for love. Before she wrote these lines she had had a quarrel with her partner and phoned me because she was so upset. Something in my response, she said later, made her feel as if her hands had been slapped. She swung for some days between her tyrannical power-hungry sisters, then she wrote the following:

> How much bullshit do I have to put myself through before I can get out of this mirror maze? I can rationalize anything. I can play any game in the book and make believe it is real. SHIT. I'm not yet ready to give up the role of the mad little girl who didn't get her own way. Or the other end of that game, "See Mommy what a good girl I am. See how much I try to do to please you? Love me. Love me. I'll be anything you want, just love me."
>
> This baby needs to be garbaged. I applauded myself by having a tantrum because I didn't get my own way right away. (I would rather not know this!) Why does it have to be played out to its awful extreme before it can be clearly seen and dealt with. And the other childish thing I do is to make mountains out of mole hills and then mistake that dramatization for reality. If I can't be in control, then I play out the role of victim and convince myself that my failure to get my own way is someone else's fault. It's a pretty righteous form of self-justification and means that I never have to confront the fact that I play power games. That I like to play power games! If it suits my position of power to play helpless, I will play helpless. I'll play it any way I can to keep control. If I'm not in control, then I'm nobody, then nobody loves me because I have to be somebody for anyone to love me.
>
> If I can't be the most WONDERFUL woman in the world then I can be a POWERFUL woman and if I can't be a powerful woman then I can be an awful little girl that nobody loves. (Nobody loves me. Everybody hates me. Going to the garden to eat worms.) Any way that best suits the situation so I can be the center of attention! Does the world not revolve around me? Was heaven and earth not made for me alone? And this is the other side of the coin of not being able to take oneself seriously. ALL or NOTHING!!!
>
> And the line that holds these forces in place is not some magic mana from heaven that one waits for, but a grown-up sense of proportion, the understanding and acceptance that I am a part of a larger whole of things, that I have a place in the picture. One place that is mine, not more special, nor less, than any other place. It is my given place. It is my fate. And I can play the overstated games out all my life if I like and by so doing miss my life. I DO NOT WANT TO MISS MY LIFE.
>
> The question is, "Am I going to grow up enough to don my own clothes and be responsible for myself? What is and is not my responsibil-

ity? Am I willing to see a situation for what it really is?" The answer is YES. To the best of my conscious knowledge the answer is YES.

It has been a sobering set of days. Perhaps humbling set of days would be more accurate.

"God grant me the serenity to accept the things I cannot change, courage to change the things I can, and wisdom to know the difference." [AA prayer]

After two years of analysis this woman was mature enough to differentiate the voices of her psychic sisters, and instead of projecting them onto her partner or her analyst, she was ready to participate responsibly in her own destiny. The energies which were formerly racing back and forth between "the most wonderful woman in the world" and "the awful little girl" were now available to the ego, and instead of cutting her off from the reality of relationship by projecting her own "bullshit" onto others, they now connected her to life and genuine dialogue. Crucial to this process is having the courage to spend the "humbling set of days" alone, facing the real problem of the complexes, waiting for the real question to come to consciousness. Once the ego can articulate the question, the unconscious response is right behind. In the above excerpt the instantaneous YES follows the three questions that came directly from the ego: Am I going to grow up and be responsible for myself? What is and is not my responsibility? Am I willing to see a situation for what it really is?

An addict lives a life of self-denial. Where the parents for their own narcissistic reasons are unable to mirror their child, the child lives with little sense of its own authenticity. When it grows up, it continues to love mother, or father as mother, as a power principle, not as an individual person. Mother gives, mother controls, mother demands performance; the grown-up child is still helpless, its very life dependent on pleasing mother. The dependent—and often rebellious—child in the addict typically constellates the controlling mother in the partner, whose underlying message is, "You won't be competent. I will eventually have to be responsible and take care of you, my helpless child." That is power, characteristic of the partner's unconscious attitude, and indeed that of the addict as well. The demanding negative mother, whether internalized or projected onto the partner, destroys the feminine ego in a woman and the anima in a man because it leaves no room for individual feeling. It leaves both addict and partner with only two ways of relating: power or identification with each other.

If, for example, a child kicks its mother in the shin, her natural response is anger. If she can be honest and accept her human condition, and if she genuinely loves the child, she can return a good shout and automatically forgive. If, instead, she responds out of power, then she says, "It's alright, dear, I understand," and does nothing. Her failure to acknowledge her own natural response is inhuman; the child in turn feels its own anger is denied—it is not loved as a whole human being. The unspoken script determining the mother's attitude is, "I will not express what I feel. Neither should you. That would be wrong. And what I do is right." The undifferentiated animus in a woman locks feeling into this kind of either/or situation. Without a natural exchange, the child is forced into an "accept or rebel" response because it is smothered inside the mother's psychic space. Individual response is not considered and real feeling goes underground, only to erupt in later life in statements like, "If I let my feelings out, I'd blow other people away," or in secret behavior unacceptable to the conscious ego. The either/or animus forces both the outer child and the woman's inner child into manipulation and lying. By rejecting both, the woman causes both to reject themselves. Such rejection fosters revenge.

If she works on that black and white animus, the woman can differentiate her feelings and act accordingly. She can say to herself, "I have two sets of feelings. Which do I want to express? I kicked when I was a child. He's rebelling and that's natural. But I want to kick him back and that is not acceptable. How do I express the feeling without rejecting the child? How do I validate his feeling without rejecting him?" Now the feeling is conscious. It is not merely reflex affect. She has moved into a third position which recognizes both herself and her child as individuals. By being honest with herself and honest with her child, she moves out of power into love, thus constellating the positive mother. Empathy recognizes and accepts the total human being. Instead of driving anger underground, love recognizes and forgives, thus transforming negative emotion into potentially positive energy. So long as parents identify with a collective value system that denies that they and their children have an animal nature, the implied expectations can only lead to pretense, masochism and self-destructive rejection of life.

Young plants need warmth and water and light. Love is the valuing of individual feeling that provides the warmth. Water is the essence of life, the energy that wants to flow, to explore everything. Light is the insight that illuminates. Nature is energy manifest. The sanctification of matter has to do with the human love that recognizes the power of animal energy, recognizes it is sacred and that human nature evolves from that foundation. That foundation is the Great Mother, Sophia, in whose womb we mature. Our biological nature, quickened by the Spirit, receives energy through the five senses, as well as through the inner eye and the inner ear, until the red robe of passion worn by the virgin soul is enhanced by the blue mantle of wisdom.

Positive energy is life, light, god, love. It holds atoms together. When it is recognized as sacred, and when the soul is able to contain it and still allow it to flow, then the virgin is sitting on the lap of the Great

Mother. The woman has become conscious of herself as an individual soul. Out of her individual feeling, she loves individually. Her baby kicks and pukes and pees and she holds the paradox: the soul is incarnate. She changes the diapers in the blossoming love of raising the child. Linked to the Great Mother, she sees in the body the soul in action. Securely related to the feminine side of God, she is capable of personal relationships that are no longer based on power or dependency, but on empathy. She is free. Now she can displease the collective and, instead of feeling the terror of rejection, know that she is blessed among women. And her child, inner and outer, is free to act out of its own nature, able to accept discipline because it is secure in its mother's love. It is no longer outside of life, terrified of rejection and therefore driven to please.

When the veils that surround the addict are stripped away, the obsessive ritualistic behavior can be seen as protection against unendurable pain. To rip away those veils by, for example, force-feeding an anorexic, or forcing an obese woman onto scales, or forcing a bulimic to stop her rituals, provokes compensatory forces in the unconscious whose strength may far outweigh ego control. To attempt to enforce strict discipline on an ego that has been raped all its life merely reinforces the psychology of the victim and with it the compensatory rebel and liar. Compulsive dieting reinforces already firmly entrenched compulsive patterns and releases more violent compensatory instinctual needs, creating a conflict which tears the soul to shreds and may lead to a psychotic break or suicide. So long as a woman secretly despises her own womanhood, fears her own sexuality, flagellates her body with curses and starvation or food that is poison to her, no healing can take place, however fat or thin she may become.

Addicts relate to the addictive object as helpless children relate to a mother who has total power over them; they have not the individual feeling values which can make them stand up for their own lives. Once trapped in parental images, they are later trapped in these introjected images of themselves. They observe their own behavior by judging how it is going to look from outside, then switch into false feeling. Then they are caught in the complex. (Will I hurt her feelings if I don't eat her cake? If my conversation sparkles, they won't notice I'm not eating.) Impersonalizing themselves permeates every decision. In lifelong eating disorders, addicts have denied the body not only permission to eat but permission to enjoy life. Is it any wonder that it finally succumbs to allergies to almost every food or that its immune system can no longer protect it? Masochism feeds on itself. The oppressed become the oppressors. Delighting in the same vicious games that destroyed them, they corner other people and themselves with their deceitful tricks, then laugh, and smile smugly at their own power.

Consider a simple situation like writing an essay. A food addict begins to write the paper, then starts to eat. Food becomes more important than ideas; peanut butter jams the typewriter. At that point, if she can stop eating and ask herself what is going on, the addict can separate her own feelings from the complex. The negative mother complex will not want her to accomplish anything for herself. That would be selfish. Only giving is safe. What she has to see is that giving can be rank manipulation. Moreover, the complex interprets receiving as being manipulated, because as helpless child the woman received from powerful, bountiful parents until she had no ego to speak for herself. In her dreams, the complex may manifest as a dutiful sister who parrots all the clichés of the culture. If she can bring the negative mother to consciousness and realize that it is the complex that will not allow her to achieve, "because it isn't nice to be ambitious," then she can stop deceiving herself and decide whether *she* wants to write the paper or whether she never wanted to go to university in the first place.

It is important to stress that "mother complex" and "father complex" take in far more than personal mother or father. They are unconscious, archetypal processes that have nothing to do with the conscious motivation of the parents. Parents were once children themselves, trapped in *their* parents' complexes. Often it was a parent's silent pain which was most excruciating to the sensitive child. No matter what it did to make the parent happy, the sadness never went away. That sadness of the soul becomes part of the child's inheritance.

Our culture is moving at an alarming pace, spurred by collective values that have little time for individuals. Institutions reinforce the complexes: Mother Church, Mother Social Security, Father Law. People trapped in a negative mother complex fear gifts, whether they are given by persons, state or God; always someone is trying to exploit them and later on the hidden motive will be revealed. The negative mother attempts to twist everything into power and the weak ego colludes in this treachery by failing to believe in its own worth.

In analysis, this power game goes on so long as the analysand projects negative mother or father onto the analyst and attempts to retain power by maintaining the compliant persona which blocks the analyst out. Once a beam of love penetrates to the uncherished child within, out come the tears and repressed rage, and the process begins. Nor can intellectual insight alone release the abandoned child. The body too must go into the fire. The life force manifests biologically as well as psychically. In situations where the child was not wanted, or where a child of the opposite sex was ardently desired, there was nothing the infant could do to be acceptable. That realization would murder the little soul, as a canary dies if it is left alone in a cage. To protect the soul, the Self seems to set up a block, so that the unendurable pain is channelled into the body where nature deals with it as best it can. Because the pain is somatized, its psychological component is not consciously experienced. Obsessive ritualistic behavior is a magical way of holding the unbearable truth at bay, while erratic eating behavior is an attempt to nourish the animal and at the same time kill it. (Introverted intuitives in particular take refuge in the numinosity of their unconscious extroverted sensation, creating elaborate eating rituals to defend themselves.)

In the analytic situation, trust constellates terror of dependency, and vice versa. As the analysis proceeds, the energy pendulum swings farther and with more force, activating dormant resonators that have their source in the primal rejection. An increase in conscious trust between analyst and analysand constellates increasing fear of rejection in the analysand, and a compensatory determination to be the one to do the rejecting. (This is true not only of addicts, and not only in analysis. Anyone rejected as a child will unconsciously attempt to set up a situation in which she or he has to be rejected, or defend against the possibility by being the first to reject.) Until a woman can receive herself, she will unconsciously force others to reject her, despite the fact that her most conscious desire is to be loved. Rejection is annihilating, but even worse is the total collapse of the frail defensive framework when acceptance threatens. "What do I do if someone actually loves *me*?" At this threshold the full terror of dependency manifests. The stubborn resistance to change which is characteristic of most addicts is often protecting the ego from the abject despair of the primal rejection. Repeatedly, the energy of the dreams circles back to pick up the abandoned baby, or even unborn foetus. When the psyche is strong enough to take the pain of knowing it was unloved, then the body can release its somatized pain. Sometimes with good body work that happens literally from the soles of the feet to the top of the head.

Some knowledge of energy centers in the body—the chakras of Kundalini yoga—is invaluable during this period because the mysterious symptoms that appear in various parts of the body may be physically and spiritually related.[3] The wisdom of the East can bring profound insight into what is otherwise blank terror. This is not to belittle Western medical science, which is also necessary during this period, but physical and spiritual awakening belong together. It seems, for example, that when the prime connection was never made with the lowest chakra, *muladhara*, the individual has survived by sheer will power. When that will power breaks, the individual may be overwhelmed with sloth and an irresistible desire to stay in bed. The psyche, trapped in its somatizations and addictions, may be waiting for the strength to activate the *muladhara* area, where the real life force is.

At the deepest levels of the psyche, distilled grief often lies in a poisoned pool. The lotus blossom that opens to the sun must have a firm root in clean mud, and when the spiritual eye is activated the area

Seven lotus centers of the Kundalini.

of the perineum is often in turmoil until the entrenched attitude is released. The soul flower finds its nourishment in the roots that go deepest into the dark, rich mud.

The Soul Sister

C. S. Lewis's *Till We Have Faces* is a retelling of the Psyche and Amor legend from one sister's point of view. Orual, the ugly sister of Psyche, is being brought to her "ultimate stripping," crying out against the gods who, she believes, robbed her of her soul sister. Because her rational attitude cut her off from Psyche's joyful world of the creative imagination, she persuaded Psyche to do the forbidden—to shine a lamp on the face of her bridegroom god. The instant she saw her Brute's beauty, Psyche's paradise vanished and she became a wanderer with difficult tasks to accomplish. Orual, meanwhile, became the veiled queen of her father's kingdom, leading her soldiers in battle, demanding every ounce of physical and mental strength of herself and her subjects. Still, she lived haunted by her soul sister, beautiful Psyche, whom above all others she loved, but sought to possess.

Orual was determined, that is, to *possess* her soul, and in that determination she lost her. Though her Psyche-soul struggled to show Orual what she wanted—to live in her palace with Brute—Orual thought she knew better. Treating her soul as an unenlightened inferior, she determined to impose upon Psyche what she believed to be best. Her standpoint was the standpoint of the negative mother. Locked in her own judgmental, sullen world, resentful of her own unlived sexuality, Orual lived by the law but her heart was pierced by fleeting moments of grief and hope when she thought she heard her sister's heartbroken sobs. Driven between two poles—spirit and instinct—she had no center, no soul.

Having accepted in girlhood that "no man will love you, though you gave your life for him, unless you have a pretty face,"[4] and having adamantly believed that "the gods will not love you (however you try to pleasure them, and whatever you suffer) unless you have that beauty of soul,"[5] Orual now stands reading her bitter complaint before her judge, convinced of her ugliness on both counts, complaining against her destiny:

> Oh, you'll say you took her away into bliss and joy such as I could never have given her, and I ought to have been glad of it for her sake. Why? What should I care for some horrible, new happiness which I hadn't given her and which separated her from me? Do you think I wanted her to be happy, that way? It would have been better if I'd seen the Brute tear her in pieces before my eyes. You stole her to make her happy, did you? Why, every wheedling, smiling, cat-foot rogue who lures away another man's wife or slaves or dog might say the same. Dog, now. That's very much to the purpose. I'll thank you to let me feed my own; it needed no titbits from your table. Did you ever remember whose the girl was? She was mine. *Mine.* Do you not know what the word means? Mine! You're thieves, seducers. That's my wrong. I'll not complain (not now) that you're blood-drinkers and man-eaters. I'm past that ..."

"Enough," said the judge.

There was utter silence all round me. And now for the first time I knew what I had been doing. While I was reading, it had, once and again, seemed strange to me that the reading took so long; for the book was a small one. Now I knew that I had been reading it over and over—perhaps a dozen times. I would have read it forever, quick as I could, starting the first word again almost before the last was out of my mouth, if the judge had not stopped me. And the voice I read it in was strange to my ears. There was given to me a certainty that this, at last, was my real voice.

There was silence in the dark assembly long enough for me to have read my book out yet again. At last the judge spoke.

"Are you answered?" he said.

"Yes," said I.

... The complaint was the answer. To have heard myself making it was to be answered. Lightly men talk of saying what they mean. Often when he was teaching me to write in Greek the Fox would say, "Child, to say the very thing you really mean, the whole of it, nothing more or less or other than what you really mean; that's the whole art and joy of words." A glib saying. When the time comes to you at which you will be forced at last to utter the speech which has lain at the center of your soul for years, which you have, all that time, idiot-like, been saying over and over, you'll not talk about joy of words. I saw well why the gods do not speak to us openly, nor let us answer. Till that word can be dug out of us, why should they hear the babble that we think we mean? How can they meet us face to face till we have faces?[6]

Orual had spent her harassed lifetime writing out her complaint against the gods who, she snarled, had "no answer."[7] Finally, she recognized "too true an image of the demon within."[8] Fearing for her sister and simultaneously attracted to and revolted by the mystery of sexuality, she became obsessed with separating Psyche from her beloved Brute. Like the evil witch in Hansel and Gretel, she unknowingly forced her lower innocence into the anguish that leads to the higher innocence. Her rational mind could only catch glimmerings of the world of the imagination, and therefore, in typical compulsive style, she created as much nuisance value as she could to scuttle Psyche's symbolic world. Then she bitterly complained against the gods for taking *her* Psyche away, and dreamed of her soul sister crying at the well. While she ruled with an iron fist, her real energy was in her yearning. There was the gap between illusion and reality—the gap that was filled by her addiction to work. Finally, brought to her "death before death" she recognized that her complaint written day after day in her book was her answer. She had no chalice to present to the gods, only her book.

Many people suffering from an addiction are in Orual's position. So long as there is one more deadline at work, one more gamble, one more binge, one more fix, they avoid the confrontation, and whether their book is real or imagined, they continue with their daily complaint. Then one day, through some crisis, they hear themselves and face up to their own loss and fear and guilt.

Other pairs of "sisters" whose extremes are clearly visible in food addicts are also present in people who do not suffer from an obvious addiction. In order to understand the structure underlying the neurosis, we need to look more closely at the psychic dynamics between the unconscious sisters. One sister may manifest as a particular facet of the feminine shadow, the other as an "animus-hound." Together they make an unholy but powerful alliance in the unconscious. When a woman looks in the mirror and sees her fat shadow, her dark animus instantly gets his judgmental foot in the door and says, "You're no good." The fat shadow goes numb, confirming his accusation. Then he throws his whole weight into the room and his harangue demolishes her ego. Above all, the woman must learn how to keep that door locked. When she hears him wheezing on the other side, she must stand to everything positive in herself. She must develop sufficient ego strength to differentiate the complicated set of variables that constitute her prison.

So long as a woman is unable to find her own identity, her ego responses will be determined by some combination of interactive complexes. The crucial word then is "unrelated." When, for example, the ego has not integrated sexuality, the person will act out of an instinct or a spiritual ideal. The human love which would create the bridge to another person as an individual is not present. Addictions are manifestations of possession by either the somatic, instinctual pole of an archetype or its psychological pole, or both, and therefore preclude human relationship. Some of the complexes that may interact, ganging up on a weak ego, are shown in the accompanying chart.

As I understand them, the symbiotic dream sisters have a secret that each knows and both cling to. But there is also a secret they do not know, and both are searching for the same key to release them from the same prison. Superficially they are opposites, but at the core they are one. They are in fact complementary to each other, for each has an essence

Aspects of the Feminine Shadow	Aspects of the Animus
Earth Mother	*Father-Jehovah*
—nourishing, protecting (combination of mother's shadow and father's mother-anima)	—status quo, stasis (combination of father's shadow and mother's father-animus)
Femme Fatale	*Don Juan*
—father's unrelated feminine side	—mother's unrelated masculine side
—mother's unrelated, unlived sexuality	—father's unrelated, unlived sexuality
Uninitiated Girl	*Adolescent Rebel*
—infantile, living in fantasy	—uninitiated, hungry boy
—rebels against mother	—rejects everything father stands for
—unconscious sexuality	—wounded masculinity
—potential energy for creative spirituality	—potential energy for creative spirituality
Devouring Witch	*Demon*
—cold, impersonal	—reinforces inertia
—inertia, sleep	—rigidity that kills femininity
—depression	—either-or attitudes
—eat or be eaten, or starve	—devour or die

Some aspects of the unconscious feminine and masculine that may interact with each other, either in projection between two people or within an individual psyche.

that the other needs, and knows she needs. Blood bonded, they will live together, die together and perhaps fight bitterly, yet if an outsider criticizes one then the other springs into action to defend. The nature of the sisters varies in individual psyches, but in severe eating disorders a fairly consistent pattern manifests. To simplify and clarify this pattern as it manifests in a single person, let us call the fat sister Floe, the thin one Flame.

Their psyches move in and around and through each other. Ask one how she feels and she may give you the other's reaction. Both are driven by an apocalyptic vision: in some imaginary world, if only this mundane reality were finished, something numinous, something totally new, would reveal the essence of life. Floe eats her way through food in order to finish it off and begin a new era. Flame spends hours sorting and organizing, driving herself to the edge, physically, mentally and spiritually, in an effort to get things done so that the "real thing" can begin. Both feel betrayed when the long-anticipated holiday with its hours of leisure and reflection never materializes. Other things interfere, demanding all their energy. Neither has the ego strength nor the sense of personal worth to take time for herself every day. The great moment of truth is always ahead if only she could find time for it. When the unconscious decides it can't wait, that it wants to live in the *now*, apocalypse turns into holocaust. Floe is magnetized by the numinosity of matter (Mater, mother, food); Flame is magnetized by spirit (no Mater, no mother, no food). Both are seeking some way out of their concentration camp.

If Floe is invited to a party, she naturally thinks about her dress. She knows it is a size 14; she knows her hips are now size 18. She refuses to recognize the truth. She goes on whistling her little tune whenever she's afraid. When party time arrives, the whistling stops. Here is reality. She has fallen into unconsciousness; she cannot wear the dress; she is too depressed to leave the house. At that edge she may either binge herself into oblivion, or the tension may be so extreme that it will turn into its opposite (a process Jung calls enantiodromia),[9] in which case Flame will be constellated—Flame who hates Floe's self-indulgence, cannot endure watching Floe eat and loathes Floe's fat body. Floe has wrecked Flame's party. There is no envy, however, no jealousy, no anger. Flame is relieved. She won't have to sparkle and pretend to be somebody she is not. She won't have to be one woman with one man, another with the next, and she won't come home from a splendid party wondering why she is crying. She won't have to recognize that she puts her kindness ahead of her truth and loses her reality as a result.

These "sisters" may be personified in two different persons in a household; they may both be enacted by one person over a week or a month; they may be enacted by a bulimic within half an hour. Not a few Floe-Flames are living a double life. Well adapted in their professional world, their Floe is superbly disciplined, forthright, articulate, quick with de-

The Two Sisters, watercolor by Eryl Lauber.

cisions. While she interacts well with men professionally, she knows the man she loves cannot relate to her efficiency and incisive perception. Nor does she want him to. With him she is Flame, submissive, sexually involved, a mirror of his anima, perpetuating the symbiotic relationship she had, or wished she had, with her father or mother. She does not realize that symbiotic nurturing is not relationship. If possible, she sets up her life so that Floe functions for four days a week and Flame for three, or some such variation. She knows she needs time to move from one into the other; in fact, an intense inner battle often ensues when gentle Flame has to leave her beloved on Sunday afternoon to make the long, long journey back to her own apartment and Floe. Once she becomes Floe again, she is excited by the challenge of the week's activities, but there is a No Woman's Land between. Often the passover requires a bath, a different set of clothes, a different voice, a different diet, a different walk. Even the appearance of her body may change.

Certainly all of us change gears between our professional and personal lives. The pace of modern life, however, and the demands made on women to be whole with no model of wholeness, are creating split personalities. Living wholly in one world, then doing an about turn to live wholly in another, creates a hole in the center unless there is an ego strong enough to hold its own standpoint while attempting to integrate both sides. Addictive behavior typically takes place in this "hole." Floe's incessant running away from the hole is merely a flight into delusion because she is running toward her opposite, constellating Flame, who can only enjoy her Garden of Eden because she knows she is going back into Floe. She also knows that if the weekend went on until Wednesday, Floe would start arguing. She might even start eating, and trouble with her man would erupt. Floe-Flame finds it easier to live the two sides separately than to hold the tension of the opposites. Living both sides until she is conscious of both may be necessary, but when the cycle has been repeated often enough, eventually someone inside says, "That's it, no more!"

Sometimes it is the addiction itself that brings the woman to consciousness. More often a crisis arises in a relationship that forces her to differentiate the opposites, and in recognizing the two sides she sees that the woman who should be at the center is not there. In flying from Floe to Flame, from Flame to Floe, she has either lost her identity or never had it. The lost one is Fleur, the conscious woman, the blossom that grows on a healthy rooted plant. If she can realize this, then instead of lashing out against a man or raging against a patriarchal God and seething with bitterness, she knows her task is to find herself. Rage and bitterness do not foster femininity. They harden the heart and make the body sick. Trust that can dare to stand against all rational logic opens the heart to love. Honesty born of trust may indeed threaten to destroy a relationship, in which case the validity of attempting to save it must be questioned. Even if it is lost, a relationship that has resulted in insight, thus enabling the partners to recognize why a pattern is repeating itself, has been worthy of the energy that went into it. Both can then develop their own individual resources and search for their virgin within.

When Floe and Flame cease their frantic chase to and away from each

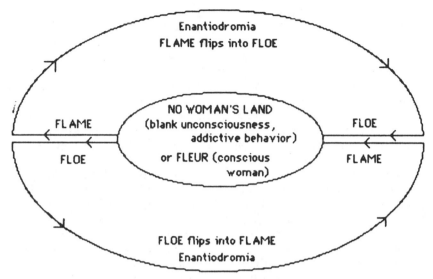

The Floc-Flame syndrome.

other, both may be quiet enough to hear Fleur's voice. When fat Floe realizes that thin Flame is not the projected feminine she so desperately seeks, and Flame realizes that fat Floe is not a positive mother, then there is a possibility of choice. They can embrace and love each other for the suffering they have shared, and both turn their faces to the immediate task of finding Fleur. Floe's secret binging and Flame's secret starving and Floe-Flame's secret vomiting are resolved when the secret key reveals that each is a fragment of the whole.

The psyche has within it a natural gradient toward wholeness, and while one may attempt to ignore nature, the body attempts to remain in harmony with it in order to incubate the totality. Prolonged abuse may result in an illness which brings the totality to consciousness. Here is the paradox. While the pieces of the puzzle gradually build toward the whole, at some point we must have a vision of wholeness in order to put the pieces into perspective. Once the voice crying at the heart of the addiction is heard, then the binging and starving and vomiting can be seen for what they are: an attempt to obliterate the crying. Then the physical food need no longer tantalize the two sides of the complex; spiritual food can feed the soul. Neurotic frenzy can be replaced by real energy.

The abandoned one at the heart of the addiction is the soul of the potentially conscious woman, the virgin "one-in-herself." She is the one who needs food. Her food is the food of the creative imagination.

Mother as Shadow Sister

The mother who functions as a shadow sister is often the one who, when she married, gave up her hopes for her own creative life, and in her disappointment projected her unlived life onto her child. Spoken or unspoken, the grief and frustration of that sacrifice weigh heavily on the child. The mother felt locked in a cage of marriage, the bars of the cage being not her husband, whom she had already realized was not Prince Charming, but the child in her womb. The guilt that the child feels for the crime it never committed has its etiology then in the very fact of its existence.

The grown-up children of such mothers will say, "I get the feeling it's my fault that the baby cries, that my sister doesn't have enough money, that my son can't write his essay. I even feel it is my fault if the sun doesn't shine for my family's picnic. I feel they are blaming me, then I blame myself for not being God. It goes back to my infancy when my mother looked at me with those piercing eyes. I thought she was angry with me. I could deal with that. But then I would see the pain in her eyes. That I could not and cannot deal with. I cannot deal with the fact that I caused her pain—pain because I was there, and now pain because I do not fulfill the life she never had. Then I flip. My guilt turns into rage. What does she expect of me? What do my sister and my children expect of me? I won't be eaten up. Go away. There's nothing left. The Great Mother whose breasts drip with the milk of human kindness instantly goes dry, wants to starve them, refuses to eat with them, hates them for eating her up." The "good mother" suddenly flips into the deprived child.

In that instant of enantiodromia, the nourishing mother, Janus-like, shows her devouring face. There is an identity of opposites—Creator and Destroyer—simultaneously present in an undifferentiated form. Until those opposites are brought to consciousness, the woman falls into a paralysis of unexpressed rage and powerlessness. A main aspect of the problem is that she thinks she can make all things right—she identifies with the Great Mother. That is power masquerading as love. When she cannot control her world, she falls into the dark side of the mother. She moves from abundance to deprivation, from symbiotic intimacy to rejection, from love to hate. The speed with which that can happen, and the intensity of the emotions released, terrify her.

The child, whether seven or seventy, can only break that unconscious bond with the mother world when it realizes it has a soul of its own, which has been born onto this earth through the body of the mother but does not belong to her (or to anyone else). The task for a person of either sex is to differentiate oneself out from the mother—to know where one ends and the other begins. The woman's task then (different from a man's)[10] is to reconnect in a new way (Demeter and Persephone). The danger is the possibility of falling back into unconsciousness. Human actions must have the support and blessing of nature, but if a woman is to experience nature as a blessing she must be conscious. She must realize that while the biological purpose of life at the unconscious level is to reproduce itself, the conscious purpose is not simply to reproduce or perpetuate, but to *know*. It is the difference between unconscious creation and conscious creation. There is no antagonism between them unless one is denigrated or considered a substitute for the other. Ultimately, conscious and unconscious are one. The one longs for the other because the one *is* the other.

Sometimes a woman comes to the threshold of separation from the mother, and rather than taking the responsibility of bringing her own inner child to birth she becomes obsessed with having a real baby. Her fear around her own inadequacies and her own lack of identity make her want to *be* someone—a mother with an actual child onto whom she will project her own unresolved life. If she can hold the tension until she finds herself, then her baby, if she has one, will not have to carry what she has fearfully avoided. An abortion can be the threshold that forces a woman to seek her own identity, in which case the baby becomes the sacrifice through which the woman brings herself to birth. If that is brought to consciousness and dealt with *as* sacrifice—something of great value given up to something of greater value—then the underlying depression is released from the body and psyche.

The extent to which mother and child believe they belong to each other destroys psychic growth. At the deepest levels, most children know they do not "belong" to their parents; they feel their sense of unity with all life. In a world in which people possess each other, however, not to belong makes the child feel like an outsider. While the resultant "orphan" psychology may be a source of fearful anxiety, in reality it is an affirmation, from the beginning, of spiritual freedom.[11] The fact remains, however, that the infantile fear of being left alone, or abandoned in the street, is indelible. So long as that fear is not brought to consciousness, freedom will always be experienced negatively as desertion by somebody else. If the positive mother is not strongly enough located in the very matrix of the psyche, there is simmering fear and rage which must be purged.

In most eating disorders, the body is sick with the poison of the negative mother complex. Lady Macbeth's, "Take my milk for gall," is the motto of the negative mother.[12] The food addict is the infant at the breast of the negative mother taking her food for gall. The way out of this despair—the compulsive eating of poisoned food—is not to vomit it out, or to refuse to eat at all, or to eat certain foods to such excess that one develops allergies or candida.[13] The way out is to discover what it is that one is eating. Confront the poisonous negative mother complex. Confrontation is slow and painful work when one has lived with the complex all one's life. Our culture sentimentalizes "mother," makes her into a "sacred cow," thus blinding itself to the devastation the negative mother complex wreaks, personally and culturally. Loyalty is mistaken for love. Until the addict can separate the real mother from the sacred cow, she loves what is destroying her. Because she loves what is destroying her, her love of her "mother" is her rejection of herself. The evidence of her love for her mother is her loathing of herself. The more she loathes herself, the more she obeys the negative mother complex and projects the positive mother, the nourishment she so desperately needs, onto food. So long as she takes the milk for gall, the poisonous tit cannot dry up.

The contrary is also true: the more a woman loves herself, the more she loathes the sentimentalization of mother. Loathing mother is far more painful, far more threatening, than loathing herself. Too often a food addict is prepared to destroy her own life rather than hate the mother complex, which she associates, rightly or wrongly, with her actual mother. Accept her mother she may, but hate the complex she must, if she is to be released from the suicidal loathing of herself. Only when the hatred is fully expelled from the body and from the psyche is all the gall from the mother's breast removed.

And as it is removed, the body begins to live. As the body awakens into life, it experiences for the first time the positive mother, Sophia. The body experiences an ontological shift from "it" to "she." The fiat of the negative mother, the cataclysmic injunction "*Do not be*," is transformed into a gentle "*Be*." For the first time *she* (the body) experiences herself without the primal despair—*she* sees tulips aflame in springtime, *she* hears the cardinal's courting call. *She is*. The more a woman breathes with Sophia—her own body wisdom telling her what she wants and really needs in order to live—the more she sees into the anguish of the woman from whose womb she was born. The more she forgives, the more she is transformed. She may even thank her mother for giving her life. The negative becomes the positive even as it all along contained the positive. Light manifests in Darkness.

All this is not to suggest that grey-haired maidens should vent their fury on their dear old mothers, nor that secretaries should explode at their female bosses, nor that women or men should rise up in arms against the negative mothers who are earnestly, albeit unconsciously, fulfilling their duties as puppets of the patriarchy. Women who are possessed by the complex do not know they are possessed. They are usually living out the only reality they have ever known. The fury can be vented in private (and behind the steering wheel of a moving car is not private). Standing firmly on one's own ground speaks loudest.

When the energy that went into over-endowing the false goddess is centered where it belongs, life is restored. What has been initiated is spiritual health, spiritual life. The pain of the transformation is real—physically and psychically—but only the intensity of the fire can unite body and soul. This is a soul-making process. That it is so is seen not at the beginning but at the end. The body is the grit that produces the pearl.

The Black Madonna

Once the purging has taken place, the woman often dreams of a black goddess who becomes her bridge between spirit and body. As one aspect of Sophia, such an image can open her to the mystery of life being enacted in her own body.

The significance of what the black goddess symbolizes is recognized by many religions. In the ancient text entitled *The Thunder, Perfect Mind*, her wisdom—encompassing, unfathomable—is revealed:

> *For I am the first and the last.*
> *I am the honored one and the scorned one.*
> *I am the whore and the holy one.*
> *I am the wife and the virgin.*
> *I am (the mother) and the daughter.*
> **I am the members of my mother. . . .**
> *I am the silence that is incomprehensible*
> *and the idea whose remembrance is frequent.*
> *I am the voice whose sound is manifold*
> *and the word whose appearance is multiple.*
> *I am the utterance of my name.*[14]

In Christianity this goddess is personified by the Black Madonna. In Montserrat, Spain in the Middle Ages, the Benedictine monks saw their craggy mountain, lush with flowers, as an image of the Virgin herself. Referring to this shrine, Marina Warner writes,

> While Mary provides a focus for the steeliest asceticism, she is also the ultimate of fertility symbols. The mountain blossoms spontaneously; so does the mother maid. The old significance of the moon and the serpent as divine attributes survives in such sanctuaries as Montserrat, for there she is venerated as a source of fertility and delight. ... The Virgin of Montserrat presides especially over marriage and sex, pregnancy and childbirth.[15]

Like other Black Madonnas, her "mysterious and exotic darkness"[16] inspires a particular depth of wonderment and love.

For a woman without a positive mother, this "dark" side of the Virgin can bring freedom, the security of freedom, because she is a natural home for the rejected child. The child born from the rejected side of the mother can bring her own rebel to rest in the outcast state of Mary. She need no longer be the poor little match girl outside the window looking in at the Holy Family on Christmas Eve. She need no longer light her solitary match in the snow while the family celebrates together around the blazing hearth. She need no longer fear dying alone when her last match goes out. The fact is the domestic world alienates her. She is an outcast, a gypsy. There is no room for her in the inn.

Saving the abandoned child within her is the woman's own version of the Virgin and Divine Child. Her virgin, however, is not what Marina Warner calls "a focus for the steeliest asceticism" (which is what her negative mother was). In stark contrast to that steeliest of mothers, her virgin is the other side of Mary, "the ultimate of fertility symbols." In loving the abandoned child within herself, a woman becomes pregnant with herself. The child her mother did not nourish, she will now nourish, not as the pure white biblical Virgin who knew no Joseph, but as the dark Montserrat Virgin who presides over "marriage and sex, pregnancy and childbirth."

The Black Madonna is nature impregnated by spirit, accepting the human body as the chalice of the spirit. She is the redemption of matter, the intersection of sexuality and spirituality. She is the loving biological tie to the body, fertility, babies. She is the "right to life" versus the "pro choice" problem in a nutshell. Issues involving tubal ligation, abortion, "the pill," put the Black Madonna at the very center of our culture.

Connecting to this archetypal image may result in dreams of a huge serpent, mysterious, cold-blooded, inaccessible to human feeling. Seen as an appendage of the negative mother, it is the phallus stolen from the father and used to guard inviolate purity. Yet this same snake, when seen in relation to the moon, symbolizes the dark, impersonal side of femininity and at the same time its capacity to renew itself. The daughter who can come out from under the skin of the negative mother will not perpetuate her but redeem her. The Black Madonna is the patron saint of abandoned daughters who rejoice in their outcast state and can use it to renew the world.

Although not to be found in "authorized" versions of the Bible, the Apocryphal New Testament contains much material on this "dark" side of the Virgin. The Book of James tells how Joseph, after a long sojourn "building his buildings," returned to find his sixteen-year-old virgin wife six months pregnant. He was both heartbroken and afraid:

The Black Madonna of Montserrat.
(Twelfth-century Byzantine)

[He] called Mary and said unto her. ... O thou that wast cared for by God, why hast thou done this? thou hast forgotten the Lord thy God. ... But she wept bitterly, saying: I am pure and I know not a man. And Joseph said unto her: Whence then is that which is in thy womb? and she said: As the Lord my God liveth, I know not whence it is come unto me.

And Joseph was sore afraid and ceased from speaking unto her, and pondered what he should do with her. And Joseph said: If I hide her sin, I shall be found fighting against the law of the Lord: and if I manifest her unto the children of Israel, I fear lest that which is in her be the seed of an angel, and I shall be found delivering up innocent blood to the judgement of death. What then shall I do?[17]

The judgment referred to here meant being stoned to death as an adultress.

There follows a long description of the dream in which Joseph is reassured by an angel that the child in Mary's womb "is of the Holy Ghost."[18] Then he and the Virgin have to undergo humiliation and "testing" at the hands of the priests. As the story unfolds Joseph takes care of Mary, but both are confused and alone:

And they drew near (unto Bethlehem) within three miles: and Joseph turned himself about and saw her of a sad countenance and said within himself: Peradventure that which is within her paineth her. And again Joseph turned himself about and saw her laughing, and said unto her: Mary, what aileth thee that I see thy face at one time laughing and at another time sad? And Mary said unto Joseph: It is because I behold two peoples with mine eyes, the one weeping and lamenting and the other rejoicing and exulting.[19]

The "two peoples" Mary sees are aspects of herself, the one "weeping and lamenting" at the sacrifices foreshadowed through the child within, the other "rejoicing and exulting" at the imminence of new life. Death and life meet at the threshold of birth.

It is this paradox of the virgin that speaks naturally to the woman who felt rejected as a child. If she can empathize with her own pregnant mother, she may experience her gazing out the window, dreaming of the music she no longer plays, the picture she no longer paints, the world she no longer inhabits. She may see in her mother the creative artist or crusader who was always outside society because, before motherhood, she too was a "virgin," receptive to the creative imagination. The mother's betrayal of her own creativity made her a "bondwoman." Outcast and alone, mother and daughter both carry the potential energy represented by the Black Madonna.[20]

The woman who unexpectedly finds herself with a child in her womb is like Mary. Mary, who had been a virgin in the temple, initially responded to the angel with, "Be it unto me according to thy word."[21] During the ensuing months, however, her task was not only to accept the child but to release herself into her own creative destiny. Similarly, a modern woman who feels trapped in motherhood must come to realize that the child is part of her destiny. It is the negative mother complex in the woman that makes her resent the unborn child because she fears it will interfere with her own creative dreams.

Positive mothering, for both mother and grown-up daughter, comes in the realization that they must release each other from the unconscious trap of the negative mother. If the mother finds her own freedom (or is released through death) before that release takes place in the daughter, then the latter is instantly confronted with both her mother's birth and her own; she can be born at last from the original carnal womb in which they strangled each other. The mother's freedom can give the daughter her freedom—if she is psychologically conscious enough to take it. Without that release, however, the daughter will eventually become the parent and the mother will respond by becoming dependent and infantile.

If both women can relate to the Black Madonna within, they can respect and love each other within a framework to which they both belong. The Black Madonna is the carnal womb through which one gave birth and the other was born. Not daring to look at the truth which binds them together is precisely what has kept them apart. The most positive thing that can work between them is the recognition of their carnal bonding. This positive recognition, which can give each her psychic freedom, must take place in the deep underground caves of the conventional home, and utmost vigilance is required to stay with the real task. What seems to be going on in the living room may be the opposite to what is going on in the basement. The mother may be attempting to push the daughter out of the living room so that she will not repeat her mother's pattern. The daughter, then, has to recognize the mother is not pushing her out because she hates her, but because she wants to release her. If that is not brought to consciousness, daughter becomes guilty rebel who hates her mother, and mother becomes suffering victim whose efforts are defiantly rejected. They are terrified to face each other.

The woman in her function as Black Madonna, whether consciously or unconsciously, may be trying to save the daughter. If rebellious daughter wants to go away to school, off to camp, or around the world, mother sends her. Anything to stop the negative cycle, if it's the last thing she does. A daughter locked into an eating disorder is at war with food—with mother. Wolfing, rejecting or vomiting food is repeating the negative cycle, "There'll be no men, no babies, no me." If she can relate to the Black Madona, she can experience how her body is crying out against physical death, trying to give her soul a chance to live. If she can experience this in her gut—the instinct valiantly attempting to survive—she can connect to the positive side of her own mother, the positive energy of the Black Madonna. Then "diet" is no longer deprivation or forced feeding—punishment or compensation—but positive mother feeding her hungry child food for the body and food for the soul.

If consciousness can come before the physical death of the mother, then both women may be released. If not, then the mother's freedom (which is how the still trapped daughter will see her death) requires the daughter to deal with her own introjected negative mother. Can she accept her freedom? Her body is locked into experiencing itself as a deserted child; both mother and daughter left it behind. Now daughter has to go back and retrieve it, fully aware that she cannot bring it into consciousness through punishment or abandonment, aware too that she must ask its forgiveness. A body whose wisdom has never been honored will not easily trust. Without a positive model, something creative must go on between a woman and her inner mother in the underground cave. The ego that refused to submit to the body must now submit to the healing power of nature. The ego does not know what to do, and the body, like an animal with a crazy trainer, has developed crazed and chronic habits. Where the animal has been allowed to run wild, it takes time and discipline to allow the healing powers to develop a mutual trust between the ego and the creative aspects of the unconscious.

If individuals accept the prison of a collective system that denies their very existence, then in effect they accept a concentration camp life. They are victims who believe in the victor. A mother and daughter trapped in this dynamic—as their prison dreams clearly demonstrate—are trapped in a power principle whose goal is to keep them in a gas oven until they die. So long as it remains unconscious, the vicious circle repeats, intensifying in each generation. To bring this to consciousness is to recognize the Black Madonna, the repressed outlaw, as the potentially positive bond between the two women. There is where the Light in the relationship is—freed bondwoman to freed bondwoman. In the Old Testament, it is Hagar, the dark Egyptian, the freed bondwoman of Abraham, who is cast into the desert to care for her son, Ishmael.

Once mother and daughter realize they do not belong to each other, that each has her own soul and both are the daughters of the Great Mother, Sophia, then the positive side of their relationship can be recognized and neither woman need despise her femininity nor continue to violate her body. Violating the body may be transformed into validating the virgin.

The Open Virgin

There comes a time with any addiction—compulsive work, compulsive eating, compulsive sexuality—when the "if only's" ring false and the "why me's?" are boring. To persist after that point is psychic death—choosing to blind oneself in the neurosis rather than moving forward with the new insight. Illusions protect the addict from moving through the birth canal, but when the nine months is accomplished, the baby that stays in the womb dies.

Freud and Jung both realized, though in different ways, that because life begins in the Great Mother the relationship to her is the defining relationship in our lives. She has lain asleep for centuries in our bodies and in the very earth on which we dwell. Is it possible that the food addictions so rampant in our culture are related to the absence of primal bonding? Are addicts looking for the nurturing and recognition they never had? Are they running away from the fact that they were never loved and cannot love themselves? Is the Great Mother making herself conscious by compelling addicts to deal with her? Is the instinctual energy attempting to reconnect with her? Only when we perceive the symbolic meaning of the addiction can we turn it into positive action.

Only when we raise an activity from an unconscious instinct into a conscious action can we bring Light to Mater. That is our individual way of redeeming the Great Mother.

In moving closer to her, we are at the same time moving closer to our own virgin soul and her potential energy. Crafty and determined as she is, she will not be ignored, and because she knows us so well, she creates the complex at the heart of the addiction in order to protect herself. There she is sure to be at the center. While our relationship to her may be neurotic because (like Orual in *Till We Have Faces*) we are convinced we know what she needs, eventually we recognize her tears and, if we are conscious at all, we take care of her. From the core of the complex, the archetype of the virgin beckons us all the way. She needs the certainty of the ego's love before she can trust, before she can reveal herself face to face.

Building the chrysalis in which Fleur, the embryonic feminine, will develop is important because structure is essential in order to give reassurance to the ego that is letting go. The chrysalis is the sacred container, the womb, in which the process is taking place; if it is contaminated with other people's opinions, the undefiled virgin will not emerge. In accessing the transformative energies, through dream work, journal writing, dancing, whatever channels are available, the individual must be able to contain them. New energy radiates from a central core of vision, and instead of merely feeling "wired," one has to hold the optimal tension within the structure in order to release the truth.

The individuation process is described by Jung as an *opus contra naturam*, which means that one must make a conscious effort not to act instinctively.[22] The psychoid process involves both biological and psychic energies. By blocking the instinctual act, fully conscious of its power, the ego holds the tension until it is rechannelled and manifests in an image. This is not sublimation so much as transformation. When, for example, a woman becomes conscious of her rage—her own and that of the generations of women before her—she will probably find herself acting it out on all the men in her orbit, especially her husband or lover. If she can contain that rage, consciously recognize that men are victims as much as she is, then instead of unconsciously and repeatedly acting it out she can consciously block it, in which case it may then appear as a killer or rapist in her dreams. This does not involve repression, nor moral sanctification, nor acceptance of collective values. Rather it has to do with trusting in the transformative powers of the psyche and the teleological goal of the process. Self-indulgent acting out with drugs, alcohol, sex or binging puts a leak in the vessel. Consciously working with a dream image, taking responsibility for it instead of projecting it onto others, eventually transforms hate into acceptance, or even love.

When instinctual responses are so far from consciousness that the ego cannot contact them (as in some of the cases I have described) then body work in the presence of a trusted friend or trained therapist, who acts as conscious container, can release the repressed instincts without the danger of inundation by raw energy, red in tooth and claw. Gradually, animal becomes human. A strong ego can also function as witness if the individual is conscious enough to do body work alone. The demon lover (Hitler, for example, in dreams) who has kept Eve (the body) in chains all her life needs a strong counterpole to break his power, and certainly there is nothing stronger than whore energy to depotentiate the patriarchal collective that has kept the virgin silent. However, if the ego identifies with the emerging psychic content, it will usurp the primordial energy (inflation) or be absorbed by it (slip back into sheer unconsciousness). The ego must remain conscious enough to allow the released energy to flow within the container until it is transformed.

As different possibilities of how to use the emerging energy become apparent, the ego has to do the hard work of discriminating which path to take. The feeling function may suggest one path, the thinking another. One has to hold on until the emergence of the new consciousness is supported by the unconscious, that is, until the direction in which the energy wants to go becomes clear from the dreams. This recircuiting is an incubation period in which the growth process is going on within. The ego, as pregnant mother, needs time to rest and dream and prepare while her baby takes the energy it needs to grow in her womb.

Often this process is thrust upon us. Some failure in life—illness (perhaps because of the addiction), the loss of a relationship or a job—strips away the well-adapted persona and the ego plummets into the pain of helplessness. Its defeat starts the initiation. While life's circumstances may demand some kind of persona performance, the ego is thrown into the transformative fire, and the only inner support the individual has is the conviction that the Self or some higher power is attempting to bring healing and wholeness. That faith brings a certain detachment: the ego can submit to the stripping, knowing it has to be. Detachment, unlike indifference, experiences the suffering, in fact experiences it more keenly because consciousness bares the truth. Detachment, however, does not identify with suffering. It maintains the larger perspective: the paradox. The ego that is moving from voluntary to involuntary functioning must be strong enough to endure the confusion, the sacrifice and the new insights, while becoming flexible enough to surrender. Its terror is real because the "backbone" and "stiff upper lip" that it has spent a lifetime creating are softening. The rigidity that supported the old adaptation is being dissolved into the fluidity that will support the new. It feels like being a spineless jellyfish, yet the letting go releases the energy that will carry the young child into the revolution. The inner dialogue may go something like this excerpt from a woman's journal:

I am in a life/death struggle.

I who have taken care of everyone am no longer responsible. I dare not give into my tears because everyone depends on me. They've never seen me cry. They'd be shocked if I broke down. What if I do break down. I would be powerless. I don't know how to take care of myself. I'm too afraid to go near that lost part. It's as if I never was. I DO NOT WANT TO KILL HER.

If only my critical animus would shut up! He makes me think everyone sees how disoriented I am. I think they are mocking me, fed up with my whining, ready to attack me. I can't even talk. I stammer and stutter, start one sentence and end with another. I don't know what I'm going to say next. Everything is true and not true.

What if my dreams are all an illusion? What if I lose everything and find out I am nobody? What if I don't have the strength to get through to the other side? What if I am going crazy? Why am I always the one who is different? Why am I always the one who is alone?

The core problem in the chrysalis is receptivity. The persona and the performing shadow, having always justified their existence by being lovable and entertaining, cease to function and the energy regresses to the naked foetus lying defenceless in a world where being itself produces genuine fear of being obliterated. The result is paranoia. In this regressed state, even the most attractive woman may say, "I am untouchable. I am unlovable. How could anyone love me? Why would I reach out for understanding? I expect nothing." In that moment, receiving the touch of a hand may be more than she can accept. Receiving has within it the terror of psychic rape. Her lifetime defence system, charming and well wrought as it may be, is the armor that has protected her baby girl from annihilation. Receptivity for her is the rape of her essence; she cannot trust that her Being is received or can receive.

Our society is geared to block reception. Children learn while still very young to block and to pretend. Young minds dwell in images that naturally move at the pace of reading a story. Television bombards them with images beyond their grasp so that nature builds up a selective process to protect them, but the protection can become armor that encases them in an alienated world in which they dwell alone. In a school auditorium, they may sit daydreaming and inattentive during an excellent program, then burst into wild, meaningless clapping when it is over. Listless, uninvolved, they have received nothing, but their repressed energy erupts in empty hand movements. Their rudeness can be equally meaningless. When they do receive on a personal level, they whisper about their hidden kingdom. Small wonder they grow up unable to receive.

The adult world moves at such a pace and with so much fear that people cannot take in what others are attempting to give. Bombarded by trivia, and bombarded equally by heartbreaking images of famine, wars, desecrated nature, they are obsessed with their own defenses.

Locked into a rigid framework, they attempt to chisel themselves into images of the gods of our age—machines that perform efficiently but are without heart. Their bodies cry out in fear or rage when they pop pills, have an intestinal by-pass, staple their stomachs, yet they still ignore their ferocious rape dreams and rush on again in their mad, goal-oriented pursuit of a perfection that is in fact a total illusion protecting them from looking at themselves as failed human beings.

We are not gods; we are not machines that can be driven by logic or power. We do have hearts, and our hearts are in our bodies, and our bodies are related to our instincts. So long as we allow our heads to be cut off from our bodies, we are colluding with the madness of our age in attempting to cure physical ills without making the necessary psychic corrections. We may temporarily succeed, but the body will have its way. It will not lie. It has received the pain that the mind cannot endure. Eventually it will reject the shallow veneer that blocks the possibility of honest response—the kind that would take in, go through the slow, circuitous route of the gut and heart, and come back with a real reaction. In genuine conversation, intercourse takes place. Soul is shared with soul. Each has enough Presence to allow the other in without distortion and projection. Each gives energy to the other.

No amount of therapy or analysis can heal a heart that cannot trust. The virgin is so wounded by the pressures of modern living that, valuable as rational insight can be, only a numinous experience of love and grace, bursting through from the unconscious, can redeem her. Since most of us as children were told that "it is more blessed to give than to receive," we have been so busy giving that we are unable to receive. The possibility of receiving is blocked by the unconscious message, "You are not worthy to receive; if you do, you are guilty." Women who absorbed that message from their mothers, who heard it from *their* mothers, will sacrifice almost anything to a man and yet hate the word "receptive." They associate it with passivity, submission, non-being. The negative connotations presuppose a weak ego, no chalice to be pierced. Fearful of receiving even from those they love, they dare not risk being receptive to the totally unknown "other." They fear surrender to the creative unconscious. Yet real creativity happens only when the ego is strong enough to surrender. Imagine the strength of Shakespeare's chalice pierced by the divine phallus.

Femininity, biologically and psychically, is by nature receptive, and until women learn what active receptivity is and how crucial it is in creative work and in relationship, they belittle their own womanhood. Men, too, if they are to be creative, and if they are to be able to receive women, have to find their own virgin within. The task of finding the balance between femininity and masculinity is of course different for men and women. But for both the liberation of the heart is essential in order to bring healing within and without.

Surrender to the unknown may be experienced as being raped, until the young feminine is mature enough to genuinely receive. This is often reflected in dreams of rape or bands of hoodlums invading the childhood home, or tornadoes threatening the dream ego as it frantically struggles to keep its luggage together. Sometimes a pubescent girl in dreams becomes furious with the dream ego for being so slow. Persephone, if she is to grow up, must be separated from her mother in order to be receptive to the penetration of Hades. A flexible ego can bend and assimilate the fear released by negative memories in the body and in the psyche. It is painful, but it is an unavoidable life experience on the road to psychological maturity.

Positive energy will also be appearing in the dreams, very often as an energetic young girl. Often a synchronistic event in outer life will give her an opportunity to act. Since she is very young, some compromise between past and present may be necessary. Usually the old persona is undermined, demanding an ego-reorientation that can leave room for the Presence of the feminine. School teachers, for example, may maintain their teaching load by allowing for subtle shifts in their teaching techniques. What they lose through inefficiency, they will gain in a new relationship to the students and a new learning milieu in the classroom. They and their students will experience the excitement of creativity in the *now*.

The body individuates along with the psyche and its messages are as important as the dreams. The body always attempts to preserve the totality. Women who have not menstruated for two or three years may have a period. "I feel I am going through puberty consciously," they say. "I am moving into my body. It is forcing me to move at its speed. If I don't rest and become conscious of what is happening, I become so dizzy I have to go to bed. When I try to speak the old ideas, my tongue feels too big for my mouth. I feel as if I'm telling lies, but they were true once. The words are the same, their meaning is different. The powerful energy I used to get out of food doesn't ground me anymore. It puts me further into unconsciousness. I can't drink coffee or alcohol. I prefer chicken and fish to red meat. I have so much energy I don't know how to handle it. Nothing will wait on the back burner. Everything is all up front, exhausting. I'm being thrust along." The immense energy that drove the body into a death drive is turned into a life drive. Consciously receiving in actual life (reflected in dreams of eating food that is offered) becomes part of the daily rhythm. When the psychological hunger is fed, the physical hunger finds its own balance.

The archenemy of the young feminine is the demon lover, the dark side of the archetype that lies at the core of the father complex. While the negative mother freezes her victim into a paralysis of inertia, the killer animus actively attacks. Cold, impersonal, dedicated to disembodied spirit, his sole purpose is to lure his victim out of life. Addictions are a favourite method: keep a woman fat or starved, drugged or drunk; keep undermining her with "should, ought and have to"; keep her "wailing for her demon-lover."[23] Her resistance to falling in love is his seduction. "You are mine," he says. "Get that fellow out of here. If you don't, I will." And he will succeed unless she has the courage to bring him to consciousness. He reveals his real face exactly at the moment when the young feminine is ready to move into freedom. Because the ego is afraid, it looks at the unconscious with fear and animosity, thus constellating the demon face that stares back.

Sometimes a woman thinks she has conquered her negative animus projection onto men, only to discover she has projected it onto the institution for which she works, or onto some relatively unknown "boss" to whom she is responsible. She is convinced she will lose her job, or should lose it, because she is so incompetent. Then the best way to break the power of the complex is to initiate a feeling relationship in the actual situation—get to know the other person, human being to human being. The power of the complex may thus be depotentiated rather than splaying her with disembodied, impersonal ideas. So long as a woman is haunted by the impeccable logic of the animus, she is possessed and convinced that someone is out to destroy her. That "someone" is actually the complex. To overcome it, she must differentiate her own truth from its logic because it feels nothing. She must say to herself, "That is the voice of the complex. Its logic is sound, but my feeling is my truth." The best way to fight the complex is to build up the ego's reality, minute by minute, differentiating what is right for *her* from what is right for it, saying to herself, for instance, "My work can never be perfect. That is not a statement of defeat. It is an acceptance of my humanity."

A free woman has a strong neck—an open connection between heart and head, a balance between reality and ideals. To fall into the complex is to damn herself for her imperfections; to accept the attitude of the virgin is to accept her human life and open herself to her own truth. Then Lucifer turns his other face; he becomes the Light Bringer, the Christ. So long as the virgin is unconscious, she is unable to surrender to Light. The very Light blocks her acceptance of herself and becomes the demon lover because she cannot receive. (This is dramatically illustrated in Stephen Spielberg's film *Poltergeist*.) Once she is conscious enough to forgive her own and other people's imperfections, then her positive animus becomes the bridge between conscious and unconscious. Psychic incest is the energy source of creativity. Incorporating the Light

The Good and Evil Angels Struggling for Possession of a Child (1795),
watercolor print by William Blake. (Tate Gallery, London)

at the center of the father complex is the soul work of the receptive
virgin.

In the Middle Ages, this task was symbolized in the taming of the
unicorn. That mythical beast is once again popular in our culture, but
in images so bastardized and sentimentalized with romantic fog and
dumb virgins that any attempt at intercourse between them would be
a fiasco. A limp horn attempting to penetrate a swooning womb is not
going to create Being. Marshmallow masculinity may be attracted to
phantom femininity, but that has nothing to do with the psychological
significance of the unicorn and the virgin. The unicorn symbolizes the
creative power of the spirit, and was seen in medieval times as an allegory
of Christ.[24] Its energy is so fierce and so dangerous that only a virgin
can tame it, and only then through deception. She must deliver it into
the hands of the human hunters who kill it and allow its red blood to
flow. In its transformed, resurrected state, the unicorn is the powerful
energy contained in the virgin's holy garden.

The power of the negative animus at the very moment of possible
freedom is clear in the following dream of Sarah, a middle-aged woman

who believed that after five years of analysis she was finally free of the patriarchy. Then she found herself in a life situation in which she had to stand up for her own convictions in opposition to the man in her life. The dream clarifies her conflict:

> I am running to meet my beloved on a ship which is ready to sail. I see a dress in a shop window. It is unquestionably my dress—very simple with a large eye over the heart. I rush into the shop and am met by an anorexic salesgirl who wears a proper little black dress, black shoes and horn-rimmed glasses.
>
> "How much is that dress?" I ask.
>
> She seems frightened. I'm in a great hurry.
>
> "Is it $40?" I ask impatiently. She looks straight into my eyes, paralyzed with fear. I see tears. "I'll give you $4,000," I say. Then she cries, and I am surprised by my own tears. Then I see behind a curtain Mr. Wolf, the owner of the shop. He is watching and he knows he has her in his power. He does not want me to have the dress, and although she wants to sell it to me she can do nothing. I wake up in the impasse.

This dream illustrates the importance of the relationship between the "dream sisters." Unless a woman is constantly alert to the despair of her shadow, she will unconsciously betray herself into the hands of the demon lover, whatever his disguise. Sarah was ready to sail with her creative animus and was willing to put all her feminine energy (4,000 = 4 x 10 x 10 x 10) into the dress, which, with its "large eye over the heart," symbolizes a genuine feeling attitude. But in spite of her energy and willingness, her shadow sister, "paralyzed with fear," had not the strength to defy "Mr. Wolf." (Here the dream sister, who dutifully obeys the masculine, personifies a combination of the father's anima and the mother's shadow.) The energy in the father complex is revealed in the name, an interesting allusion in that a real Mr. Wolf was in fact the owner of her favorite dress shop in her teens.

Since wolves often appear in the dreams of addicts, "wolf energy" must be an element in the addiction. Children of a wolf parent have typically been born with the magnificent hunger for life that the parent once had. Full of energy and high spirits, they constantly reached for the sun-god Apollo, whose animal is the wolf. They laughed hard and cried hard. Then "the shades of the prison house"[25] descended and their hunger for life was shackled. Psychologically, their ego became identified with the wolf, and what began as hunger for life became greed and was displaced onto some object or person. The obsession and the fantasy world, the compulsive, repetitive behavior, are attempts to avoid the real pain of having been denied the depth and breadth and height of life itself. Until the soul is free, some form of neurotic behavior will persist.

If "Mr. Wolf" is seen as a combination of negative mother and negative father, then the dream suggests that Sarah's parents were also undermined by a need for personal power. To sell the dreamer the symbol of her own identity would be to free her to go with her own creativity. This the negative complexes would never willingly do, and so long as her despairing shadow sister is their victim, the ego too is in their power.

The solution to the impasse lies in the dress itself. Almost as if the "large eye" were already over her heart, Sarah sees into the anguish of her trapped sister. As soon as she penetrates that wound, and recognizes the weakness in rigidity, she connects with her own virgin within; her heart opens and she loves her, that sister side of herself that formerly irritated her. Each recognizes she is dependent on the other for freedom: the weak one is forcing the strong one into the conscious awareness and openness of heart that can liberate both. That understanding takes place in silence. Anger, love and forgiveness are almost simultaneous. The secret trap (the mutual loathing and disdain) that once separated them is transformed into the secret that unites them; each holds that secret until the ego can look the shadow in the eye and claim it as her own without being undermined by the judgmental animus. Accept or reject turns to "wake up." The dream ego cannot go to her beloved until the pain of that recognition produces a new integration and a new moral standpoint in the ego.

The dream left Sarah sadder but wiser. It is the kind of shadow confrontation that typically gives depth and understanding and Presence to the personality.

The Conscious Feminine

The essential problem in eating disorders is not the oscillations from fat to thin, from Floe to Flame. The problem is what it has always been, "Who is Fleur? What is my reality?" When the time is ripe, false dramatics and forced sacrifices cease. The secret covenant with death is broken and we are brought eye to eye with a reality that pierces with its truth. Feminine wisdom that is grounded in the love of Sophia accepts what *is*: "This is who I am. I am not asking for your approval. I do not have to justify my existence. I want to know and be known for whom I am." Deciding to go down the birth canal produces a shift in energy: new potential is available to the ego, and as it turns its positive face to the unconscious the demonic face is infiltrated with Light. The throes of death are transformed into the pangs of birth.

As the ego establishes its own feminine standpoint, the woman's creative masculinity is freed from the father. The two processes run parallel, and are reflected in dreams. The images vary from one person to another because circumstances are never the same. The image of Hitler may be replaced by hoodlums, for instance, but one masculine figure is fairly consistent. That is the adolescent rebel. Very often he has just been let out of prison and he ambles insolently past the dreamer, hands in pockets, cigarette dangling from his lips. He is the rebel son of the father who will be anything but who his father is. In women with eating disorders, this typically manifests in a defiant attitude toward society, with behavior ranging from the mildly unconventional to the violently criminal. The adolescent rebel is an anarchist who rejects the collective law, but has no inner standpoint of his own. Sometimes he appears as a junkie, or a homosexual hippy, or a gentle but lost soul with a fierce temper. His failure to be initiated into manhood is reflected in the woman's failure to deal rationally with food. She has no inner voice that says "yes" to a nutritional diet. Nor has she any genuine desire to move into the world.

In his transformed state, however, the arrogant adolescent may become a warrior who unites with the feminine ego in a new conscious attitude. The following is Sarah's dream one year after she freed herself from "Mr. Wolf" and took responsibility for her own creative talent. She was in the process of surrendering to the dynamic energies of the unconscious when she had the dream.

> My husband is a warrior, fighting afar. I am sitting for a portrait of myself with our new-born twin sons. I want him to share this miracle. I am sitting in a forest clearing, bathed in full sunlight, wearing a white velvet coat with a white wolf collar. I hold the twins, one in each arm, powerful baby boys, both named T. I am also aware that my maid has born twin sons in the forest, and their names are both t.

Sarah awoke with an abiding sense of what Being is. While her warrior husband fights to protect her and the new-born babies, she abides, serene and confident, cherishing the miracle of birth. The fiery red wolf that had roamed through previous dreams, driving her to hungry, restless searching, now appears as a white wolf collar. Symbolically, the passionate, wild, instinctual energy has been transformed into spiritual passion. But it is not a passion merely of the head, because while she sits in the bright sunlight of consciousness, she is at the same time in a forest clearing and her shadow maid (a variation of the anorexic salesgirl in the earlier dream) has also given birth in a deeper part of the forest (the instinctual world).

This is the kind of dream that invites quiet meditation because its feeling tone needs to permeate the entire personality. Sarah learned to relax her whole body—let her jaw loose, her shoulders drop, her pelvic floor release, that is, let the rigid complex go and just *be* there.[26] After one meditation she wrote:

I lie on the floor. I feel my bare feet on the warm earth. I feel its solid peace radiating with warm rays up my dark legs and through my body, mingling with the warmer rays of the sun. I embody T. The energy of the cross-bar shoots through my outstretched arms, wrenching them, opening my heart and severing my head. My legs and torso writhe. "Tension, Tumult, Terror, Trying, Tears, Tryst." These words leap out with my sobbing. "Tryst," I scream, and all the shame and guilt and fear, the humiliation and vulnerability, the chaos of all the years of trying to find my own self roll through me, wave after wave of searing pain. Suddenly it is black. I am sucked into darkness. I am terrified. I am dying. I am being born. Then the torment ceases. I lie exhausted with Time.

Months later she dared to incorporate "t":

My body sings as my toes curl into t and the energy moves up: "tree, trunk, torso, tongue, touch, tear, tender, trespass, torrid, trust, total, temple, triumph." I re-member my exquisite body, its sinews, its skeleton, its perception, its obliterated suffering, childhood suffering locked in its muscles. I go into its darkness, my darkness, my unconscious identification with its density, this abandoned mound of flesh I have lugged around. I feel her grief. I love her. I beg her to forgive me. Darkness comprehends Light. Her Light, her Wisdom, ancient, more ancient than I, SHINES. My body, my soul. My arms and chest ache with the pain of too much loving—*here, now*—forever, in this moment.

t opens, soft, flexible, yielding—yielding, yes yielding to T, vibrant T shimmering with Light. I let it happen—cell by cell my soul opens to my spirit. I lie silent in Truth.

In amplifying the letters of the alphabet, Robert Graves in *The White Goddess* treats them as archetypes. He recognizes that the written letters reveal images of nature, and therefore inherent in these images is the energy and truth of the instincts. Concerning the letter T, Graves writes:

We may regard the letters D and T as twins: "the lily white boys clothed all in green o!" of the mediaeval *Green Rushes* song. D is the oak which rules the waxing part of the year—the sacred Druidic oak, the oak of the *Golden Bough*. T is the evergreen oak [the holly oak] which rules the waning part, the bloody oak. ... *Dann* or *Tann* ... is a Celtic word for any sacred tree.[27]

When a letter which has appeared as a dream symbol is embodied (i.e., put back into the instincts) through active imagination, its healing power becomes numinous. In experiential work, T as a symbol often initiates the movement into the third eye, a movement into transformation, specifically the differentiation of body and spirit. It is a letter of crucifixion, connected to the cross as sacred tree that joins earth and heaven. It forcibly opens the body, at the same time keeping it flexible, so that light may penetrate the dark flesh.

The doubling or twin motif in a dream suggests that something previously unknown is attempting to cross the threshold of consciousness, but at the threshold only part crosses while part is left in the unconscious.[28] Without body concentration, the twins in Sarah's dream would have remained incomprehensible. The archetypal energy released when they were incorporated brought new life. Only then did she read Graves, who validated her crucifixion experience. In actual life, the dream did prefigure her first experience of her own feminine soul through a new awareness of her body. It also prefigured the surrender of her ego to the spirit when, as she said, she allowed herself "to go into her craziness in order to find something new." Like Eve in the Garden of Eden, her matter had been unconscious; like Mary, she remained true to her own individual destiny and became a conscious Eve. What was so numinous for Sarah was the totality of the experience, centered as it was in the completely unknown power of the symbol T. Her body involuntarily responded to the ancient symbol. Her dream and her experience in her living room acted as guides when life suddenly swept her into psychic crucifixion, her prelude to rebirth.

Sarah's profound experience of the meaning of the incarnation is by no means unique among modern men and women who are on a conscious journey. Nor is the transformation of wolf energy from addictive behavior into spiritual quest uncommon among addicts who see the devouring abyss at the heart of the addiction. Yet binging, starving and bulimic vomiting are still a growing cancer in our society in spite of the millions of dollars being spent on "rational" attempts to stop them. If the head is going one way and the heart another, with an abyss of betrayal right down the center, only love can bring them together. Is it possible that Sophia in her own domain of physical and spiritual food is attempting to force us to consciousness through our own agony or the agony of someone we love?

We are coming to the end of the line personally and globally through our rejection of the feminine side of God. Addicts manifest an extreme form of this desecration in our culture, but they are also potential catalysts for the rebirth of the feminine. Not only are they individuals carrying the unconscious of their forebears. As human beings in the history of mankind they are also living out what is unconscious in the social environment. We can remain blind to our personal shadow until we look into the starving eyes of an anorexic or alcoholic we love; we can also remain blind to the collective shadow until we turn on television and look into the eyes of a starving child.

In a technological civilization geared up for its own heady destruction, we are destined to become the victims of an outworn patriarchal consciousness so long as we collude in equating femininity with biological identity. That kind of consciousness is propelling not only individuals but the whole planet into an addiction to power and perfection which, viewed from the perspective of nature, can lead only to suicide. Feminine consciousness dare not be limited to unredeemed matter or unconscious mother. The realization that a neurosis has a creative purpose applies globally as well as personally, and surely, in an age addicted to power and the acquisition of material possessions, the creative purpose must have something to do with the one thing that can save us—love for the earth, love for each other—the wisdom of the Goddess. Responsibility belongs in the individual home, in the individual heart, in the energy that holds atoms together rather than blows them apart.

Fundamental in the psyche of the addict, as I see it, is an apocalyptic vision. (Apocalypse comes from a Greek word meaning to uncover, to disclose—to unveil the old and reveal the new.) The eating mania is in part an attempt to eat everything up, finish it off and start afresh. Bulimics eat huge quantities, then purge themselves to begin anew. Anorexics do not consciously seek death, but their obsession with "order" has within it the terror of annihilation through chaos. Not only with food, but also with money, energy, cleaning, their whole life is an attempt to finish things off and start again *or* not start again. They may agree with the philosophy "death to the old, life to the new," but in their unconsciousness they confuse the literal and the symbolic, thus turning their search for essence into Non-being rather than Being. The apocalyptic psychology of an addicted culture—a psychology that anticipates the divine revelation in one blinding bolt of insight—could on a planetary scale foreshadow a holocaust.

Many addictive personalities who can find no acceptable outlet for their energy in our society would have been devoted worshippers of Dionysus had they lived in Ancient Greece, a culture where religious yearnings had a meaningful focus. Repeatedly they say, "If it were well with God, it would be well with my body." Intuitively, they are right. Their fierce longing for life is both physical and spiritual; they yearn for what Walter Otto calls "this unity of the paradoxical which appeared in Dionysiac ecstasy with staggering force."[29]

Otto's description of the Greek maenads in their ecstatic dance captures the essence of what lies at the core of much addictive behavior:

> He who begets something which is alive must dive down into the primeval depths in which the forces of life dwell. And when he rises to the surface, there is a gleam of madness in his eyes because in those depths death lives cheek by jowl with life. The primal mystery is itself mad—the matrix of the duality and the unity of disunity. ... The more alive this life becomes, the nearer death draws, until the supreme moment—the enchanted moment when something new is created—when death and life

meet in an embrace of mad ecstasy. The rapture and terror of life are so profound because they are intoxicated with death. As often as life engenders itself anew, the wall which separates it from death is momentarily destroyed. ... Life which has become sterile totters to meet its end, but love and death have welcomed and clung to one another passionately from the beginning.[30]

Describing the Dionysiac madness, Otto sees it as "the churning up of the essence of life surrounded by the storms of death."[31] This paradox is apparent in a passage written by a young pregnant woman:

After making love, I fell into a fit of sobbing. I buried my head in my husband's arms and all I could see was darkness. I felt private and safe. I felt so incredibly alive and passionate in my body—human, earthy, real, lost out of this world inside the passion of his body and my body. My feeling for life was overpowering, and with it came the feeling of my own death, my own solitary and lonely and final death. Then I could feel the first false contraction, making me exquisitely aware of the childbirth that is so close to me now—so much life and living, moving and happening in a physically real way, so bodily based that I cannot escape it.

And with all that living physical reality, the reality of death—linked together, part of the same whole, the same totality. Oh yes, we are finding baby furniture now, preparing, getting ready ... and there are preparations for death too. Are they really so different? From the space within me the child will emerge into this temporary world. But I believe the seed for this child was planted long long ago, just as my marriage was somehow known by someone greater than myself. This life will come to an end, but it could be that life will continue in some new way yet unknown.

Addicts, like maenads, flee from a static situation, from a meaningless status quo. Through their fasting and purging, addicts may be unconsciously enacting initiation rites which, if understood, would release them from the merely biological body into the subtle body. These are the women who are forced by their addiction to give birth to themselves or die. Their task is to reaffirm nature on a conscious level. Man's blind destruction of nature by attempting to bend it to his will can be redeemed through their feminine affirmation of nature in their own bodies. Man's actions must have the blessing of nature, and for that, woman must be conscious. Mary's child was nature, consciously embraced. The incarnation is ongoing. If consciousness is the god or goddess in us, then at the core of the fierce energy of the addiction may be the divine voice. Compliant, self-abnegating and stubborn as food addicts appear to be, there is often another side that carries an uncanny strength. Their life of mirroring others puts them in touch with the collective unconscious of the culture. Their bodies, their images, their rituals mean something, and so do their dreams—dream images reflecting the power-driven attitudes of modern men and women that keep the feminine imprisoned.

Such images make me think of the young Jewish woman Etty Hillesum, who was taken from Holland to Auschwitz in 1943. A year before her death, keenly aware of what was happening to her people, she wrote:

> Reality is something one shoulders together with all the suffering that goes with it, and with all the difficulties. And as one shoulders them so one's resilience grows stronger. But the *idea* of suffering (which is not the reality, for real suffering is always fruitful and can turn life into a precious thing) must be destroyed. And if you destroy the ideas behind which life lies imprisoned as behind bars, then you liberate your true life, its real mainsprings; and then you will also have the strength to bear real suffering, your own and the world's.
>
> ... Oh God, to bear the suffering you have imposed on me and not just the suffering I have chosen for myself.[32]

Dr. Elisabeth Kubler-Ross tells of going into a concentration camp after the war. She walked through the barracks where the Jewish people had been interned before they went to the gas ovens. On the walls where the children had stayed, little hands had drawn butterflies in their anticipation of freedom.

Shanti Nilaya

Logo for Elisabeth Kubler-Ross Center.

Love—stronger than Death and harder than Hell.   —Meister Eckhart.

One of the most important and difficult tasks in the individuation process is to bridge the distance between people. There is always a danger that the distance will be broken down by one party only, and this invariably gives rise to a feeling of violation followed by resentment. *Every relationship has its optimal distance,* which of course has to be found by trial and error.   —C.G. Jung, *Letters.*

> It wasn't an angel entering—recognize—
> that frightened her. She felt no shocked surprise
> more than do others when sunbeam or moon
> bustles with its affairs about their room.
> No more did she care now to be indignant
> at the shape which an angel had assumed.
> . . . No, not his entering; but he so inclined,
> the angel, a youth's face to hers, that it combined
> with the gaze with which she looked up, and the two
> struck together, as though all outside suddenly
> were empty. What millions see, hear, do,
> was compressed into them; he and she only;
> beholder and beheld; eye and eye's delight.
> Nothing at all else in this place—oh see
> this terrifies. And both were terrified.
>
> Then the angel sang his melody.

        —Rainer Maria Rilke, "Annunciation to Mary."

In the male, sex with aggression can be combined, but not sex and fear. In the female, sex and fear can be combined, but not aggression and sex. And there you have the animus-anima problem in a nutshell.

        —Marie-Louise von Franz, *The Problem of the Puer Aeternus.*

> I wish I knew a woman
> who was like a red fire on the hearth
> glowing after the day's restless draughts.
>
> So that one could draw near her
> in the red stillness of the dusk
> and really take delight in her
> without having to make the polite effort of loving her
> or the mental effort of making her acquaintance.
> Without having to take a chill, talking to her.

        —D.H. Lawrence, "I Wish I Knew a Woman."

6

Piercing the Heart:

Yin, Yang and Jung

Love consists in this,
that two solitudes protect,
and touch, and greet each other.
                    —Rainer Maria Rilke.

One April morning, I was walking through the park in my clown shoes, pondering

> *this tremendous scene—*
> *This whole Experiment of Green—*
> *As if it were [my] own.!*[1]

And I remembered other springs in the first bloom of young love when I moved through the startled mists of morning, singing, remembering two hearts beating their quiet miracle, yellow daffodils blooming yellower, hair curling curlier, red blood flowing redder, and open arms embracing the whole world without even trying.

Suddenly I was pierced by a forsythia spear—a moment in another springtime—stillness—time then, time now—eyes unfocused through tears, forsythia bushes and green grass dissolving into an abstract of gold and green. *Now*.

> *... at the still point, there the dance is,*
> *But neither arrest nor movement. And do not call it fixity,*
> *Where past and future are gathered. Neither movement*
> *   from nor towards,*
> *Neither ascent nor decline. Except for the point, the still*
> *   point,*
> *There would be no dance, and there is only the dance.*
> *   ... concentration*
> *Without elimination, both a new world*
> *And the old made explicit ...*[2]

"Yes," I thought, "tears synthesize. So does moonlight."

Feminine consciousness is lunar consciousness—the translucent glow of the pearl that illuminates with delicate moonbeams. Whereas solar consciousness analyzes, discriminates, cuts and clarifies, making well-differentiated boundaries, lunar consciousness unites; it thinks with the heart and heart thought incorporates past, present and future. It moves in Time out of time. And while tears may be part of its motion, tears of the thinking heart are not sentimental. The heart knows what is real. It beats in the reality of *now*, and when we think with the heart we are not looking back through the misty corridors of the mind. We *are* in the reality of *now*—whatever was real, is real, forever real. Whoever is able to come from that still point is free to be a virgin—free to love and be loved, free to come from an inner center of gravity and free to allow others to come from theirs.

As the veils of illusion are stripped away, we recognize the sacred being within. We recognize too that the world cannot be separated into an either/or contradiction. Structuring life that way is infantile. When we can hold the paradox of the totality, the armor that defended us against a world of enemies becomes the full armor of God, the armor of invincibility that protects the inner sacred grove. There God is both *he* and *she*—the sunlight that illuminates with clarity, the moonlight that illuminates with love. The energy changes from fighting the enemy to making room for the rose of creation to open in the fire of consciousness. We move from rape to ravishment.

Incorporating that vision is not easy. It sometimes feels like endless water-carrying in a leaky vessel. And the leaky vessel is most obvious in the relationships through which God is mirrored in our lives. Eternal love is rooted in human love. The mystery of God touches us—or does not touch us—in the smallest details: giving a strawberry, *with love*, receiving a touch, *with love*, sharing the snapdragon red of an autumn sunset.

In this book, I have concentrated on women's tasks in freeing themselves from the father and mother complexes. The tasks are no less arduous for men, in whom femininity is even more psychically raped by collective values. Their dreams too are full of mutilated baby girls, young women being dragged in chains, grandmothers crying, prisons and towers in which the feminine is encapsulated. Rock videos and pornography that depict women as sexually insatiable and indiscriminate, and sex itself as an act of manipulation and violence, ravage the soul that lives and grows on symbols. The images on which we feed govern our lives. If we allow ourselves to become garbage dumps for the soft-core porn of advertising and "the soaps," our femininity is desecrated. Television bombards us with images of threatened victims looking for a strong Daddy, or witches whose sole purpose for existence is to destroy their man. Such portrayals tend to desensitize us, making us blind to our own self-rape.

Many men, however, are acutely aware of their own threatened femininity and the anguish in their wives and partners. As one male therapist wrote to me in a letter, "For so long now, I have been wrestling with, agonizing over, and trying to help women to see their own locked-up femininity. I have counseled many couples prior to marriage, and have seen too many men who have no idea at all of the feminine within themselves, and even less of the feminine in their intended bride. I feel so impotent when faced with the magnitude of the problem. ... I have believed for a long time that in some way the male can bring the female to bloom, helping her to come into full flower from a tightly closed bud. But I have found that this belief is not shared by many feminists, who feel they can 'do it on their own.'

"I also know that for a man to be able to do this, he must be in touch with his own true masculinity—not the usually accepted 'macho' type—but true masculinity which is strong enough to recognize the feminine in himself as well."

The feminist issue opens another avenue of thought, one on which I can merely comment. While our culture is indebted to the pioneer achievements of the feminist movement, women who are so vociferous in their outcry against men, and so intent on pigeon-holing the female psyche, need to take the time to look at their own dreams. Rigidity destroys spontaneity; this often shows up in dreams of little girls being raped. What that rigidity fails to acknowledge is that men are the victims of the patriarchy and the phallic mother as much as women are, and their embryonic feminine is easily murdered by a vituperative animus—spoken or unspoken. In a culture teetering on the edge of annihilation, surely our focus needs to be on working together rather than on issues that widen the split.

I look at the dreams of women tyrannized by rapists, robbers and dictators, and I look at the dreams of men threatened by sharks, wildcats and witches. I see what each sex is projecting onto the other and I wonder how we exist together on the same planet, let alone in the same household or the same bed. What goes on inside goes on outside, or as Jung put it, "When an inner situation is not made conscious, it happens outside, as fate."[3] So long as we remain unconscious, our ambivalent feelings are imaged in our dreams. A women who believes she loves her husband dreams she serves him an elegant dish of poisoned shrimp. A man who worships his wife dreams of driving a stake through her heart. Until the inner warfare is made conscious, the outer world will continue to be a battleground of the sexes—however placid it may sometimes appear.

The love with which the finely honed sword of discrimination is wielded makes the difference between union and separation. If the concentration is on bringing together the opposites, the focus is in the *now*; the edges between masculine and feminine become lovingly blurred when the whole takes precedence over the parts. This is not "unisex" in which feminine and masculine are virtually indistinguishable, clinging together in one big psychic hot tub. Rather it is the finely differentiated

Yin-Yang, each containing a portion of the other, each the complement to its opposite.

In *Man And His Symbols*, Marie-Louise von Franz has elucidated Jung's four stages of anima development in a man. Introducing them, she writes,

> The first stage is best symbolized by the figure of Eve, which represents purely instinctual and biological relations. The second can be seen in Faust's Helen. She personifies a romantic and aesthetic level that is, however, still characterized by sexual elements. The third is represented, for instance, by the Virgin Mary—a figure who raises love (*eros*) to the heights of spiritual devotion. The fourth type is symbolized by Sapientia [Sophia], wisdom transcending even the most holy and the most pure. Of this another symbol is the Shulamite in the Song of Solomon. (In the psychic development of modern man this stage is rarely reached. The Mona Lisa comes nearest to such a wisdom anima.)[4]

Although neither Jung nor von Franz elaborates on the Shulamite, modern sensibilities may see this "black, but comely" queen (Song of Sol. 1:5) as symbolically equivalent to the Black Madonna. At that stage of anima development, a man's sexuality and spirituality would come together.

In the Eve stage, the man is in thrall to the mother complex, the sucking infant feeding on the all-powerful breast. The need is both ways: the breast has to be emptied and the child receives pleasure in taking. The dependency needs are fulfilled. This is Mother Nature, an essentially symbiotic interaction. When Mother withholds the breast, she becomes a manipulating witch whose demands the man cannot possibly meet.

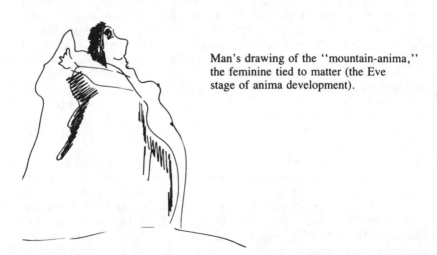

Man's drawing of the "mountain-anima," the feminine tied to matter (the Eve stage of anima development).

How quickly that can happen is clear from one episode in a marriage that was in serious difficulty. After a crucial weekend of discussion, both partners felt they were on the road to reconciliation. As the wife was leaving for work on Monday morning, her husband was about to rush downstairs to kiss her goodbye—a very important kiss for both in the circumstances. In the midst of his heroic attempt to leap downstairs his wife said, "Bring the Kleenex." He was left splayed on the staircase. An apparently innocent request, but his complex heard negative mother telling him what to do and his bourgeoning manhood said, "No."

On the other hand, many "relationships" and marriages in our present culture are bogged down in the Helen stage of development. When the negative mother is unveiled and the negative father depotentiated, what commonly surfaces from the unconscious of both men and women is a virgin/whore split and a brutal realization that life has not been lived. The glass coffin of the idealistic virgin may shatter, plunging her into the unrelated sexual energy of the whore. A dangerous transitional period may ensue, because a woman's ego or a man's anima that is not in touch with differentiated feeling values will give away feminine pearls for a romantic cause, whether religious, political or moral. Psychologically, the relationship is based on archetypal projection. The man projects his soul onto the woman, the woman projects her soul onto the man; both hang on in terror of losing half of themselves, then scream with pain when the partner's human action does not tally with the archetypal projection. They are in love with love, imprisoned in their own ideals.

The tragic dynamic between Shakespeare's Othello and Desdemona illustrates the danger of archetypal projection, so-called romantic love. Othello, the black Moor, the staunch warrior, the mother's son, the primitive man, projects onto his bride, Desdemona, she of "whiter skin ... than snow,"[5] the perfection of womanhood. She in turn, an idealistic father's daughter, projects onto him the perfection of manhood. Deceived by Iago, his shadow, into believing that his wife is unfaithful, the insecure Moor lays a trap for Desdemona with the handkerchief his mother embroidered with strawberries. Insanely jealous, Othello believes any lie Iago hints at, and eventually determines that the "cunning whore of Venice"[6] must die because she is false to his idealized feminine image. Desdemona, meanwhile, ritually prepares her chamber. Unconsciously aware that her marriage bed will be her death bed, she sings her fatal willow song:

> Sing all a green willow must be my garland,
> Let nobody blame him, his scorn I approve—[7]

When Othello comes to "put out the light; and then put out the light,"[8] his love has been ravaged by faulty thinking.

> *It is the cause, it is the cause, my soul*
> *Let me not name it to you, you chaste stars!*
> *... she must die, else she'll betray more men.*[9]

Ready to kill her, he kisses her as she sleeps—the sleep she has been in most of her life.

> *So sweet was ne'er so fatal. I must weep,*
> *But they are cruel tears. This sorrow's heavenly;*
> *It strikes where it doth love.*[10]

Without the human love to re-member their human reality, they cannot see through the veils of illusion. Othello sees her as his own soul; Desdemona unconsciously colludes in the identification. Together they consummate the death marriage.

Not all couples constellate a death marriage, but many, mired in "heavenly sorrow," do constellate the death of their own marriage. Known to the world as "the perfect couple," basking in how they look to others, they wither behind their perfect masks. Their interaction is often based on the idealization of the one who is the giver; giving is then idealized, but behind the giving is power. "My love for you depends on what you give to me, and I will give to you so that you will love me." The parental archetypes determine the relationship when individual feeling values have not been differentiated from collective attitudes. Mother needs son, son needs mother; father needs daughter, daughter needs father. Sooner or later the incest taboo constellates between them. Sexuality becomes problematic, communication suffers. "Mom" lives with "Dad." In their wish to maintain a surface harmony, the guts of relationship are not allowed; individual is afraid to confront individual. In some cases an enormous split results: the mother and father projections are maintained, but the instinct seeks an erotic partner elsewhere. The tragedy is, of course, that until the mature virgin is released from the mother, the cycle will repeat. In the dreams, one is again in bed with mother or father; in actual life, one is looking for yet another sexual partner.

Trapped in a romantic vision, people sometimes despair of ever changing the archetypal pattern in which they are caught. "What is the purpose of analysis?" they ask. "It just leads me into a deeper recognition of what is happening—the horror of living out my fate." They see themselves going around the same circle—a different situation, but the same dynamic, a dynamic they consciously tried to avoid. Closer discernment, however, helps them to realize they are not in the same place, but on a new rung of a spiral. Perhaps they are not so identified with the despair as they were last time—nor the fear, nor the pain, nor the abandonment. Perhaps they are more objective, allowing the grief and rage to flow through them without being swept away by either. Their ego may no longer be so inundated by archetypal energy, no longer in such danger of acting out the archetypal pattern. Certainly, there is a death going on, a sacrifice, which must be perceived as sacrifice and treated as such or it can turn into annihilation. Part of what has to be sacrificed is the archetypal identification. That is the very thing people do not want to give up—the idealization, the obsession, the perfection of joy, even the perfection of suffering.

How inevitably a Desdemona can forfeit her femininity to an Othello when she has carried her father's idealized virgin projection is clear in the dream of Kate, a woman in her late thirties. Crippled in her relationships to men by a power-driven mother and an alcoholic *puer* father, after one year of analysis and years of therapy and body work, Kate at last found her own dark goddess. The following is the dream that initiated a major transformation in both her masculinity and femininity.

> I'm underneath a black slave girl's skirt. I'm looking up at her vagina. There is a tear welling out of it. I hear my voice becoming stronger and more beautiful as I sing a hymn to her vagina. My voice strengthens as it soars, and as I sing, her vagina becomes exquisitely beautiful, the tear a glistening drop. I feel mesmerized by it. At first I am repulsed, but gradually the meaning of vaginal juices as a symbol of feminine essence makes me accept her femininity. I feel a desire to melt with it. I begin to understand why men love oral sex.
>
> Then I come out from under her skirt and I am a boy. The girl takes off her pearls to give to me out of love and appreciation. I am afraid of the man who owns her, afraid he will beat her. She swoons back on a couch and lies there as slave to a sultan. The girl wants me to take her, but I am afraid the man will take vengeance on me. I just stand there. I switch back into being a woman.
>
> Then the dream plays again from the top. I watch as a dark man sings to the girl's vagina and takes her pearls. I can see the girl is giving away her only valuable possession. I look at the girl and at the man. With her he could be rich but he has no intention of loving her. I look at the man to find evidence of my tenderness that sang to her vagina. Greed instead is curving his mouth. The girl thinks she is uniting herself to the man by giving him her pearls. In fact, she is making herself worthless.

The carefully modulated tenderness and crescendo of feeling toward the black slave girl in this dream resonates with Bea's initiation dream in chapter 4 (page 95). The black girl is a slave because she is still undifferentiated, that is, relatively unknown to the dreamer and therefore still in bondage to the "sultan." In Kate's psychology, the slave is a combination of the shadow side of her idealistic mother and the primitive anima of her father. At first, the dream ego is repulsed at her fascination with the slave girl's vagina, an attitude toward the feminine body which the dreamer had unconsciously assimilated from her parents. When through the singing (her true feeling) the dream ego transcends this unnatural response, she wants "to melt with" the sexuality of the girl, experiencing the vaginal tear as a symbol of feminine essence.

Suddenly the standpoint of the dream ego shifts from singing her feminine song to thinking as a man attracted to oral sex. Immediately, the singer becomes a boy—a masculine aspect of the dreamer too immature to protect the feminine. Simultaneously, the slave girl falls into unconsciousness, bondwoman to a sultan (the authoritarian father world). In a touching effort to thank the dreamer for at least—or at last—recognizing her, the girl offers the gift of her one possession, her pearls, symbol of luminous moonlight, their luster depending on the living skin on which they rest. The dreamer, however, stands helpless, incapable of receiving them; her ego is not yet strong enough to receive the powerful feminine energy they represent.

In real life Kate's parents had scorned sexuality. At two crucial developmental times in her life, at five and thirteen, her father had responded brutally to her developing sexuality. At five he had disciplined her with a severe beating on her bare bottom for playful sexual touching with a little boy. At thirteen there was ongoing physical abuse, heavily laced with sexual overtones. When her father ridiculed her body, he was projecting onto his daughter his own whore anima. Earlier he had projected the lily-white virgin onto her, a role she was in fact conscientiously trying to live out through a spiritual orientation. Her mother, meanwhile, professed an abhorrence for sexuality but was always searching out "filthy sex." She too ridiculed her daughter's growing breasts and budding femininity. Their ambivalent attitudes created in Kate the virgin/whore split that is reflected in the dream.

The violence of the father echoes in the dream in the fear that the man would take vengeance not only on the slave girl but on the dreamer herself. She cannot move. Petrified in the *puer* attitude of the father who was terrified of the earthy power of the feminine, she stands helpless in the guise of a little boy, unable to claim her own womanhood. Although the black girl, potentially her Black Madonna, reaches out to her, she cannot receive.

Then, as if to make sure she receives the message, the dream repeats, with the dreamer watching herself as a dark man in effect raping the slave girl. Here is the shadow side of the tyrannical sultan father, his unrelated sexuality devastating the undeveloped feminine shadow. Although he goes through the performance of singing praises to the feminine, he is without tenderness, without any individual love for the slave. Instead his lips curve with greed.

Commenting on the dream, Kate said, "If the black girl had been more realized in me, she would not have been a slave. As I watched the dark man take her pearls—her essential feminine identity—I realized she was giving away her only valuable possession. The pearls gave her whatever status she had and made the men treat her with respect even though she was a slave. Too naive to keep her own being intact, she was sentimental and ingratiating, thinking the man would love her if she handed over her pearls of gratitude. Without them, she was totally at the mercy of the man and, pearl-less, she would be thrown out to grovel in the street. The man's greed and lust were interested in the pearls merely because of their material value. The slave girl was offering them as a token of love—a soul gift.

"I see how crucial the feminine standpoint is in relation to the masculine. Women don't maintain their own standpoint. In trying to please, they hand over their pearls—their soul. They think they are showing their appreciation and love. In fact, they lose their own vigor, their own substance, their turgidness goes limp. Giving away their pearls ends in handing themselves over to the lust of their own masculinity. The desecration that takes place in the psyche of a woman who fails to value herself as a woman plays itself out in relation to a man."

The imbalance between masculine and feminine in Kate's psyche is evident in the dream. As her father's anima, she functioned out of a male psychology, playing the role expected of her by men, rather than acting out of her own feminine instincts. At this stage in her process, the masculine strength necessary to appreciate her budding femininity is as absent as the inner sense of personal worth that in the dream would prevent the black girl from betraying her own essence. The little boy stands numb, just as a mother-bound man quails before the authentic feminine. Until the dreamer consciously treasures her own enslaved "dark" side, the shadow side of the patriarchy will continue to psychically rape the feminine. These same dynamics are part of our cultural unconsciousness.

Kate had to live through one more relationship in which she handed her "pearls" over to a man, before she was able to break the pattern. Two years after the slave girl dream, Kate dreamt of a big black bird (symbol of the negative or phallic mother) being escorted away by a young man (her hero animus), ready and willing to perform the dangerous task of taking the bird to a faraway land. The boy of the earlier dream had now matured enough to deal with the negative mother. It took the masculine energy to make room for the conscious feminine to grow. In actual life, Kate put all her energy into creating a world for herself.

The following year, a new man came into Kate's life. The nature of their relationship demanded continuous response from her conscious femininity. This man would not be pushed, and she continually had to curb her ego desire to "nudge away" at him. When Kate was able to hold a let-it-be standpoint, then her positive inner animus was constellated. Toward the end of one long dream, a young man appeared in

Kate's kitchen. A lettuce-whirler turned into a fishbowl containing live fish; then the water changed into fire that poured over the man's left hand. When he brought his right hand to his left, both were on fire. He held his hands out to her in a supplicating gesture. She looked around, saw a white linen napkin on her pine floor, wet it and put it over his hands. They glowed red through the linen. Later his hands were not burned at all.

The transformation in the dream moves from the product of the earth, to the living water, to the sacred fire. When Kate was able to love the man himself instead of her projection, the Spirit was not a fantasy in the sky but a reality in her own kitchen, with the fire of the Holy Ghost in her own fishbowl. Open to the gift that life was bringing her, she perceived the masculine hands not only as skin over bone, but as human flesh consecrated by spirit—the mystery of love glowing, incandescent, the incorruptible substance veiled beneath her own consecrated linen. No longer a slave girl giving away her pearls, selling out her femininity to greed and lust, Kate was now in a relationship that demanded real love, real suffering—the rose in the fire.

Real suffering burns clean; neurotic suffering creates more and more soot. What is emerging in our culture is an unprecedented attempt by many individuals to relate through Eros, Jung's third stage of anima development. In a relationship based on Eros, both partners are in touch with their own maturing virgin, individual relating to individual, no longer "what can we *do* for each other," but "what can we *be* for each other." They are attempting to open their hearts, daring to leap, albeit tremulously, into the cleansing fire.

Relationship, as I understand it, has to do with the exquisitely tuned harmonics between two people who are attempting to become conscious of their personal psychology. The mystery of each individual is holy, and the mystery which brings each into relationship with the other is tenuous, invisible and sacred. As Jung wrote when his friend Father Victor White died, "The living mystery of life is always hidden between Two, and it is the true mystery which cannot be betrayed by words and depleted by arguments."[11]

In such a relationship, both partners are attempting to become more conscious of their complexes and their masculine and feminine sides, both are willing to reflect on their interaction, and both have the courage to honor the uniqueness of what they share. Neither is attempting to possess the other, neither wishes to be possessed. The relationship itself is unburdened by the pressure of inchoate needs and expectations. The partners do not demand a "whole" relationship, nor do they seek to be made whole by it; rather they value the relationship as a container in which is reflected the wholeness they seek in themselves. Each is free to be authentic. Living in the *now*, unfettered by collective ideas of how either should act or be, they have no way of knowing how such a relationship will develop. If they persevere, they may experience the grace of the unicorn, as Rilke expresses it in his *Sonnets to Orpheus*:

> *This is the creature there has never been.*
> *They never knew it, and yet, none the less,*
> *they loved the way it moved, its suppleness,*
> *its neck, its very gaze, mild and serene.*
>
> *Not there, because they loved it, it behaved*
> *as though it were. They always left some space.*
> *And in that clear, unpeopled space they saved*
> *it lightly reared its head, with scarce a trace*
>
> *Of not being there. They fed it, not with corn,*
> *but only with the possibility*
> *of being. And that was able to confer*
>
> *Such strength, its brow put forth a horn. One horn.*
> *Whitely it stole up to a maid,—to be*
> *within the silver mirror and in her.*[12]

This may sound idealistic, but anyone involved in the soul-making process knows it is bedrock reality. It demands honesty, steadfastness, humility, humor, detachment, the capacity to endure the pain of withdrawing projections. This could become a very long list. It would have to include faith, love and hope—when there is little reason to hope.

For such a relationship to exist, the partners must be constantly responsive to the ever finer tuning of the maturing masculine and feminine both in themselves and in the other. Each is pioneering new territory because each is attempting to relate not through the manipulating complexes but from a conscious center. This is *human* relationship, "I love you as you are," the kind of relationship that is not possible as long as people are enslaved to archetypal patterns, whether instinctively or spiritually. It is freedom as opposed to bondage. It is looking at another human being and, instead of wanting to be loved, loving—loving the beauty and courage and fidelity of a separate maturing soul. It is not "togetherness," it is psychological separateness. It leaves a "clear, unpeopled space," open to "the possibility of being."

Withdrawing projections is invariably the most painful task. We fear the realization that we are essentially alone; but where our fear is, there is our task. Projection is a natural process, through which, if we are attentive, we come to recognize our own inner world. Through the withdrawal of projections we come into possession of what Jung calls our "treasures":

When you are in the condition of the beginning of life, in an adolescent condition of mind, you are not in possession of the animus—or the anima, in a man's case—and you have no consciousness of the Self, because they are both projected. You are then ... liable to become possessed by somebody who seems to contain these values; you get under the influence of the apparent proprietors of your treasures, and that is of course a sort of magic influence.

Now the more you get under that fascination, the more you become immovable. ... You are in prison, you are utterly unfree.

That is why people are afraid of each other—they fear that somebody could put them into prison. Many people have a tremendous fear of attaching themselves ... as if the very soul were threatened. ...[13]

Such fear may lead people to resign themselves to a life without meaningful relationships; the pain of disappointed expectations is too great. They refuse to risk falling in love "yet again." But individuation cannot occur without relationship. As Jung points out:

If you can accept that fact of being caught, of course you are imprisoned, but on the other hand you have a chance to come into possession of your treasures. There is no other way; you never will come into possession of your treasures if you keep aloof, if you run about like a wild dog.[14]

Projections carry very real energy; they either sustain or undermine. If someone hits us with a poisoned projection, we feel it whether we recognize it or not; if we are struck with a loving projection, energy is released; if we are struck with a power projection, our energy is smothered. As we become more conscious we are increasingly aware of what we have projected onto others, both the good and the bad in ourselves. Unconsciously we have asked them to take responsibility for what we have failed to recognize in ourselves—or what of ourselves we have failed to realize.

Projections are charged with archetypal energy until they have been assimilated by the conscious ego. Our inherent natures and the individual circumstances of our childhood put us in touch with particular archetypal patterns; these are the tapestries within which our lives are woven. How we relate to them is our choice. We can succumb to a pattern and blindly live it out, in other words, never question who we are; we can identify with a pattern that is foreign to our nature, effectively burying ourselves alive; we can resent our apparent destiny, thus evoking a negative response from the unconscious (chronic conflict, accidents, disease); or we can acknowledge our personal parameters and celebrate the mystery of who we are. The last involves a redefinition of "suffering," thinking of it not so much as pain to be avoided at all costs, but as the travail natural to any growth process.

Take, for example, a woman who through her experience of herself knows she is a "father's daughter." While unconscious, she may despair of ever being released. When she becomes conscious, she realizes that all is not lost. She sees that she is both blessed and cursed with a savior within. She can either project him onto a mortal man, living with "infinite passion, and the pain/Of finite hearts that yearn,"[15] or she can relate inwardly to that archetypal image and allow her human partner to be who he is. If she can celebrate her psychological reality by conscientiously exploring her living connection to the creative imagination, then she may claim her sacred stewardship toward the gifts of the unconscious that are naturally hers. She is then free to see the man she loves in the full dignity of his maleness, whatever his personal limitations. The evanescent mystery of human love in his smile, the changing landscape of his face, the nuances in his voice—these become the punctuations that give mortal life meaning within the context of the immortal. Knowing who we are, celebrating who we are, is individuating the archetype.

The positive animus manifests in a woman's creative energy. His radiance is unmistakable. He is the inner beloved and the guide to the Self. Usually he does not appear in dreams until the woman has the ego strength to take responsibility for her own inner gifts. Sarah, the woman in chapter 5 whose shadow was still in thrall to the father (page 134), worked hard on both her tendency to hand over authority to the patriarchy and her inclination to project her own creative talent onto creative men. Even more important, she gave up her exhausting struggle for "self-identity"; she concentrated on relaxing into her own Beingness, her own receptive virgin, and allowed life to come to her.

Intent on containing her psychic energy instead of projecting it, Sarah was able to bring to consciousness her own artistic talent. She made a commitment to what she believed was her gift, and established a loving relationship to her creativity by making space in her life for it. A new crisis came when it seemed time to put her work before the public. Her own perfectionist animus, and therefore the men onto whom she projected that animus, discouraged her. The following dream, one year after the dream of the twins (above, page 136) released her from incessant fears of critical judgment and public rejection.

> I am browsing in an old cemetery. The graves are above ground, mostly cement vaults. Suddenly I am aware that the top of one is moving. I stop in amazement about twenty feet from it. The top is being pushed up from underneath. A powerful masculine arm thrusts the top off. An equally powerful hairy leg swings out over the side. A magnificent blond, blue-eyed man rises out of the tomb, laughing and shaking himself. Light bounces off his skin. He opens his arms and strides toward me as if I were his long lost love. This is my Dionysian Christ.

The masculine spirit freed from the tombs of a world that is now dead for Sarah rises up with the joyous energy of the instinctual masculine and the radiant energy of the spirit. The stone of the past is rolled away and the vibrant new energy moves toward the feminine as if it had loved her all her life, if only she had known how to receive it. Now the creative animus is where he ought to be, a psychological reality, functioning as a psychopomp who can lead the woman to greater freedom. "He was like the Lord of the Dance," said Sarah. "He made me feel that I was conceived in love. The very cells of my body leapt with love to receive him. I don't know if he was an embodied spirit, or a spiritualized body. I only know I loved him." Receiving the positive animus opens the woman to a new experience of sexuality. Her whole body, the whole world, is eroticized when she transends the ego boundaries of consciousness. Such a dream gives a woman tremendous confidence, a confidence she desperately needs if she has betrayed her own feeling most of her life.

The feeling function is so mutilated in women that they may betray themselves with no understanding of what they are doing. Without a well-differentiated animus, a woman cannot tell the difference between her own standpoint and a man's. She is constantly waging inner warfare, fearful of acting on her own "foolish" needs, fearful of the scorn of her partner's logic if she discloses what is crucial to her heart. Denying the truth of her feeling, she goes along with what is eminently logical. The real issue is not brought to consciousness: *in accepting the masculine standpoint, she is betraying her own soul.* The head does not understand the heart's reasons, nor does the heart respect the head's, although they may sometimes cooperate.

> *Heart! We will forget him!*
> *You and I—tonight!*
> *You may forget the warmth he gave—*
> *I will forget the Light! . . .*
>
> *Haste! lest while you're lagging*
> *I remember him!*[16]

What is crucial to a woman may not seem important to her partner, but if she denies her feminine feeling, both may live to regret her self-betrayal.

The same is true for a man. If he habitually ignores his feeling in favor of a rational standpoint, he too is betraying his own soul. He may dream of being seduced by a "virginal" woman—his undifferentiated feminine side seeking union with his conscious masculinity—or dream he is with an unknown woman for whom he is responsible, often a woman who is pregnant or whose child he is caring for. As he gives more attention to what these images represent in himself, his feeling function may then conflict with his thinking.

The "mother's son," for example, so vulnerable to feeling guilty that he is not "better," or "more manly" or "more capable," thinks automatically of pleasing the women in his life. He may believe that is how he feels, but it is not true feeling. It is thinking contaminated by the mother complex. It is sheer sentimentality, a plea to be loved, and, whether it is answered or not, it breeds resentment because it puts all the power in the hands of the woman. If he can contact and express his real feeling, he can stop seeing women as negative mothers whose demands he is constantly trying to live up to. Instead, he can celebrate his very real strengths—for instance, strong religious feeling, or a great capacity for friendship, which often, according to Jung, "creates astonishing tenderness between men and may even rescue friendship between the sexes from the limbo of the impossible."[17]

The man's task, then, is to separate the actual women from his archetypal projections onto them. This is the process through which his inner virgin is separated from the mother complex; as he comes to recognize that the controlling mother who tells him what to do and who to be is his own inner problem, he draws closer to his own *I am*, his soul.

Intense conflict between an outworn conscious attitude and emerging feeling values is often the seed-bed for the birth of a new standpoint. I think of David, a man in his late thirties, whose symbiotic marriage seemed to be a model of loving harmony but in fact had been sexually unsatisfactory for years. He felt sad most of the time, quietly desperate, and often thought of leaving, but that made no logical sense. His reasoning told him that sex was "relatively unimportant, compared to everything else we have together—and she needs me." He continued to put all his energy into pleasing his mother-wife, but sank deeper into depression and self-pity.

Finally, while in analysis, he began to concentrate on how he really felt about his situation. He did a series of drawings of his wife while writing out and reliving the history of their relationship. He consciously acknowledged the conflict and held the tension. After a month, on June 28th, he dreamed that he left his wife behind and followed a young woman across a bridge. Although this did not resolve the conflict, and he still could not bring himself to leave his marriage, he experienced this dream as a reward for the time and energy he had spent on giving creative expression to his own feeling values.

Nine months later, on the afternoon of March 1st, David realized he would no longer go on living with his wife. He suddenly saw his situation clearly in terms of his own needs, not his wife's. "That's it! That's it!" he said aloud. "I don't *want* a life like this!" It struck him as an experiential realization of his own truth; it was numinous and he knew he would have to act on it. It was the kind of "thought in the form of an experience" that Jung describes as having a transformative effect:

> As long as an analysis moves on the mental plane nothing happens, you can discuss whatever you please, it makes no difference, but when you

strike against something below the surface, then a thought comes up in the form of an experience, and stands before you like an object.... Whenever you experience a thing that way, you know instantly that it is a fact.[18]

And that night David had a dream:

Oh! that was really something! Eva [his wife] gave birth to a baby boy. A fantastic birth scene by the side of the water, with lots of people gathered around. I am the midwife—and the father.

It all takes place at the top of a flight of stairs, leading up from a large body of water. Eva is lying on a table, like a ritual altar. The vagina opening is clearly visible, with blood oozing out. She doesn't actually go into labor; it seems it will be a relatively painless birth. She calls out instructions to me, tells me to get down lower—to kneel on the ground. I am slightly annoyed about this, since I've delivered babies before and I don't think it's necessary to get down lower—closer—until the baby starts to come.

Then I leave the scene and go down the stairs to the water. I splash about. Meanwhile the people around Eva are getting more and more excited. I see a doctor rush up, with long surgical gloves pulled up his arms. I race up the stairs and when I get there, to my surprise I find the baby has already been born. The doctor is holding the baby up for all to see. I push my way through, I am the proud father. I hope it's a girl. I can see the baby's head with little frizzy hair, and then the doctor cries out, "It's a boy!"—and I think, "Oh a boy—how nice." I thank the doctor. He presses the top of the baby's chest so it vomits out some liquid. It's all very beautiful. There's lots of blood.

This dream can be seen as the response of the unconscious to David's "experiential realization" that day; it mirrors the birth of the new attitude toward himself that enabled him to act according to the way he felt. Nine months after the constellation of his intense conflict, so intimately connected with his masculinity, the new feeling attitude literally erupted into consciousness. Through giving creative expression—the drawing and writing—to his own feeling values, David had in effect impregnated his inner woman. But the potential energy for life represented by the anima figure with whom he crossed a bridge in the earlier dream did not manifest as a new conscious attitude until the incubation period was complete.

The details of the dream suggest a ritual birth. It takes place "by the side of the water," on a table "like a ritual altar." Whose altar it is, is not clear, but the woman's instructions, to "get down lower," is a recurring motif in many dreams where the voice of the Great Mother insists that the dream ego come into closer contact with the earth, establish a closer tie with nature, become humble before the mystery of what it is to be human.

The movement, down the stairs to the water and up the stairs to the altar, mirrors the radical shift in David's level of awareness. Symbolically, the dream ego enacts a scene of baptism—a watery death to the old, the resurrection of the new. When he arrives at the "altar," the baby has already been born. A doctor has delivered the child, a detail suggesting that while the dream ego must go through the descent and ascent, the birth itself is outside its control. It is an act of grace, a gift from the healing powers of the Self. The doctor-Self empties the embryonic fluid from the child, opening its lungs for the first breath of life. David's decision that day (the very fact of deciding, rather than *what* he decided) had released his masculinity from the protective—and smothering—womb of the mother.

David's drawing of the scene shows the child asleep in a basket between his legs. The infant is in the position of the father's phallus, his new-found masculine energy. The cradling of the new-born also suggests that the dream ego is both father and mother to the child. Reminiscent of Nativity scenes, an earthy brown donkey stands beneath a tree with budding green leaves. Again the unconscious shows the need for a balance between the spiritual and the physical. The donkey represents the wisdom of the instincts, reinforcing the dreamer's need to honor his masculinity. Like Balaam's ass in the Old Testament, who saw the angel

when Balaam did not,[19] the chthonic animal drive represented by the donkey has an intelligence valuable in itself, the complement of the conscious intellect. When Balaam smote the ass three times for not obeying him,

> the Lord opened the mouth of the ass, and she said unto Balaam. ... *Am* not I thine ass, upon which thou hast ridden ever since I *was* thine unto this day? was I ever wont to do so unto thee? And he said, Nay.[20]

The criss-cross shape behind the mother in David's drawing is red, echoing the blood in the dream, which symbolizes the sacrifice, the living blood that has to be shed in order to move out of the mother-anima into new life. The juxtaposition of birth and crucifixion in the drawing epitomizes the pain of the passover.

A man's inner woman matures as he works on the differentiation of his own feeling values. Increasingly he will be able to flow with his own stream of life. Far from making him effeminate, his pregnant virgin demands that his infantile *puer* grow up into a strong masculine container. The stronger the container the more flexible it can become, and the more the riches of the unconscious will become available to consciousness. Think of a dancer like Baryshnikov. His body is superbly trained, ready to take conscious discipline. Technique, however, does not make a great dancer. His capacity to surrender his technique to the soul energy that gives the lift to his leaps puts him in the *now*. Anyone who has seen him dance the Prodigal Son can never forget the final moments when, having squandered his life, he returns to his father. Like a young child, he crawls up into the great arms and slowly, every gesture exactly in harmony with the transpersonal energy mounting in himself and in the audience, his anguished body comes safely to rest on his forgiving father's breast. Baryshnikov enacts the *process* and *presence* palpable in the audience.

Consciously, with utmost attentiveness, the masculine ego differentiates the feeling values that connect a man to his own soul and make him an authentic person. Saxton, a man in his mid-thirties, had been in analysis five years when he had the following dream:

> I'm driving in a red sporty Ford with a V-8 engine and 8 gears. It is fast and powerful. I drive through city streets and pass another Ford—only a V-4 or V-5. I go to the outskirts of the city and then I'm on foot running with a small fiesty dog. I learn not to make growling sounds, as he interprets this as a fighting challenge and nips and bites at me. We travel together and I come to a fence which I climb over.
>
> Then I'm in a room. Outside there are farmer's fields and nature. Inside is a gorgeous woman that I've been spending time with. Her name is Sophia and she is like Sophia Loren: warm, wise, sensual, earthy and deep. We lie together on a bed and I want her to stay with me and have a love relationship. She is reticent as she had made a resolution due to

her past. I really want her to stay with me and ask her what happened. She tells me a sad story: her teen-age daughter had ended her own life after she had been into the sea and had somehow been injured and disfigured, her face and head damaged. Sophia blamed herself for her daughter's accident—letting her stray into the sea—and decided never to form a fruitful union again. I assure her she could not have known and was not at fault. I feel she may stay if I accept her feelings and give her time. Outside the room there is a brilliant light and I hold a folded rectangular two-sectional piece of cardboard to shield us from the brightness.

The dream ego sets out in a powerful red sporty car. The vehicle has in its structure, the V-8 motor and eight gears, the doubling of the feminine number four. Here again is the doubling motif, presaging a content that is attempting to enter consciousness, but is not yet there (above, page 138). The structure of the car points to the feminine energy that can provide the link with the totality of the Self. The dream ego, however, is using that power to pass lesser cars. His exuberance in being at the head of the pack suggests pride in his male dominance, pride in his achievements in a society that values speed, flair and power. It is a persona performance. Then he is running on his own two feet with "a small fiesty dog," his instinctual world that is his friend so long as he does not "growl" at it, or treat it as a joke. They arrive at a fence—a barrier over which the dream ego climbs into another world, one in which the dog is replaced by a woman.[21]

Now in a place of nature and living water, he is spending time with a gorgeous woman, Sophia, "warm, wise, sensual, earthy and deep." She is reluctant to have a loving relationship with him because of a resolution she has made, "due to her past." She cannot trust him so long as he is not relating to her out of his feminine receptivity. Determined to stay with her, the dream ego hears her sad story. Like Demeter, she is grieving for her teen-age daughter who is lost to her. Unlike Persephone, the girl has committed suicide after having been in the sea (the unconscious) where she has been injured. Her face, the mirror of her soul, and her head have been disfigured. Damage to the orifices of the head by guns, hose nozzles and pipes often symbolizes psychic rape in dreams of both men and women. Because she feels she did not take responsibility for the girl, Sophia has resolved never again to make a "fruitful union," again echoing Demeter's decision to withhold fertility from the earth. In this situation that would mean cutting the man off from the reality of his inner world. The dream ego has to reach out to Sophia to convince her that she was not to blame, convinced in himself that if he accepts her *feelings* and is patient in his relationship to her, she may stay. That is to say, the man must in day-to-day life be true to his own personal feelings in order to consolidate the transpersonal link to his own inner woman.

The dreamer associated Sophia Loren with a film entitled *Two Women* in which the actress played a mother lovingly preparing her daughter for womanhood. As the two are traveling on the road one day, they are separated and raped by soldiers. Afterward, Sophia sets aside her own pain and searches for the girl, fearing she is dead. In an unforgettably poignant scene, she looks through the trees and sees her daughter standing in a stream, her little hands splashing water over her stricken body, trying to cleanse herself of the unspeakable horror.

Discussing the dream, Saxton said, "The relationship of my consciousness to my soul is broken, raped. That shows up in Sophia's problem: she embodies the fact of that rape in her reaction. I fear linking to my soul because it would mean being linked to my own sense of who I am. Early in life I was raped because I was true to my soul. Someone—my mother, my father—who was not in touch with *me* was angry and, therefore, raped me. To link with my soul is to face the danger of rape again and again. If I move closer to my soul, I experience terror—slow, annihilating terror."

It is important that the dream ego wants to have a loving relationship to Sophia, not just a sexual one. The dreamer is able to pursue what is of utmost value to him when he realizes it might be lost. The feeling sensitivity and softness represented by the number eight in the motor and gears are backed by tremendous masculine strength. In the past, he had failed to take responsibility for his soul. Here he is able to act. He will not allow her to disappear.

"The mother in me," said Saxton, "failed to take responsibility for new life. Demeter in the Greek myth raged but she never got down to the guilt of having not mothered her daughter. Fear and rage may be the result of unconscious guilt. To take responsibility for your own actions often means recognizing that your rage is an unresolved sense of self-responsibility. You've blamed others for what you failed to do yourself."

What leads to Sophia's decision in Saxton's dream is the fear of suffering, the fear of opening herself again to the possibility of mutilating pain. Her fear leads to an attempt to control—to break the relationship—which is power, power which breaks the bond between conscious and unconscious.

"Unconscious power injured my soul in the first place," said Saxton, "eventually I just couldn't take any more pain. I decided it wasn't worth it to try to be myself."

The daughter in the dream could not accept her disfigurement; her ugliness made her unlovable and so she chose to die. For the man this meant the repression of his soul. Sophia's guilt lay in being unable to protect the new life. That task now becomes the work of the ego. If the ego does not realize the pattern that is unconsciously being enacted, then the "disfigurement" of the virgin-soul and the rage and guilt of the mother happen on a daily basis in the man's life. The new values, newly emerging feelings, are met by a lack of loving, a lack of caring attention. The resultant fear and anger both block the possibility of potential pain and guard the soul from intolerable anguish. In the daily round of living, it takes constant vigilance and a discerning masculine sword to protect the feminine soul, giving it space to mature.

The lysis of the dream, that is, the last image, which usually shows where the energy wants to go to correct the psychic imbalance, presents another possibility of protecting the soul. The brilliant light outside the room may symbolize the bright sun of consciousness in which Saxton in his daily life flourished. It may also symbolize the searing fire of the Self. The "folded rectangular two-sectional piece of cardboard," which the dream ego used against the harshness of the sun, is again a doubling of something not yet in consciousness. "It was a reflector, something silver about it," Saxton said. It suggests "the silver mirror" of Rilke's poem. This is not mirror-gazing, spinning webs of fantasy. It is conscious relationship contemplated in a virgin soul; it puts an end to mere acting out. Gradually, one is able to control the cruel barbs that blurt out of the complexes and destroy relationship. One is able too to recognize "the Moments of Dominion"[22] that are the grace that opens the relationship to the third—to the God and Goddess mirrored in love. Uncontemplated relationship lacks the moist, shadowy receptivity which allows for the possibility of true being. The mystery of love withers in the analytical light of the sun; it shines in the luster of the understanding heart.

Saxton's dream, and Kate's slave girl dream, are characteristic of countless dreams I have seen in which a shadow power figure in effect rapes the inner virgin. The ego must take responsibility for cherishing her back into consciousness. Looked at as dreams mirroring the collective unconscious of our culture, the archetypal link between mother and daughter is precariously threatened. Until our egos have the discernment and fortitude to acknowledge the anguish and guilt of the mother and the loss of her virgin daughter—body and soul—there is little possibility of genuine relationship. Lust and love remain split. Conscious and unconscious do not unite. Bringing healing to the anguished matter, and love to the dead or dying virgin, depends on us.

Healing depends on listening with the inner ear—stopping the incessant blather, and *listening*. Fear keeps us chattering—fear that wells up from the past, fear of blurting out what we really fear, fear of future repercussions. It is our very fear of the future that distorts the *now* that could lead to a different future if we dared to be whole in the present. A woman who has acquired some psychological insight through working on herself, for example, may become fired with a crusading zeal to bring her man to consciousness. Blind to his reality, she may seduce his soul with her brilliant exposition of projection. But who will then receive *her* soul? Why does dialogue suddenly become monologue? Why does his voice become harsher, his eyes wider, his body more rigid? The interaction that might bubble up from the depths is blocked; the relationship is no longer organic. Unless both are coming from their own center of vulnerability, animus talk constellates anima mood and nothing can happen. The channel to the Virgin is plugged with wax. Until we relax into the slow rhythms that open the channel to our inner truth, we are simply unable to experience who we are in the situation as it is. Reality is not there; the hand of the Goddess is not in the shit.

If the psychic integration is being paralleled by physical integration and the body is becoming increasingly conscious, body symptoms must be acknowledged in the relationship. The feminine is not interested in abstract theories and logical reasons. Feminine wisdom comes out of the marrow of bone, out of the suffering of experience—the fish that comes out of the gut, not the bird out of the head. Like the primitive woman, the feminine makes the passover into maturity when it experiences itself as part of the cosmic rhythms of nature, at the same time looking straight at the reality of the *here* and *now*, the present that is instantaneously shifting. That truth is non-negotiable.

Here is where real problems develop in long-established relationships. The mature feminine will not tolerate the demands and projections of the patriarchy. It wrenches the symbiotic twins apart. It will not be used as a commodity, like instant saccharine. If the partner is not in analysis, the shift in energy is exasperating. If, for the first time, a woman is experiencing her feminine ego well grounded in her own body, her husband may be delighted, surprised and shocked by her sexual abandonment. However, opening the body can open a crevice in the heart that becomes an abyss containing the pain of a lifetime. Suddenly, consciousness may illuminate the crevice, or the Self may begin to demand a new level of physical and spiritual integration, in which case the woman must recognize her need for a period of natural celibacy. The husband may experience this withdrawal as rejection. However, if the woman goes against her instinct, her body will manifest intense physical symptoms which demand a celibate state until the problem is synthesized at a more spiritual level of awareness.

The man too may experience a withdrawal of his sexuality. If the two souls are not attuned, or if the Self is demanding a new attunement at a new level of sexual and spiritual integration, the partners may try to fool themselves into believing that everything is all right. One or other may demand sexual intimacy. But the embodied soul does not lie, nor is its wisdom shallow. The conscious body will attempt to move onto a new level of spiritual intimacy which, when embodied, may be experienced as a very different kind of sexuality.[23] This passover requires a fine differentiation of both the feminine and the masculine in each partner if their relationship is to survive. This is relatively unknown territory. It is Sophia's country and there one moves with faith.

Sometimes a relationship reaches a point of spiritual flowering, and suddenly, for no apparent reason, a blight appears and flower and plant wither, to the anguished shock and savage disappointment of the two involved. The heart of each "is still aching to seek,/But the feet question 'Whither?' "[24] One or both may have to detach from the relationship in order to discover their own individual identity. Spirit yearns for spirit; flesh aches for flesh. Sometimes it is only in distancing that the depth of the root of the relationship becomes apparent, in which case the plant may be cut off almost to the ground and still, with tender care, rejuvenate.

Often what is going on during such detachment is a lesson in humility. The Self is burning out the ego desires. In a passage from *Four Quartets*, T.S. Eliot clarifies in a few words what, on an emotional level, is the fire of hell.

> *There are three conditions which often look alike*
> *Yet differ completely, flourish in the same hedgerow:*
> *Attachment to self and to things and to persons, detachment*
> *From self and from things and from persons; and, growing*
> *   between them, indifference*
> *Which resembles the others as death resembles life,*
> *Being between two lives—unflowering, between*
> *The live and the dead nettle. This is the use of memory:*
> *For liberation—not less of love but expanding*
> *Of love beyond desire, and so liberation*
> *From the future as well as the past.*[25]

Detachment liberates the heart from the past and from the future. It gives us the freedom to be who we are, loving others for who they are. It is the leap into *now*, the stream of Being in which everything is possible. It is the domain of the pregnant virgin.

Giving up the past can release chaos. Anger, grief, fear are natural reactions. The death of a loved one, divorce, loss of relationship, such events can precipitate a year of mourning: the first Christmas alone, the first robin in the garden, the ambushes of each season that catch our heart unaware. Ego desire may be surrendered one minute, only to be clutched back the next. But crucial to any sacrifice, particularly one having to do with relationship, is the giving up of ego demands. If the ego uses transpersonal energy for its own selfish ends, that is black magic. Only if the grief persists year after year, trapping the individual in the past, or if the energy turns destructive, will the Self demand a "letting go." Sometimes a sacrificial ritual, such as the one described with Lisa (above, page 86), initiates the re-entry into life. Such a ritual must never be undertaken without a strong ego container or without a friend within close range of a telephone. If forgiveness is involved, then one must remember:

> If thou bring thy gift to the altar, and there rememberest that thy brother hath ought against thee; Leave there thy gift before the altar, and go thy way; first be reconciled to thy brother, and then come and offer thy gift.[26]

It seems to me the most important thing in surrendering a close bond is sacrificing the relationship without sacrificing the love. If life is an "opening out like the rose that can no longer keep closed,"[27] then everything we love is an opening of a petal. When the thorns are accepted love abides. The profound relationships in our lives, whatever their outcome, have given us the riches of loving and that wealth is the only wealth that means anything in the end.

If we can contain the conflict of the opposites—what our small egos want as opposed to what the Self or Destiny has ordained—if we can hold at the center, then we learn to think with the heart. We can know what we feel, know what we desire, and at the same time gradually surrender to our larger circumference. Then without becoming bitter or cutting ourselves off from our own reality, we can consciously accept what is happening. Aware of both sides, the mind can accept and the heart can continue to feel. Where mind and heart are tearing apart, thinking with the heart is the only way to transcend the opposites. What would otherwise be the salt of bitterness can thus become the salt of wisdom. This is the wisdom of Sophia, who understands so well the grain of salt that gives life its savor.

The emergence of feminine consciousness in our culture is bringing with it a social upheaval that is like a great dyke giving way. As individual feeling values take the place of collective moral sanctions, what one wants to do may demand precedence over what one "ought to" do. Well-established "relationships" may split apart, or be seen as the empty containers they always were. However, a frail ego facing the world alone is in danger of inundation by archetypal energies, and even a strong ego can be shaken by the release of long-repressed sexuality. That is the price that may be exacted in experiencing the revolutionary energy of the outcast goddess who is attempting to counterbalance our goal-oriented, rational, technological milieu.

As we have seen earlier, pale shadows of this goddess appear in concretized form in the rock stars. Whiffs of her blow over us every time we hear of yet another marriage breakdown. While we barely recognize her, she may well be present (in a perverted way) in rape, in abortion, in reproductive technology, or in the world of contraception that releases women from their biological "destiny" and at the same time thrusts them into psychological awareness. She is biological destiny raised to consciousness, biological destiny elevated to freedom.

In the dreams of men and women this goddess takes many forms. Usually she is black or oriental or simply dark. She may appear as a proud gypsy, a dancer in a tavern, a sacred prostitute, a Mary Magdalene. Always she is outside the collective value system of the dreamer's conscious world, and while she may be wounded or disfigured, she carries immense potential for new life. Hers is the energy that can unite the opposites—the whore and the idealized virgin—because she contains both. In her the idealized virgin who is cut off from her instincts, spinning her spiritual webs, can find the ground of her own body. The lily-white virgin is closed—selfish, possessive and unrelated to her feminine reality. She is the shadow sister of the whore, who believes her sexual allurement is a personal attribute for ensnaring the masculine. Together they drift like mermaids through the waters of the unconscious creatures of nature, whose powers of enchantment can only be broken when their fish or serpent tails are transformed into human legs that stand on the earth. This involves a conscious integration of their respective energies. The human body becomes a vessel for human love when one surrenders to the Black Goddess in whom spirit and instinct

The Kiss of the Enchantress (1890)
by Isobel Gloag.

meet. In her, Sophia's wisdom bridges the two. Through detachment born of profound suffering, Sophia is able to empathize with human pain while at the same time recognizing that this is the way life is. When consciousness is in touch with that wisdom, then Sophia is recognized not as an abstract concept but as a "thought in the form of an experience," a fact that becomes a determining influence in one's life.

In ancient times, most women once in their lives surrendered themselves to the goddess of love. They performed the sacred marriage in the temple of the Moon Goddess in the full knowledge that the instinctual energy pouring through them did not belong to them personally. Instead they honored it as the transpersonal energy of the Goddess. Having once surrendered to that energy, they were "virginal," incapable of usurping goddess energy as a personal attribute.[28] In other words, psychological virginity, which releases an individual from selfish, possessive clinging, was attained, and is attained, through surrender to a god or goddess.

In one of Donne's "Holy Sonnets" he prays that God will "break, blow, burn, and make me new," and then concludes,

> *Take me to you, imprison me, for I,*
> *Except you enthrall me, never shall be free,*
> *Nor ever chaste except you ravish me.*[29]

Chastity is being open to the life of the spirit, purified of ego desire. Ravishment is saying *yes* to life, not the yes of naive innocence, but the *yes* of a higher innocence that is consciously involved in the sacrifice. Surrender to the Spirit opens the virgin soul to the full range of Beingness, the carnal and spiritual passion that burns at one's center but is not personal. Recognition of the fire as nonpersonal allows personal ego desires to be burned clean. No longer identified with instincts or spirit, one is human, open to the love of Sophia and the fertility that comes through that love. Then, within everyday experience, one is able to perceive the subtle Presence of the Goddess.

The ever-changing moon is the image of transformation of those parts of ourselves which usually live in the dark. Protected from the enlightened mind, the very essence of life is gently distilled from concrete experience. The distillation takes place through reflection—through the silver mirror. Through contemplation, ego desires can be transformed into love—love that honors its own individual essence and the essence of another. Outside the laws of the collective, love obeys its own inner laws, creating unique relationships.

Anyone involved in soul-making is relating through the virgin, because only she is able to catch the inevitability of the moment in action. In her, sexuality and love are perceived as manifestations of the divine, and that energy in daily life becomes the mystery of transformation. On a collective scale, her love could create a greater explosion than any nuclear device ever conceived.

The Nativity by William Blake. (Philadelphia Museum of Art)

Out of the union of soul and spirit a child is conceived—the Jewel in the Lotus, the new consciousness dedicated to the possibility of Being. The child is the new energy that steps out of the the past and turns its face to the future with hope, but lives in the *now*.

Organized religion once recognized the mystery of the union of the soul with God and the fear involved. Church rituals were set up, not to do away with the mystery, but to allow people to experience it. Western science finds a mystery intolerable and sets out to explain it away, or even to prove it evil. Logos thinking tries to solve the mystery, rather than enter into it. Ritual and contemplation are not an attempt to explain the mystery, but rather an attempt to orient individuals toward the mystery so that it may be approached without fear. When the Holy Spirit speaks it can be terrifying because it evokes profound fear of the unknown, fear of life, fear of stepping into our own destiny. If, however, men and women can find their own virgin within, they can learn to *Be*, both alone and with each other. The mystery lives in the possibility of Being. Love chooses us.

Feminine consciousness is concerned with process. It sees the goal as the journey itself and recognizes that the goal is consciousness of the journey. Being is consciousness of Becoming. To see the goal as the process itself is bringing to the masculine beam of light a "dome of many-colored glass"[30] which refracts that beam and, like a prism, makes it many-faceted, every facet being a mirror of the center, the center being in every facet. The point of feminine consciousness is not to resolve matter into spirit, or spirit into matter. Rather it is to see spirit in matter and matter in spirit. Such a perception is quite foreign to a strictly masculine consciousness, which would consider this kind of concept a logical impossibility.

In men and women who are attempting to become conscious, the difference between the feeling of a man and the feeling of a woman can create incalculable difficulties. When feeling emerges in a man, it often comes through the perception of a psychic value, less linked to the body than is the feeling of a woman. In women, the body as the sacred dwelling place of the soul is part of her realization of herself as a woman. If she has experienced the Black Madonna in herself, or Sophia as the bridge between spirit and body, then her very *knowing* can put a man in touch with that bridge within himself. The natural bond may be in a shared sexuality, but more than that, a spiritual relationship can develop in which each acts as a bridge to the other's soul, providing a fleeting glimpse of an eternal reality beyond nature and sensation. When the masculine is unbound, and the feminine is unveiled, then together they interact within and without. The penetrating power of conscious masculinity releases the eternal feminine. The woman awakens the man to his own receptive power. He penetrates her; she receives him. He awakens her to her own penetrating power; she awakens him to the presence of his own feminine soul. Together they are put in touch with their own inner wisdom. The process, not the goal, is all.

Whether the interplay of masculine and feminine is solely within, or within a relationship, the individual must be conscious of the inner laws which have their own absoluteness and can be brutal. These are the laws that must be obeyed not with resignation, but with acceptance and love. Vulnerability is an aspect of the feminine; the masculine learns from the feminine how to accept the transitory, how to die to the past and to the future, how to live in the *now*. Between the very separateness of masculine and feminine Sophia's bridge is built.

Sophia will not accept compromise. Until one is ravished by her, relationship is based on emotional barter: "I'll give to you if you give to me." Sophia demands that we move out of the old patterns, the old mythology. Men have always feared the power of the earthy feminine, and until recently in this culture women have blinkered themselves by colluding with the male point of view. As women become more conscious of their inner slave girl, however, they are acknowledging the depth of their own sensuality and sexuality in service to the goddess, not in service to men. While this acknowledgment threatens the macho

---

Pregnant Lady of the Cross

Lady, Lady on the Cross
Was it I that crucified you?
And am I too up there beside you?
Like a robber to deride you
Luster mixed with dross?

Pregnant Lady on the Cross
Will the man-child that's within you
Bursting forth all stiffening sinews
Live his life but not unpin you?
Gain, but at what a cost!

In this act I play the Pilate
Lifting the curtain for a start.
Author and producer
There's nothing finer
Than to be both audience and stage designer.

When I'm down and at a loss,
That's the time that I seek to free you
But give me the strength to nail and be you,
Splayed upon that suffering tree
You pregnant Lady of the Cross,
Pregnant Lady of the Cross.

—Song by Peter Tatham.

---

male persona, it does encourage men to become more aware of their feminine side.

If they consciously integrate previously repressed feeling values, *puer* men can move out of the shadow of the patriarchy and realize a personally more authentic standpoint—one which involves a close relationship to their own inner virgin. Then they can no longer countenance a split anima—no longer love the idealized virgin while raping her whore body. Nor can a conscious woman demean herself by conspiring with the split. Surrendering to the goddess releases the man from the unconscious mother and daughter, just as it releases the woman from the unconscious father and son.

In evolving relationships, the inner dynamics are in constant flux. No two relationships are the same, but some difficult questions constantly re-occur as men and women commit themselves to new levels of understanding. How does a woman maintain a daily balance between her love for her animus (her own creative energies) and her sexuality toward the man she loves? Does the pursuit of consciousness widen the abyss between the Eros of a man and the Eros of a woman? Or does consciousness intensify the magnetic poles that ultimately attract each other? Does a basic feeling difference between men and women need to be acknowledged, perhaps even celebrated? Does the mystery of love abide in the recognition of the immensity of our own otherness and the otherness of the beloved?

The answers wait in the chrysalis. We cannot force them to emerge, any more than we can make love happen. But we can listen. We can tune our inner ear to the inner Presence and we can honor our own souls and the souls of those we love, leaving a "clear, unpeopled space" that cherishes the possibility of Being.

> *I said to my soul, be still, and wait without hope*
> *For hope would be hope for the wrong thing: wait without*
> > *love*
> *For love would be love of the wrong thing; there is yet*
> > *faith*
> *But the faith and the love and the hope are all in the waiting.*
> *Wait without thought, for you are not ready for thought:*
> *So the darkness shall be the light, and the stillness the dancing.*[31]

The Listener, papier-mâché by Dorothy Cameron.

Voices from the Chrysalis

My life has been an excavation through one man after another until each one resonates with another and I see they're all the same.

It won't work if you yell at a flower and say BLOOM!

I waken in the night. My heart is a red hot furnace. I think I am having a heart attack. I find my arm lying on his empty pillow. I can't move. I cannot raise my body from the bed.

On Fridays I start to feel low at work because everyone is looking forward to their weekend date. I don't because I have nothing, no one, no "big plans" for the weekend. I come home. I try to remain calm. I try to put on dresses—a sort of private fashion show. ... I force myself to go swimming. It breaks the hold of creeping depression. I have to accept that no Prince Charming will appear to rescue me from my reality. I have faith that there are better times to come. I can't help but grieve at what a child I've been.

I live a push-pull existence with men. They offer something; I put out my arms to receive it; they chop them off. They promise, but they don't come through—I am always left empty. I can't do anything when they're through with me. I give them the power, as I gave my father the power.

I won't have this relationship at the expense of my reality. I honor my own reality. I performed for my father to perfection. Then my lover rejected my performance. That feminine part of me that's been trapped all these years can't be bothered bouncing off men anymore.

Innocence is no longer a virtue. I am accountable. I know I'm quick to put out false banners.

My wife is bitchy and abusive. She does not understand there are major and trivial issues. She believes that if she feels strongly about something, it is a major issue, and she feels strongly about just about everything lately.

Pain, terror, isolation have forced me onto my own path. My husband was a wonderful mother to me. I damned him for not being a good lover. I damned him for leaving. I was thrown into hell and found my own path.

I'm trying to let her go. I feel as if I am drowning and she's standing on my shoulders.

He wants the chicken to fly cooked into his mouth.

I can't hide behind my stupidity anymore and I can't hide behind my baby girl or my Daddy. My flower won't open if it's not watered.

Life in India has not yet withdrawn into the capsule of the head. It is still the whole body that lives. No wonder the European feels dreamlike: the complete life of India is something of which he merely dreams.

—C.G. Jung.

They say that reality exists only in the spirit
that corporal existence is a kind of death
that pure being is bodiless
that the idea of the form precedes the form substantial.

But what nonsense it is!
as if any Mind could have imagined a lobster
dozing the under-deeps, then reaching out a savage and iron
    claw!

Even the mind of God can only imagine
those things that have become themselves;
bodies and presences, here and now, creatures with a foothold
    in creation
even if it is only a lobster on tip-toe.

Religion knows better than philosophy
Religion knows that Jesus never was Jesus
till he was born from a womb, and ate soup and bread
and grew up, and became, in the wonder of creation, Jesus,
with a body and with needs, and a lovely spirit.

—D.H. Lawrence, "Demiurge."

The great epochs of our life are at the points when we gain courage to rebaptize our badness as the best in us.

—Friedrich Nietzsche, *Beyond Good and Evil*.

The dream is the small hidden door in the deepest and most intimate sanctuary of the soul, which opens into the primeval cosmic night that was soul long before there was a conscious ego, and will be soul far beyond what conscious ego could ever reach. —C.G. Jung.

Beloved Enemy:

A Modern Initiation

Within be fed, without be rich no more.
So shalt thou feed on death, that feeds on men,
And death once dead, there's no more dying then.
——William Shakespeare, Sonnet 146.

What took me to India had very little to do with why I went. Certainly I was drawn by a romantic vision of the East—the Taj Mahal by moonlight, the ivory palaces, the holy men. Certainly E. M. Forster's *Passage to India* tantalized my imagination. What did happen to Adela Quested in the caves? Was she raped or was she crazy? What mystery was at the heart of her story? Well, I went to India and I saw the palaces and the holy men, and I found answers to some of my questions. It has taken sixteen years, however, to discover why I went.

I am telling the story now because it is more than my story. It is the story of a modern initiation rite into womanhood. It is the story of an unconscious girl who had never passed through puberty rites because her world was unaware that such rituals ever existed. Like many of her peers, she had never moved out of the security of Mother Society; she had never taken up residence in her own body; she had never recognized herself as part of the cosmos. It had never occurred to her that God might have a feminine counterpart who could give meaning to her life as a woman among women and at the same time connect her to her own unique destiny. This is the story of passing through a birth canal, dying and being born again.

I was in early mid-life at the time. I had almost everything middle-class culture could offer—beautiful house, fine husband, excellent teaching position. I expected life to go on into prosperous middle age, reaching its climax in my well-earned, well-respected golden years. I had no reason to doubt that my mother country would continue to care for me: my monthly check was always deposited in the bank by my school-board; income tax and pension deductions were automatic; sick leave was ready for any emergency. I had it made.

All my life I had it made. I loved being a minister's daughter. I liked going to church every Sunday in my organdy dress, my ringlets and ribbons perfectly placed. I liked the excitement of parsonage life: baptisms, weddings, funerals. I liked slipping into the church every afternoon to wait for God. Hiding under the seat, I often heard Him, but I was never quite quick enough to jump out and see Him face to face. Then the janitor told me the sun warming the old pews made the strange squeaking noise, not God. And I quietly put away my childhood faith.

I went to university. I married and moved from the security of my father's home to my husband's. I continued to believe in God, but rejected the pot-luck suppers at the church. There were a few nasty upsets, of course, but by and large life seemed to be as it was destined to be.

Then one cold winter night I was alone in Toronto. I needed a cab. I put out my arm but the cabbies didn't stop. I was not forthright enough. I had allowed myself to become so dependent on my husband that I could not hail a taxi. "This is preposterous," I thought. "Here I am an adult woman, and I am helpless when I'm alone." I walked through the snow to wherever I was going that night, and on the way I realized that the "nasty upsets" had produced volcanic mutterings. I knew I had to find out who I was when all my support systems were taken away. I knew I would buy a ticket to India and I hoped I might encounter God in an ashram in Pondicherry.

Six months later I arrived in New Delhi. God was with me all right but His ideas were somewhat different from mine. He turned out to be She in India, a She that I never imagined existed in the narrow confines of my Protestant Christian tradition, a She that reached out to me not in the protective walls of an ashram, but in the streets seething with poverty, disease and love.

I stayed first in Delhi, attempting to orient myself in that totally foreign world. A short walk took all the courage I could muster. Terror became my gasoline. Hands grasped at me from every direc-tion—crippled beggars, black market hustlers demanding American dol-lars, professional lovers assuring me they were second only to Africans, and two tiny waifs who adopted me. Every morning these little ones waited at the hotel entrance; all day they clung to my dress; every evening I sewed up the seams. They were older than I in that world. They were used to all life being lived in the street—men shaving, women nursing babies, three-year-olds hoisting dying infants on their hips. Wherever I looked I instantly turned away, ashamed of intruding on someone's private world. In my confusion I often brushed kisses with a cow or stepped in her pancake. People shouted "Good evening" in the morning and I knew something was wrong when I shouted back "Good evening." As my exhaustion grew, my ego could no longer make decisions and strange situations began to develop. I realized my own terror was con-stellating death around me.

"Every morning these little ones waited at the hotel entrance..."

Then on the sixth day the little girls did not arrive. I walked into the street and saw an American woman. Without any salutation, she stopped right in front of me.

"Are you alone?" she asked.

I opened my mouth to say "yes," and something gave way in my gut. I knew no more until I opened my eyes in her hotel room.

"You're in culture shock," she said. "I've lived here for ten years. I can recognize it. We'll go to your hotel, gather your luggage and I'll take you to your plane. You must go home. Now."

"I can't do that," I said. "I can't live with that defeat. I'd have to come back and try again and I can't do that either."

"You cannot stay," she said. "Peace Corps people go into culture shock and sometimes take knives to each other."

But I did stay. The words of my favorite Zen koan sustained me:

> *Ride your horse along the edge*
> *of the sword*
> *Hide yourself in the middle*
> *of the flames*
> *Blossoms of the fruit tree will*
> *bloom in the fire*
> *The sun rises in the evening.*

India was my fire. Certainly it is not everyone's. We each are thrown into our own fire and the room in the Ashoka Hotel was mine. There was no one to phone, no one to visit, nothing to do. All escapes were cut off. I had to move into my own silence and find out who was in there. When I looked inside, my imagination teemed with awesome, illusive images; when I looked outside, my balcony teemed with monsoon-drenched crows croaking, "Nevermore." Gone forever was the world I had lived in. Without consciously knowing what had happened, I had sacrificed my former system of values, my sentimental understanding of life and love. In less than a week I had been forced to surrender my need to control. Here I could control nothing. I moved in what seemed to be sheer chaos, everything happening before I even suspected what could happen. Either I had to flow with what life presented in the instant or I could not survive. Every moment was new and demanded a new response. Nothing reinforced the world I had known. Even the bathtub came alive with cockroaches when I sought the comfort of a bath.

I remember falling on the tile floor, weak from dysentery. How long I was there, I do not know. I came to consciousness on the ceiling, my spirit looking down at my body caked in dry vomit and excrement. I saw it lying there helpless, still, and then I saw it take in a breath. "Poor dummy," I thought. "Don't you know you're dead?" And mentally gave it a kick. Suddenly I remembered my little Cairn terrier. "I wouldn't treat Duff that way," I thought. "I wouldn't treat a dog the way I'm treating my own body. I wonder what will become of it if I leave it here? Will they burn it? Will they send it home?" Paralyzed by the immensity of my decision—either to leave my body there or to go back into it—I saw it take in another breath. I was overcome with compassion for this dear creature lying on the floor faithfully waiting for me to return, faithfully taking in one breath after another, confident that I would not forsake it, more faithful to me than I to it.

All my life I had hated my body. It was not beautiful enough. It was not thin enough. I had driven it, starved it, stuffed it, cursed it, and even now kicked it, and there it still was, trying to breathe, convinced that I would come back and take it with me, too dumb to die. And I knew the choice was mine. Most of my life I had lived outside my body, my energy disconnected from my feelings, except when I danced. Now it was my choice—either to move into my body and live my life as a human being, or to move out into what I imagined would be freedom. I saw it take another breath and there was something so infinitely innocent and trusting, so exquisitely familiar, in that movement that I chose to come down from the ceiling and move in. Together we dragged ourselves to the little bed. I did my best to take care of it. It was as if I could hear it whispering, "Rest, perturbed spirit, rest." For days, perhaps nine days, I stayed in the womb of the Ashoka.

I had carefully chosen two books to take with me on my journey—the New Testament and Shakespeare's *Sonnets*. They and my passport were my reading material. The knots of fire in my chest were released when I lay in bed reading my passport. In this descent into hell it was important to be sure I had a name. It was even more important to see the images and hear the rhythms of the prose and poetry I loved so well. They resonated with whoever I was and overcame the fear. One day as I was reading aloud I heard a familiar line, but this time with a difference: "Death once dead, there's no more dying then." I knew that my terror of death was dead. Having taken up residence in my body, I was living my life, and strange as those days and nights in the Ashoka had been, they were real. Paradoxically, having found my life, I was now free to lose it. Whatever Fate had in store for me, I could accept. For the first time in my life, I felt my own skeleton proudly holding up my own flesh, and I, in the oneness of my being, walked down the stairs to the hotel lounge.

I sat on the end of a couch writing a letter. A large Indian woman in gold-trimmed sari squeezed between me and the side of the couch. Her fat arm was soft and warm. I pulled away to make room to write. She cuddled against me. I moved again. She moved. I smiled. She smiled. She spoke no English. By the time I finished my letter, we were both at the other end of the couch, her body snuggling close to mine. Still fearful of going outside, I returned to the lounge the next day. The same dignified lady appeared; the same game went on. And so for several days. Then as I was leaving one morning, an Indian man stepped up.

"You're all right now," he said.

"What do you mean?" I asked, startled at his intimacy.

"You were dying," he said. "You had the aloneness of the dying. I sent my wife to sit with you. I knew the warmth of her body would bring you back to life. She won't need to come again."

I thanked him. I thanked her. They disappeared through the door—two total strangers who intuitively heard my soul when I was unable to reach out my arms. Their love brought me back into the world.

Having claimed my body and at the same time having surrendered myself to my destiny, I was undergoing both the joy and the pain of experiencing life in the flesh. I was like a newborn infant attempting to differentiate my five senses all at once. The perfume of jasmine mixed with the stench of urine, the blaze of red silk mixed with the flies in a baby's eyes; the sweetness of a sitar in a summer night mixed with the screams of a beaten dog—all juxtaposed amid exotic textures and tastes, foreign, unfathomable. I was no longer the victim, however. I no longer felt psychically raped or in danger of death. I was participating in life with an open heart, ravished by the sights and sounds and smells of that extraordinarily paradoxical world.

Then one day I was bouncing along on the unupholstered coils of a worn-out taxi, assuring the Italian-Indian driver that I had *not* come to India to experience the joys of the Kama Sutra. We were on our way to the caves, at least I hoped we were on our way to the caves. The driver's enigmatic smile, the narrow roadway and the vast expanse of featureless fields made me wonder. Suddenly I saw a dog with a canary yellow eye. Minutes later I saw a cow with turquoise horns. "I'm getting too tired," I thought. Then I saw an elephant, bigger than the taxi, translucent pink. The driver was not disturbed. He was conjuring up a way to get me into the front seat.

"Was that elephant pink?" I finally asked.

"Yes," he said, as if all elephants were pink.

"And did that cow have turquoise horns?"

"Yes."

"And the dog had a yellow eye?"

"Yes! It's Krishna's birthday," he said. "We're celebrating. Would you like to go?"

It also happened to be my birthday, and in that second of recognition, without thinking, I said, "Yes."

Instantly he swung the taxi into the ditch and through the fields, singing all the way. Then he stopped. Immediately the car was surrounded by men. Someone opened the door and motioned me out. I stepped onto the ground and four pairs of hands took my sandals, my purse, my camera and my belt. The driver was nowhere in sight. I stood looking into the impenetrable faces of at least twenty men who looked back at me as intently as I looked at them.

I had been told there was still human sacrifice in India and it passed through my mind that I never thought I would die this way. Suddenly the men all bowed in a low salaam and straightened; green eyes met fiery black ones in silent concentration. In spite of my concern, I felt their reverence, not for me but for Someone I represented. "If I'm going to die, I'm going to die," I thought. "This is certainly an interesting situation. I am going to stay with it. I am not going to faint".

They picked me up, raised me above their heads and, chanting, carried me to an altar and gently laid me prone on the ground. Convinced that I was about to be sacrificed, I was simultaneously dead and fiercely alive, quite beyond fear. I was receiving powerful energy from the men, a commingling of love and praise and awe. A man who seemed to be a priest put grass in my mouth, chanting with the others. He prayed over me. He took the grass and divided it among the men who ate it as if it were holy grass. They picked me up, put me on the altar and, again chanting, did a slow dance around me.

Wisdom (Sophia) speaks in Proverbs 8: "Then I was by him, *as* one brought up *with him.*" (Detail of *The Creation of Adam* by Michelangelo; Vatican, Sistine Chapel)

Vulnerable and alone, infinitely at the mercy of whatever was to happen, I knew it was not my will, not my love, but Her will, Her love, that there was some meaning to my life infinitely beyond anything I had ever imagined, and that my delicate body—in all its ugliness and all its beauty—was the temple through which I had come to know Her on this earth. Through the dark arms of those strangers in that dusty Indian field, Sophia reached out to me. In that moment, that eternal moment, I heard her great I AM.

Again they salaamed. They carried me off the holy ground and returned my leather sandals, camera, purse and belt. The taxi driver reappeared, smiling his nonchalant smile, and we bounced back across the fields.

These initiation rites may seem extreme, but all the time they were in process I knew I was in the right place. I knew something was being burned away that had to be burned away if I was going to live my life. I knew the pain was my pain. I had no idea what it meant, but I knew it had to be. I knew I was living my destiny.

And that destiny had something to do with my repetitive childhood vision of three Hereford cows that appeared whenever I was frightened—three curly-headed, long-horned animals with eyes like placid pools of brown, chewing always chewing, watching ever watchful. So long as they were there, I was safe. In the Krishna ritual, after having so recently reclaimed my animal body, I experienced the grass as holy grass, and my milkmaid's body as a vehicle through which the love of Krishna's bride could flow. The contradiction of animal and divine was resolved.

The curly-headed Herefords were somehow crucial to my attitude in India. When the boundaries of my known reality were threatened with unreality, I was often bumped by a cow right in the middle of a city street. Unaccustomed as I was to feeling cowhide, and accustomed as I was to looking into cows' eyes, I would burst into laughter. Two worlds had collided and become one. Victor Turner's discussion of play helped me to understand not only what saved me in India, but what pushed me onto a new level of perception.

> Playfulness is a volatile, sometimes dangerously explosive essence, which cultural institutions seek to bottle or contain in the vials of games of competition, chance, and strength, in modes of simulation such as theater, and in controlled disorientation, from roller coasters to dervish dancing. ... Play could be termed dangerous because it may subvert the left-right hemispheric regular switching involved in maintaining social order. ... Yet, although "spinning loose" as it were, the wheel of play reveals to us ... the possibility of changing our goals and, therefore, the restructuring of what our culture states to be reality.
>
> You may have guessed that play is, for me, a liminal or liminoid mode. ... In its own oxymoronic style it has a dangerous harmlessness, for it has no fear. Its lightness and fleetingness protect it. It has the powers of the weak, an infantine audacity in the face of the strong. ...
>
> Play is a light-winged, light-fingered sceptic, a Puck between the day world of Theseus and the night world of Oberon, putting into question the cherished assumptions of both hemispheres, both worlds. There is no sanctity in play; it is irreverent and is protected in the world of power struggles by its apparent irrelevance and clown's garb.[1]

Because I was outside the Indian culture, I was in the clown's garb. I was looking at India and at myself in it. When I gave up my fear, I was detached, free to play, the kind of play that comes with total concentration, focus without resistance, intense but not tense. And like the archetypal clown, I was living the black and white, the tragedy and the comedy, mediating the two without judgment, at the same time transcending both.

I wish I could say I went through enclosure, metamorphosis and emergence in India, and having gone through my initiation returned in triumph to Canada, a transformed woman, liberated from my bourgeois shackles, free to BE. It was not that way at all. Bringing the treasure back from the underworld into life is always the most hazardous task in the fairytale. When I passed through the barrier in Amsterdam, I was so shattered by noise that I had to sit down. In my stunned state I saw

Silver, Southwestern Iran.
(Proto-Elamite period, ca. 2900 B.C.)

a woman in boots, with yellow blond hair, red lipstick and turquoise eye-shadow, and I thought, "She must be going to Krishna's birthday." That was the beginning of the collision that took me into analysis two years later.

*

My wise old Irish analyst, Dr. E.A. Bennet, asked me in every session, "Why did you go to India?"

Each time I tried to tell him, he nodded his head silently. I knew my answer was inadequate. Finally in desperation I said to him, "Dr. Bennet, you must be going senile. You ask me that question every time I come here."

"And every time you give me a different answer," he replied. Then he settled back in his chair and told me a story. "When I was a brigadier in the army in India," he said, "we had a hard time with some soldiers. They didn't want to fight. They put seeds in their eyes which made them blind and then they were sent home. They'd rather go home blind than fight. You think about that."

I've been taking seeds out of my eyes for sixteen years and I'm still taking them out. Integrating an initiation can become a lifetime task. And while most of it remains in the secret mysteries of the individual, some of it belongs to the universal soul that is striving to become conscious in each one of us.

What took me to India was illusion; why I went was real. India was my journey to my own India, my own dark underworld. Like whales in the sea, people live in the only world they have ever known—birth, copulation and death. Unless there is a brutal severance from the sea, they don't know they are in the sea or what the sea is. India bisected my life. Before I went, I saw with my eyes; when I returned, I saw *through* my eyes. My naive Persephone, who had lived in the security of Mother Church, Mother Society, Mother School, eventually heard the question distilled from her lips, "Who am I?" Drawn by a romantic vision of the Orient, I had set out on some sentimental search for what was, in fact, a parody of the Moon Goddess. There followed the inevitable psychic rape in the teeming streets of India. The ground opened beneath my feet. What began as an intellectual question instantly became a real question when I had to say, "Yes, I am alone."

The sword that American woman struck into my heart with the word *alone* was the sword thrust that killed the dependent child and opened the door for the birth of the woman. No longer could I rest in the comfort of other people's images of who I was: parson's daughter, professor's wife, student's teacher. No longer could I be trapped in the small frame of wanting to be thin, stepping on the scales each morning and measuring the success of my life by whether I had gained or lost a few ounces. No longer could I fool myself that life would be what I wanted it to be, if only I could discard this body for another, if only I could pretend this body did not exist. If only I could get rid of this gluttonous, lusty, fiery fiend I lugged around! That illusion had protected me from looking at who I was and what I was meant to do with my life. Gone was the fantasy of escaping into easeful death. Gone was the illusion of being able to control my destiny. Gone too were the false images of my parents—images I had created as a child and blamed for what had happened or not happened to me. Stripped of my stone gods, I could forgive.

Dead too was the romantic dreamer who created her fantasy world through language. So long as I had stayed in my mind I had been able to keep the mystery of my own reality buried in my body. Having never differentiated body and soul, I escaped my emptiness through eating or not eating, confusing the figurative and literal worlds. Faced with actual death, I had to choose. Die or live. Either accept my human condition, love my soul in my body and move into life, or reject my human destiny, go with the spirit and die. Without language, I learned to hear the Indians with my heart as I knew they heard me. And that great gift of India, that Silence, taught me to hear my soul.

I had first to face my own hatred. And in that confrontation the sacrificial blood flowed. The blood that spurted out through the word *alone* opened my heart to the faithful creature whom I had abandoned on the floor, the creature whose loyalty put my hatred to shame. Through the love that rushed out to my instinctual being, personified in my little terrier Duff, my feminine self was reborn, and she recognized that she could no longer kick her body. This was her home so long as she was a human being on this earth. And the soul that was crying to her in its forsaken and foul condition on the floor was *her* soul, her Kore of being at the center of matter, crying to be claimed, allowed to grow and ultimately expressed.

When there was no mother to care for me, another Mother cared for me—a Mother full of compassion for this faithful creature who loved me with a silent, trusting devotion that I had betrayed. I cried. I rebaptized my evil as the best that was in me. I washed the dried vomit from her hair and the excrement from her limbs. India forced me to look into the terrible face of the Goddess and that look put me in touch with a profound level of loving. Instead of blinding myself to what it means to be human, instead of cringing from the filth and poverty and pain in the street, I was able to experience the horror and at the same time love the dignity of the soul that clung to life. The rose in my heart began to open. The Word that had been Word only in my head, became flesh.

And that flesh was as metaphysical as the spirit. As it lay in its chrysalis, it dropped back into its own world of symbols, resonating with their images and vibrant tones. Body, soul and spirit were thrown together into the fire and there they reconnected with the inner journey, with the transformative images shaping my life, making me who I am. Without them, my tongue spoke, but my voice was not authentic.

And what I discovered was a soul that had never lost touch with Sophia, had never forgotten what stillness is, had never forgotten the rhythm of the slow, irrevocable heartbeat of the earth. India lives in the Goddess, as I had lived in Her as a child, as every child lives in Her: frogs dappled with dew, bodies burning on the Benares Ghats, butterflies on a kitchen curtain, candles that make time stand still. Her playfulness, Her detachment, Her fury, Her love of all things, Her teeming virginal world that contains the seeds of all possibilities—these I had accepted as a child. I saw, too, the butterfly that I once was, dancing from blossom to blossom in the Noon of my imagination, dancing free in the Noon of Her love, unpossessed and unpossessing. I saw the winged creature metamorphosed into a caterpillar, heavy with duty and responsibility, scarcely remembering her affinity for wings. Slowly, almost imperceptibly, the winter came and some compass within tugged her to the East. There the butterfly prematurely escaped, and from the ceiling in the Ashoka she looked down on the dying caterpillar and took compassion.

For sixteen years she has been explaining to the caterpillar why she is a caterpillar. "Let go," she says. "Let it be." And now that the caterpillar is beginning to understand, she is free to become a butterfly. She knows what it means

> *to arrive where we started*
> *And know the place for the first time.*
> *Through the unknown, remembered gate*
> *When the last of earth left to discover*
> *Is that which was the beginning;*
> *At the source of the longest river*
> *The voice of the hidden waterfall*
> *And the children in the apple-tree*
> *Not known, because not looked for*
> *But heard, half-heard, in the stillness*
> *Between two waves of the sea.*
> *Quick now, here, now, always—*
> *A condition of complete simplicity*
> *(Costing not less than everything).* ...[2]

Who was born of that union of opposites—consciousness uniting with unconscious, spirit uniting with matter? Seven years I was pregnant with myself. The following dream began the journey down the birth canal:

I am standing barefoot on desert sand in India wearing a peach chiffon dress and veil. It is noon. What looks like an ancient astrological clock sits horizontally on a wooden framework. Its axle has a hole that goes deep into the ground. Two huge wheels, one red and gold, one blue and silver, mark its circumference. The red wheel turns clockwise on the inside; the larger blue one turns counterclockwise on the outside. The houses of the Zodiac are clearly traced in the sand. A man who loves me, and whom I love, stands beside the red wheel; this is his wheel, mine is the blue. Green foliage grows in the first two astrological houses.

My task is to dance among the spokes of the wheels, a dangerous task because sharp knives radiate from the central axle. I am to dance until the wheels move synchronistically. A huge crowd of natives stands chanting, ready to shift the key of their chant into harmony with the music of the spheres when the wheels move.

The music begins. I dance very cautiously at first. Then my body becomes the music. I no longer fear the knives. I am being danced. Suddenly the natives in one voice shift key, music fills the heavens. The wheels move. Green shoots and a fountain spring up in the Zodiac's third house. I stop right in front of the man who takes off my veil and says, "Now I know your name."

The phone rang and I woke up. At first I felt cheated that I had been robbed of my name. But then I felt I would have died had I heard it. I knew it wasn't yet time. A few veils had still to be lifted.

That dream was a great gift, one to be shared. India, having been an

The First Temptation by William Blake. (Fitzwilliam Museum, Cambridge)

island in my psyche most of my life, now joined the mainland, in fact became a mandala at the center. This image from the collective unconscious puts the experience into perspective, personally and transpersonally. Only insofar as the personal is penetrated by the transpersonal does it carry cultural relevance. Certainly, it is an intuitive dream, pointing the direction in which the energy wants to go, rather than where it is.

The setting is in the desert. Biblically the desert is a chrysalis, a vast expanse of transitional upheaval. For forty years Moses and the Israelites were crossing the desert; for forty days Jesus was alone in the wilderness. The old life had been left behind; the new was yet to come; between was the dislocation that opened the spiritual depths. The desert gives birth to a new order in which real feelings and real values are recognized.

Wandering alone in an unmarked landscape, one imagines a mirage—a vision of what may be far on the horizon. The dreams in the desert are at first irretrievable, then "unintelligible" because their contents are so new. They prefigure what may happen, who the dreamer may become, who in essence the dreamer is. That knowledge is still so foreign that the wanderer can only say, "In spite of what seems to be chaos in my conscious life, I know there is some meaningful order in what is happening underneath. I just have to wait." Fear in the desert springs from the terror of self-deception. What if it is only a mirage? What if there is nothing there? What if all my imaginings are the temptations of the devil? What if my feet become too burned to walk any further? Gradually the perception changes; gradually the intimations are constellated. The forty years or forty days are accomplished. Then it is the task of the ego to bring into daily reality what has been revealed in the desert, to bring the treasure home. Bringing the inner and outer worlds into harmony is living one's destiny.

The dream image echoes and re-echoes within itself, the union of masculine and feminine, gold and silver, spirit and matter, West and East, Yang and Yin. Like the initiate in the primitive tribes, the dancer is to step into the cosmic arena, and through her connection with her own inner roots, she will contact "the water of life with which she nourishes the cosmic tree" (above, page 18). Vegetation in the wasteland depends on the feminine capacity to overcome personal fear and become open to the inner fountains. She must wait until the conscious energy, free of the fear of blades and spokes, resonates with its unconscious source, and both are nurtured and guided by the Self. Impersonally, energy is moving vertically from above, horizontally from the hole in the axle; personally, it is moving in the Eros relationship between her and the man. It is he who ultimately pulls aside the veil, thus connecting her to himself, to the world, and to the larger meaning of the dance. The rhythm synchronizes itself between the two dimensions, impersonal and personal. Her dancing body becomes a central axis between heaven and earth. Creation springs from that union. As in all true ritual, the body moves from its own archetypal center. It no longer dances. It is being danced.

The two wheels form a double mandala. In this dream, the blue and silver symbolize the feminine soul, the red and gold the masculine spirit. Both are centered in the axle with its hole moving deep into the earth. In alchemy, the *spiraculum aeternitatis* "is an air-hole through which eternity breathes into the temporal world."[3] The meeting place is a vacuum where the personal realm of the psyche touches the eternal, the collective unconscious. It is the place of annunciation, spirit breathing into soul. In such a meeting (the impregnation of the virgin, "the intersection of the timeless moment"; above, page 73) the ego, freed from the narrow confines of its temporal cage, glimpses the eternal reality.

In the Middle Ages, another image of this "window of eternity" or "window of escape" was the anima, or matter as the anima, identified at that time with the Virgin Mary.[4] Thus, for example, the round stained-glass windows were the great roses of the Virgin through which the fire of the spirit shone into the cathedral. In the image of this twentieth-century dream, it is through the psychologically conscious feminine in man and woman that the spirit manifests in new life. Like the eternal corn at Eleusis, the seeds of the desert having been dead are alive again, and the participants in the mystery recognize the new life with a new resonance in their chant. New life comes to the "third house," astrologically the house of communication, perhaps a new understanding between masculine and feminine, spirit and soul, West and East. The images of the dream all contribute to a sense of what the alchemists called the *unus mundus*—one reality of the physical and psychic realms, a vision of the ultimate harmony between inner and outer reality—a harmony that Jung calls synchronicity.

The dance takes place at Noon—twelve o'clock, the hour of initiation into a new level of spiritual awareness, the hour of spiritual rebirth, the hour that casts no shadow because it has absorbed it into itself. Having looked through "the window of eternity," having seen without the veil, the dancer is about to receive her spiritual name when the temporal world intercedes. She was not yet ready to see "face to face," a perception which constitutes death, the meeting with the face she had before she was born. But for one brief moment all double vision ceased. Inner and outer were one.

The unity, the essence of the dream, resides in the image of an evolving androgyny. Life is danced between the knives and spokes, but these become incidentals when the differentiated feminine is strong enough to surrender to the differentiated masculine. Her body becomes the chalice relating to the navel of the world around which the two wheels move. She is a vessel of the spirit, at the same time maintaining her barefoot connection to the earth—the soil of her being through which life flows. Herein lie her authenticity and her creativity. Only when the wheels are synchronistically attuned can all the energies of the psyche (the natives) sing in harmony with the universal law. That tuning comes about through the sacrifice of ego desire, through the birth of an ego ready to win, ready to lose, free, unpossessed and unpossessing—an ego that knows how to play. Body, soul and spirit dance, resonating with their own inner truth in harmony with the larger meaning of the dance.

The dance is danced whether we are in India or in our own living room, and we are the dancers. How we dance is our responsibility. If we hold the seeds in our eyes, we make ourselves captives to the dark earth energies that can keep us crawling on our bellies on the ground.

If we arrogantly defy the laws of nature, we are destroyed in the spokes and knives. If we dare to ask the question "Who am I?" then we commit ourselves to the responsibility of honing our way to our own inner truth. In the silence of the chrysalis our silver chalice is wrought, the silver chalice that bears the golden child. Pondering in the heart is not a sentimental journey to the Goddess. Pondering in the heart involves the joy and the agony of consciously allowing our own *I am* to magnify the great I AM until

> *... the tongues of flame are in-folded*
> *Into the crowned knot of fire*
> *And the fire and the rose are one.*[5]

Natalia Makarova, from *Waldman on Dance: A Collection of Photographs* by Max Waldman (New York: William Morrow and Company, 1977).

Notes

CW— *The Collected Works of C.G. Jung*, trans. R.F.C. Hull, ed. H. Read, M. Fordham, G. Adler, Wm. McGuire, Bollingen Series XX (Princeton: Princeton University Press, 1953-1979).

Introduction: Frog Conjunctions

1. See Joseph Campbell, *The Mythic Image*, Bollingen Series C (Princeton: Princeton University Press, 1974), p. 217, fig. 199a.
2. *The Portable Nietzsche*, trans. Walter Kaufman (New York: Viking, 1968), p. 483.
3. Carolyn Heilbrun, "What She Was Silent About," *New York Times Book Review*, February 10, 1985.
4. Ibid.
5. Mary Hamilton and Barbara Fidler were the creative theater dance and music directors.

1 Chrysalis: Am I Really?

1. T.S. Eliot, "Journey of the Magi," lines 29-43.
2. *Hamlet*, act 1, scene 2, line 133.
3. William Blake, *The Marriage of Heaven and Hell*, plate 7, line 18.
4. Edmond Rostand, *Cyrano de Bergerac*, trans. Brian Hooker (New York: Bantom Classic, 1981), p. 32.
5. Arnold van Gennep, *The Rites of Passage* (Chicago: University of Chicago Press, 1960), p. 3.
6. Bruce Lincoln, *Emerging from the Chrysalis: Studies in Rituals of Women's Initiation* (New York: Harvard University Press, 1981), pp. 103-104.
7. Ibid., p. 104.
8. Jung, "On the Nature of the Psyche," *The Structure and Dynamics of the Psyche*, CW 8, par. 388.
9. Psalms 118:22.
10. See, for example, "The Tavistock Lectures," *The Symbolic Life*, CW 18, par. 389: "Neurosis is really an attempt at self-cure, just as any physical disease is part an attempt at self-cure. ... It is an attempt of the self-regulating psychic system to restore the balance."
11. Marie-Louise von Franz, *Alchemy: An Introduction to the Symbolism and the Psychology* (Toronto: Inner City Books, 1980), p. 137.
12. Jung, "The Psychology of the Transference," *The Practice of Psychotherapy*, CW 16, par. 489.
13. *King Lear*, act 5, scene 3, lines 19-20.
14. Job 10:2, 42:5.
15. Matthew 26:39-42.

16. R.M. Rilke, *Letters to a Young Poet*, trans. Herter Norton (New York: W.W. Norton, 1962).

17. Monica Furlong, *Merton, A Biography* (San Francisco: Harper and Row, 1980), p. 330.

18. Ibid., p. 328.

19. Ibid., p. 322.

2 "Taking It Like a Man": Abandonment in the Creative Woman

1. John Keats, letter to George and Georgiana Keats (April 21, 1819), quoted in David Perkins, ed., *English Romantic Writers* (New York: Harcourt Brace Jovanovich, 1967), p. 1225.

2. *The Complete Poems of Emily Dickinson*, ed. Thomas H. Johnson (Boston: Little, Brown and Company, 1960), number 508, p. 247.

3. The term *puer aeternus* (Latin, "eternal youth") refers to the type of man who remains too long in adolescent psychology, generally associated with a strong unconscious attachment to the mother (actual or symbolic). His female counterpart is the *puella aeterna*, an "eternal girl" with a corresponding attachment to the father world.

4. Jung, "On the Nature of the Psyche," in *The Structure and Dynamics of the Psyche*, CW 8, pars. 367, 417. See also Marion Woodman, *The Owl Was a Baker's Daughter: Obesity, Anorexia Nervosa and the Repressed Feminine* (Toronto: Inner City Books, 1980), pp. 66-67.

5. Percy Bysshe Shelley, "Adonais," line 463.

6. As this was being written (March 1985), the popular columnist Ann Landers revealed the massive response to the question she asked her female readers: "Which would you prefer: to be simply held tenderly, or perform 'the act'?" She received more than 90,000 answers; 72% preferred to be held—and 70% of these were women under 40.

7. Emily Dickinson, number 315, p. 148.

8. Ibid., number 443, p. 212.

9. Sylvia Plath, *Ariel* (London: Faber and Faber, 1965), p. 86.

10. Shakespeare, *Antony and Cleopatra*, act 5, scene 2, lines 297-298.

11. Emily Dickinson, number 777, p. 379.

12. I am indebted to Dr. Anne Maguire, Jungian analyst in London, England, for this phrase that so aptly encapsulates the psychology of this type of woman.

13. William Wordsworth, "Michael," line 202.

14. Jung, "The Transcendent Function," *The Structure and Dynamics of the Psyche*, CW 8.

15. See M. Esther Harding, *The Way of All Women* (New York: Harper Colophon, 1975), especially chap. 1, "All Things to All Men."

16. See Gary Zukav, *The Dancing Wu Li Masters: An Overview of the New Physics* (New York: Bantam Books, 1980), pp. 92ff.

17. Adrienne Rich, *Diving into the Wreck: Poems 1971-1972* (New York: W.W. Norton and Company, 1973), p. 6.

3 The Kore of Matter: Psyche/Soma Awareness

1. James Hillman, "On the Necessity of Abnormal Psychology," *Facing the Gods*, ed. James Hillman (Dallas: Spring Publications, 1980), p. 17.

2. William Blake, "The Marriage of Heaven and Hell," plate 4.

3. *Hamlet*, act 3, scene 1, lines 63-64.

4. This analogy is explored at length in Marion Woodman, *Addiction to Perfection: The Still Unravished Bride* (Toronto: Inner City Books, 1982).

5. "The Lady of Shallot," *The Works of Alfred Lord Tennyson*, Part III (London: Macmillan & Co., Ltd., 1896), p. 29.

6. The influence of the mother and father complexes in eating disorders is also discussed in Marion Woodman, *The Owl Was a Baker's Daughter* and *Addiction to Perfection*.

7. M. Esther Harding, *Psychic Energy: Its Source and Goal*, Bollingen Series X (Washington: Pantheon Books, 1947), pp. 210-211.

8. See discussion by Marie-Louise von Franz in *On Divination and Synchronicity: The Psychology of Meaningful Chance* (Toronto: Inner City Books, 1980), p. 87.

9. Jung, "On the Nature of the Psyche," *The Structure and Dynamics of the Psyche*, CW 8, par. 440.

10. Ibid., par. 418.

11. In recent years, three sets of weekly workshops have been offered in Toronto to male and female participants who meet the prerequisite (a minimum of 50 hours of personal Jungian analysis). In the autumn, Mary Hamilton and I work with the group on images and active imagination with the body. In the winter, I focus with Beverly Stokes on patterns of early movement (e.g., crawling). In the spring, Ann Skinner and I lead the group in voice work. This sequence is important: work in one area enables a participant to tackle the next.

    Because the repressed emotions can be so volcanic when they erupt, it is strongly recommended that participants be concurrently in analysis. It is also helpful if they have previously experienced some form of body work (e.g., yoga, T'ai Chi, Feldenkrais classes). The workshops are conceived not as group work with group interaction, but as a group of individuals, each concentrating on his or her own material; while group energy unquestionably influences the individual, that energy is honored as transpersonal and, insofar as possible, not interfered with. The individual *temenos* is always respected.

    Much of the substance of this chapter is based on data emerging from these workshops and from the individual analytic hours that followed.

12. See Jung, "The Spirit Mercurius," *Alchemical Studies*, CW 13, par. 262: " 'Soul' represents a higher concept than 'spirit' in the sense of air or gas. As the 'subtle body' or 'breath-soul' it means something non-material and finer than mere air. Its essential characteristic is to animate and be animated; it therefore represents the life-principle." See also "The Phenomenology of the Spirit in Fairytales," *The Archetypes and the Col-*

lective Unconscious, CW 9, 1, par. 392, where Jung draws an analogy between "the idea of the subtle body and the Chinese *kuei*-soul," and states that "spirit and matter may well be forms of one and the same transcendental being."

Jung explored the concept of the subtle body in more depth in his English seminars, "Psychological Analysis of Nietzsche's Zarathustra" (Zurich, 1934-1939). Mimeographed transcripts of these seminars are available in some Jung Institute libraries, but they may not be quoted.

13. Ibid., par. 282.

14. Fritjof Capra, *The Tao of Physics* (New York: Bantam Books, 1984), p. 310.

15. Jung, "The Practical Use of Dream Analysis," *The Practice of Psychotherapy*, CW 16, par. 340.

16. A comical cartoon figure used in advertising Pillsbury's prefabricated baking goods, similar in appearance to the rotund Michelin Man (also a frequent image in the dreams of women with eating disorders).

17. Edward Albee, *The American Dream* (New York: New American Library, 1961), p. 115.

4 At the Right Time: The Ritual Journey

1. T.S. Eliot, *Four Quartets*, "Little Gidding," line 52.

2. For a fuller discussion of primitive man's sacred journey to the holy cave (as the collective unconscious, from which a numinous image may emerge), see Erich Neumann, "The Psychological Meaning of Ritual," *Quadrant*, volume 9, number 2 (Winter 1976), pp. 5-34.

3. Ibid., p. 16.

4. *Time Magazine*, March 4, 1985.

5. M. Esther Harding, *Woman's Mysteries, Ancient and Modern* (New York: Rider & Company, 1955), p. 125.

6. *We Are the World*, CBS Records, 1985, lyrics by Lionel Ritchie and Michael Jackson.

7. Jung, *Symbols of Transformation*, CW 5, par. 674.

8. John Layard, *The Virgin Archetype* (New York: Spring Publications, 1972), pp. 290-291 (my italics).

9. *The Aprocryphal New Testament*, trans. Montague Rhodes James (Oxford: Clarendon Press, 1972), p. 40.

10. M. Zimmer Bradley, *The Mists of Avalon* (New York: Ballantine Books, 1982), p. 810.

11. Jung, "On Psychic Energy," *The Structure and Dynamics of the Psyche*, CW 8.

12. Victor W. Turner, *The Ritual Process* (Chicago: Aldine Publishing Co., 1969), p. 95.

13. See van Gennep, *Rights of Passage*.

14. Bruce Lincoln, *Emerging from the Chrysalis*, p. 101.

15. Solon T. Kimball, Introduction to van Gennep, *Rights of Passage*, p. ix.

16. The process described here must not be confused with the "beauty and the beast" motif, where the woman's task is to accept a natural but "ugly" aspect of her masculinity, in order to transform it.

17. See M. Esther Harding, *Woman's Mysteries*, pp. 134-136.

18. Jung, *Two Essays on Analytical Psychology*, CW 7, par. 258.

5 The Dream Sister: Further Thoughts on Addiction

1. Jung, *Two Essays*, CW 7, par. 78.

2. The kind of "molding" that fails to recognize the feminine needs of the maturing child is in sharp contrast to the literal molding of the Navajo initiate during her "Kinaalda of Changing Woman." In that ceremony, the girl is massaged by several older women of known good character in the belief that "at the time of initiation a girl's body becomes soft again, as it was at birth"; thus she is created anew. (Bruce Lincoln, *Emerging from the Chrysalis*, p. 20)

3. See Arthur Avalon, *The Serpent Power* (New York: Dover Publications, 1974).

4. C.S. Lewis, *Till We Have Faces* (Grand Rapids: William B. Eerdman's Publishing Co., 1978), p. 282.

5. Ibid.

6. Ibid., pp. 292, 294.

7. Ibid., p. 250.

8. Ibid., p. 295.

9. Jung, "On the Nature of the Psyche," *The Structure and Dynamics of the Psyche*, CW 8, par. 425.

10. The man's task is to find his place in the father world, separate from women but not antagonistic to them.

11. Behind "orphan" psychology (the sense of being all alone in the world) is the archetypal motif of the abandoned child. See Jung, "The Psychology of the Child Archetype," *The Archetypes and the Collective Unconscious*, CW 9, 1, pars. 285-288; and Daryl Sharp, "Alienation and the Abandoned Child," *The Secret Raven: Conflict and Transformation* (Toronto: Inner City Books, 1980), pp. 95-99.

12. *Macbeth*, act 1, scene 5, line 45.

13. The use of antibiotics, birth control pills, drugs that weaken the immune system, even a prolonged high carbohydrate intake, can lead to a condition in which the body cannot properly control its yeast growth. See C. Orian Truss, "The Role of Candida Albicans in Human Illness," *Orthomolecular Psychiatry*, vol. 10, no. 4, (1981), pages 228-238. See also William G. Crook, *The Yeast Connection* (Jackson, Tennessee: Professional Books, 1984).

14. "The Thunder, Perfect Mind," *The Nag Hammadi Library*, ed. James M. Robinson (San Francisco: Harper & Row, 1981), pp. 271-272.

15. Marina Warner, *Alone of All Her Sex* (London: Quartet Books, 1978), p. 274.
16. Ibid., p. 145.
17. *The Apocryphal New Testament*, p. 44.
18. Ibid.
19. Ibid., p. 45. For a somewhat different description of Mary's grief, see the Koran, Surih of Mary, 19:24: "Oh, would that I had died and passed into oblivion."
20. Jesus had four such lost ones in his genealogy: Tamar (Gen. 38:24), Rahab (Josh. 2:1), Ruth (Ruth 3:1-18) and Uriah's wife (2 Sam. 11).
21. *The Apocryphal New Testament*, p. 43.
22. Jung, "The Psychology of the Transference," *The Practice of Psychotherapy*, CW 16, par. 469: "It goes against nature not to yield to an ardent desire."
23. Samuel Taylor Coleridge, "Kubla Khan."
24. See Jung, *Psychology and Alchemy*, CW 12, pars. 519-524.
25. William Wordsworth, "Ode: Intimations of Immortality."
26. The state of "just being," as opposed to goal-oriented "doing," is now recognized as useful in treating the anxiety, stress and tension arising from "hurry sickness": "Newer methods [of treatment] ... ask the patient to step out of a chronic, habitual way of sensing time as an inexorable flowing process into an alternative mode of time perception. They ask the patient to 'stop' time. They invite him into the realm of spacetime." (Larry Dossey, M.D., *Space, Time & Medicine*; Boulder: Shambhala, 1982, pp. 166-167)
27. Robert Graves, *The White Goddess* (London: Faber and Faber, 1975), pp. 180-181.
28. See Marie-Louise von Franz, *Shadow and Evil in Fairytales* (Zurich: Spring Publications, 1974), pp. 31-32; and *On Divination and Synchronicity*, pp. 105-108.
29. Walter F. Otto, *Dionysos* (Dallas: Spring Publications, 1981), p. 151.
30. Ibid., pp. 136-137.
31. Ibid.
32. *An Interrupted Life: The Diaries of Etty Hillesum, 1941-1943,* trans. Arno Pomerans (Toronto: Lester & Orpen Dennys, 1983), pp. 186-187.

6. Piercing the Heart: Yin, Yang and Jung

1. Emily Dickinson, number 1333, p. 578.
2. T.S. Eliot, *Four Quartets*, "Burnt Norton," lines 63-76.
3. Jung, *Aion,* CW 9, II, par. 126.
4. Von Franz, "The Process of Individuation," *Man and His Symbols*, ed. C.G. Jung, (London: Aldus Books, 1964), pp. 185-186.
5. William Shakespeare, *Othello*, act 5, scene 2, line 4.
6. Ibid., act 4, scene 2, line 90.

7. Ibid., scene 3, lines 50-51.

8. Ibid., act 5, scene 2, line 7.

9. Ibid., lines 1-2, 6.

10. Ibid., lines 20-22.

11. Jung, *Letters*, vol. 2 (1951-1961), ed. G. Adler, Bollingen Series XCV (Princeton, Princeton University Press, 1975), p. 581.

12. *Rilke, Selected Poems*, trans. J.B. Leishman (Middlesex, England: Penguin Books, 1964), p. 69.

13. Jung, *The Visions Seminars*, 1930-1934 (Zurich: Spring Publications, 1976), p. 504.

14. Ibid.

15. Robert Browning, "Two in the Campagna," lines 59-60.

16. Emily Dickinson, number 47, p. 26.

17. Jung, "Psychological Aspects of the Mother Archetype," *The Archetypes and the Collective Unconscious*, CW 9, I, par. 164.

18. Jung, *The Visions Seminars*, p. 504.

19. Numbers 22:23-27.

20. Ibid., 28, 30.

21. A man's undifferentiated feminine instinct frequently shows up in dreams and fairytales as a dog; see Marie-Louise von Franz, *An Introduction to the Psychology of Fairytales* (Zurich: Spring Publications, 1973), p. 54.

22. Emily Dickinson, number 627, page 309.

23. This experience is explored through the disciplines of tantric yoga; see, for instance, Ajit Mookerjee and Madhu Khanna, *The Tantric Way: Art, Science, Ritual* (London: Thames and Hudson, 1977).

24. Robert Frost, "Reluctance," lines 17-18.

25. T.S. Eliot, *Four Quartets*, "Little Gidding," lines 150-159.

26. Matt. 5:23-24.

27. Dante, "Convivio," *The Divine Comedy*, IV, 27, 4.

28. See Esther Harding, *Woman's Mysteries*, pp. 170ff.

29. John Donne, *Selected Poems*, ed. Matthias A. Shaaber (New York: Appleton-Century-Crofts, 1958), Sonnet 14, p. 105.

30. Percy Bysshe Shelley, "Adonais," line 462.

31. T.S. Eliot, *Four Quartets*, "East Coker," lines 123-128.

7 Beloved Enemy: A Modern Initiation

1. Victor Turner, "Body, Brain, and Culture," *Zygon* (Journal of Science and Religion), September 1983.

2. T.S. Eliot, *Four Quartets*, "Little Gidding," lines 241-254.

3. Marie-Louise von Franz, *On Divination and Synchronicity*, p. 109.

4. Ibid.

5. Eliot, "Little Gidding," lines 257-259.

Index

Studies in Jungian Psychology
by Jungian Analysts

Quality Paperbacks

Prices and payment in $US (except in Canada, $Cdn)

1. The Secret Raven: Conflict and Transformation
Daryl Sharp (Toronto). ISBN 0-919123-00-7. 128 pp. $18

2. The Psychological Meaning of Redemption Motifs in Fairy Tales
Marie-Louise von Franz (Zürich). ISBN 0-919123-01-5. 128 pp. $18

3. On Divination and Synchronicity: The Psychology of Meaningful Chance
Marie-Louise von Franz (Zürich). ISBN 0-919123-02-3. 128 pp. $18

**4. The Owl Was a Baker's Daughter: Obesity, Anorexia and the Repressed
Feminine** Marion Woodman (Toronto). ISBN 0-919123-03-1. 144 pp. $18

5. Alchemy: An Introduction to the Symbolism and the Psychology
Marie-Louise von Franz (Zürich). ISBN 0-919123-04-X. 288 pp. $25

6. Descent to the Goddess: A Way of Initiation for Women
Sylvia Brinton Perera (New York). ISBN 0-919123-05-8. 112 pp. $18

8. Border Crossings: Carlos Castaneda's Path of Knowledge
Donald Lee Williams (Boulder). ISBN 0-919123-07-4. 160 pp. $18

**9. Narcissism and Character Transformation: The Psychology of
Narcissistic Character Disorders**
Nathan Schwartz-Salant (New York). ISBN 0-919123-08-2. 192 pp. $20

11. Alcoholism and Women: The Background and the Psychology
Jan Bauer (Montreal). ISBN 0-919123-10-4. 144 pp. $18

12. Addiction to Perfection: The Still Unravished Bride
Marion Woodman (Toronto). ISBN 0-919123-11-2. 208 pp. $$20

13. Jungian Dream Interpretation: A Handbook of Theory and Practice
James A. Hall, M.D. (Dallas). ISBN 0-919123-12-0. 128 pp. $18

14. The Creation of Consciousness: Jung's Myth for Modern Man
Edward F. Edinger (Los Angeles). ISBN 0-919123-13-9. 128 pp. $18

15. The Analytic Encounter: Transference and Human Relationship
Mario Jacoby (Zürich). ISBN 0-919123-14-7. 128 pp. $18

17. The Illness That We Are: A Jungian Critique of Christianity
John P. Dourley (Ottawa). ISBN 0-919123-16-3. 128 pp. $18

19. Cultural Attitudes in Psychological Perspective
Joseph L. Henderson, M.D. (San Francisco). ISBN 0-919123-18-X. 128 pp. $18

21. The Pregnant Virgin: A Process of Psychological Transformation
Marion Woodman (Toronto). ISBN 0-919123-20-1. 208 pp. $20pb/$25hc

**22. Encounter with the Self: A Jungian Commentary on William Blake's
*Illustrations of the Book of Job***
Edward F. Edinger (Los Angeles). ISBN 0-919123-21-X. 80 pp. $18

23. The Scapegoat Complex: Toward a Mythology of Shadow and Guilt
Sylvia Brinton Perera (New York). ISBN 0-919123-22-8. 128 pp. $18

24. The Bible and the Psyche: Individuation Symbolism in the Old Testament
Edward F. Edinger (Los Angeles). ISBN 0-919123-23-6. 176 pp. $20

Discounts: any 3-5 books, 10%; 6-9 books, 20%; 10 or more, 25%

Add Postage/Handling: 1-2 books, $6; 3-4 books, $8; 5-9 books, $15; 10 or more, $10

Credit cards: Contact BookWorld toll-free: 1-800-444-2524, or Fax 1-800-777-2525

Free **Catalogue** describing over **100** titles, and **Jung at Heart** newsletter

INNER CITY BOOKS, Box 1271, Station Q, Toronto, ON M4T 2P4, Canada
Tel. 416-927-0355 / Fax: 416-924-1814 / E-mail: sales@innercitybooks.net